Short Takes

Short Takes
Model Essays for Composition

Fifth Edition

Elizabeth Penfield
University of New Orleans

HarperCollins *CollegePublishers*

Senior Acquisitions Editor: Patricia Rossi
Project Coordination and Text Design: Ruttle, Shaw & Wetherill, Inc.
Cover Design: Mary McDonnell
Electronic Production Manager: Angel Gonzalez Jr
Manufacturing Manager: Willie Lane
Electronic Page Makeup: Ruttle, Shaw & Wetherill, Inc.
Printer and Binder: RR Donnelley & Sons Company
Cover Printer: Phoenix Color Corp.

Short Takes: Model Essays for Composition, Fifth Edition

Penfield, Elizabeth, 1939–
        Short takes : model essays for composition / Elizabeth Penfield. —
5th ed.
            p.   cm.
        Includes index.
        ISBN 0–673–99463–5 (student's edition)
        ISBN 0–673–99464–3 (instructor's edition)
        1.   College readers.   2.   English language—Rhetoric.   I.   Title.
PE1417.P43   1996
808'.0427—dc20   95–3786
                                                                    CIP

95 96 97 98 9 8 7 6 5 4 3 2 1

Contents

"*Over the past twelve years I have learned that a tree needs space to grow, that coyotes sing down by the creek in January, that I can drive a nail into oak only when it is green, that bees know more about making honey than I do, that love can become sadness, and that there are more questions than answers.*"

"*Her head hangs as though she hasn't the strength or need to lift it. Hidden beneath a dingy pile of polyester, she drags her fingertips across the leather of her face, which she shifts slowly, side-to-side, as her lips scrunch roundabout as if she's talking to someone. But no one is there.*"

"*From the center of downtown Tucson the ground slopes gently away to Main Street, drops a few feet, and then rolls to the banks of the Santa Cruz River. Here lies the section of the city known as El Hoyo.*"

"*Widowed, alone, children and grandchildren flung wide from California to New England, she fills her days with little things.*"

7 Cause and Effect   181

Thematic Guide

People and Animals

The Individual

Groups

Scenes and Places

*I*deas and Issues

Education

Language

Science and Technology

Popular Culture and the Media

The Individual and the Law

Society

Preface

*T*his fifth edition of *Short Takes* remains a collection of short, readable, interesting essays, and the commentary continues to focus on reading and writing as interrelated activities. But much is new. Each chapter of *Short Takes* now includes a student essay, and more than half the professional essays are new. Charts and lists augment the introductory material in each chapter, and "Pointers for Writing" and some suggested writing assignments follow. As for the essays, the background material on each author has been expanded, and each essay is now preceded by "What to Look For," a brief description of a notable feature of the writer's style. "Key Words and Phrases," a feature of the first three editions, is back by popular demand, as is "Freeze Frame," the initial essay that sets the tone for the book by emphasizing reading and writing as active and interrelated processes, presenting an interactive model reinforced in each chapter's introduction and apparatus. Just as each chapter includes pointers, so too does "Freeze Frame," which concludes with pointers for both reading and writing.

The overall organization of the book remains the same, but the chapters that focus on analogy and on argument have been changed. Because analogy is so closely related to comparison and contrast and rarely in composition courses is treated as a separate kind of essay, the two have been combined into one chapter. And because many composition courses place more emphasis on exposition than on argument, the number of essays in the chapter on argument has been reduced. Argument, the kind of writing that students are apt to find the most difficult, comes last. Similarly, the other chapters are sequenced so that the more accessible patterns of development come first, with each chapter building on the previous one and leading to the one that follows. Within each chapter, the essays are also presented in order of difficulty. All the supplementary information—the chapter introductions, background information, notes on style, key words and phrases, questions on the essays, and suggestions for writing—try to balance process and product, working on the premise that the two, like reading and writing, are so closely interrelated that one cannot be considered without the other.

THE ESSAYS

To write is to choose among alternatives, to select the most appropriate organization, persona, diction, and techniques for a given audience and purpose. Each of the essays included in this edition was chosen because it exemplifies the author's choices, and the apparatus emphasizes those choices and alternatives. Thus the essays serve as illustrative models of organization and stylistic techniques available to the writer. The essays were also chosen because their authors represent different genders, ages, and cultures; as a result, subjects of the essays are accessible and their perspectives are lively, qualities that also allow them to serve as sources of invention, as jumping-off places for students to develop their own ideas in their own styles.

This edition contains 52 essays, 28 of which are new. All are indeed short—about 1000 words at most—and as such should easily lend themselves to scrutiny and emulation, since most of the papers assigned in composition courses fall in the 400- to 1000-word range. The essays also represent complete pieces, not excerpts, illustrating the basic aims of discourse and standard rhetorical modes.

RHETORICAL MODES AND THE AIMS OF DISCOURSE

Yet anyone who has used a reader with essays arranged by mode has likely run into two problems: first, few essays are pure examples of a single mode; second, most collections of essays treat argument—an aim of writing—as though it were the equivalent of description, comparison/contrast, and so on. *Short Takes* addresses these inconsistencies by emphasizing the difference between mode—how an essay is organized—and purpose—how an essay is intended to affect the reader—and by pointing out how essays frequently blend two or more modes.

Because essays usually employ more than one mode, the essays here are grouped according to their *primary* rhetorical pattern; the questions that follow each essay go on to point out the subordinate modes. As for the aims of discourse, the essays represent the various purposes for writing. The writer's self-expressive, informative, and persuasive purposes are underscored in the discussion questions. In addition, connections between academic writing and the kinds of writing one finds outside the classroom walls are emphasized.

Example, description, or other standard modes are used in develop all kinds of nonfiction prose—self-expression, exposition, and argument. Of those three types of writing, self-expression is the easiest and argument the most difficult. For that reason argument has its own special chapter. Of the eight essays in that chapter, six focus on different topics, and two address the some problem—the role of African-American studies within the college curriculum—from very different perspectives. And while chapters 1 to 8 contain some essays intended to persuade, those in Chapter 9 exemplify the classical appeals: to reason, to emotion, and to the writer's credibility.

APPARATUS FOR READING AND WRITING

The apparatus makes full use of the essays. Each chapter begins with a brief introduction that depicts the mode or purpose under discussion, showing how it can be used in formal essays and in practical, everyday writing tasks. The introductions go on to point out specifically how the modes can be shaped by considerations of audience, purpose, particular strategies, thesis, and organization, ending with advice on finding a subject, exploring a topic, and drafting a paper. This division of the writing process approximates the classic one of invention, arrangement, and style, but is not intended to imply that these are separate stages.

To emphasize both what a text says and how it says it, each essay is preceded by background information on the author and the text, a brief discussion of a stylistic strategy, and a list of the words and phrases that the reader may not know. Two sets of questions—"Thesis and Organization" and "Technique and Style"—come after the essay, followed by ideas for writing. Throughout, process and product as well as reading and writing are interrelated, as is the recursive nature of the act of writing. Writers constantly invent, organize, and revise; the lines that distinguish those activities are narrow, if not downright blurred.

The suggestions for writing following each essay contain a number of options related by theme, organization, or ideas to the work the writer has just read. The assignments allow a good deal of flexibility: some lend themselves to general information or personal experience essays, some to research papers, and some to the classic technique of imitation. Once the writer selects a subject, *exploring the topic* is the next step; the questions in that category are shaped so that no matter what type of paper may be involved, the writer can generate information about it. *Drafting the paper* then helps organize the material and points out some of the pitfalls and advantages inherent in the particular mode.

ACKNOWLEDGMENTS

For their help in bringing this book to publication, I have many to thank: Leslie Taggart for her good advice and flexibility; Gabrielle Gautreaux for sending students my way; John Cooke for providing time in a tight budget year; Hope Rajala and Theodora Hill for their sound recommendations, patience, and assistance with the more boring aspects of preparing a manuscript. Sharon Blackstock, Stark Technical College; Margaret Borden, Willmar Community College; Joan G. Brand, Cincinnati Technical College; Margaret Brofman, San Diego Mesa College; Lawrence A. Carlson, Orange Coast College; Charles H. Kinzel, Renton Technical College; Lia F. Maimon, Montclair State College; Sandra Petree, Fort Hays State University; Joanie Richtig, Northern Michigan University; and David Weiser, Hostos Community College-CUNY, all provided guidance and advice that improved the manuscript. And, as usual and most of all, I wish to thank my own students, who have taught me at least as much as I have taught them.

ELIZABETH PENFIELD

Freeze Frame: Reading and Writing

This Book

1   *I*n filmmaking, a "short take" is a brief scene filmed without interruption. Short essays are similar in that they move quickly, without interruption, toward their conclusions. This book is a collection of short essays that explain, argue, express the writer's feelings, or simply entertain. The essays carry out their purposes in a variety of ways, drawing on description, narration, example, division, comparison, process analysis, causal analysis, and definition—patterns of organization that you will be learning about. These essays can serve as models for you when you write your own papers.

2   And just as the essays collected here are "short takes," this essay is a "freeze frame," as though you had stopped the film on one particular shot to get a better look at the details. That's just what this essay will do, stop and take a close-up look at what goes on when you read and when you write.

The Writing Process

3   Essays, like most written work, are deceptive. What you see on a printed page resembles the writer's work about as much as a portrait photograph resembles the real person. What you don't see when you look at printed pages are all the beginnings and stops,

the crumpled paper, the false starts, the notes, the discarded ideas, the changed words. Instead, you have a finished piece—the result of the writer's choices. Don't let that result intimidate you. The process most writers go through to produce their essays is very like your own. The writer Andre Dubus puts it another way: "There is something mystical [about writing] but it's not rare and nobody should treat it as though this is something special that writers do. Anybody born physically able in the brain can sit down and begin to write something, and discover that there are depths in her soul or his soul that are untapped."

4   Both writers and readers tap into those depths, depths that help make meaning of the world we live in. The essays contained in this book, together with its explanations, questions, and suggestions for writing, reinforce a basic assumption: reading and writing are highly individual processes that are active, powerful, and inter-related ways to discover *meaning*. To check out that statement, think of one day within the last week when something memorable happened to you. Isolate that incident so it's clear in your mind. Now think of all the other details of the day, from the time your eyes opened in the morning to the time they closed at night. That's a lot of detail, and most of it insignificant, meaningless. Those are the bits and pieces of information you would probably discard if you were to write about that day. What you would be left with is that memorable thing that occurred and a few details directly related to it, some preceding it, a few following. In writing about that day, you would reshape events, evaluating, selecting, and re-creating what happened so that what was most meaningful comes through clearly. As a result, someone reading your description would be able to experience at a distance what you experienced firsthand. To write, then, is to create and structure a world; to read is to become part of someone else's. And just as reading makes a better writer, writing makes a better reader.

The Reader

5   What's a good reader? Someone who interacts with the words on the page. Just as the writer reshapes, evaluates, selects, and re-creates events, so too the reader reshapes, evaluates, selects, and re-creates the text on the page. After all, as a reader you have your own world, one made up of your experiences, family, culture—all

of which you bring with you to what you read. An essay about why people love to walk on beaches, for example, will remind you of any beaches you know, and your associations will probably be pleasurable. As you begin the essay, you discover that the writer's associations are also pleasant ones, and they in turn reinforce yours. You read on, constantly reassessing your ideas about the essay as you add more and more information to your first impression. Now and then, you may hit a sentence that at first doesn't make much sense, so you stop, perhaps to look up an unfamiliar word, perhaps to go back and review an earlier statement, then read on, again reevaluating your ideas about what the author is saying and what you think of it. The result is analytical, critical reading—not critical in the sense of being a harsh judge but critical in the sense of questioning, weighing evidence, evaluating, comparing your world to the one the writer has created on the page.

6   If you've done much writing, the process summarized above must sound familiar. Most people find that writing is a form of discovery, that writing about an idea helps clarify it. In your own experience, you have probably found that you usually don't have a clear grasp of your thesis until you've written your way into it. Odds are you start with an idea, a general focus, but that focus becomes clearer as you rethink your choice of a particular word or reread what you've put on the page to get a sense of what should come next. And on you go, sometimes speeding, sometimes creeping, constantly revising, until you finish. Even the idea of finishing is a shaky notion; many writers will continue to revise right up to their deadlines. This idea of revising and tinkering seems natural to writing but less so to reading. Yet just as you tinker and wrestle with your own writing, you should do the same with what you read. You should scribble, underline, question, challenge. Reading in this way, reading critically with pen or pencil in hand, will give you a fuller appreciation of what you read and a better understanding of how to write.

7   If you're not used to reading in this manner, it may seem foreign to you. After all, what's printed on the page should be easy enough to understand. But because words only stand for things and are not the things themselves, different readers find different meanings. If, for instance, your only memory of a beach was of nearly drowning in the Atlantic Ocean, then you would have to suspend that association when you read an essay that praises

beach walking. And if also your skin turns bright red at the mere mention of the sun, that adds one more obstacle to understanding why others enjoy the seashore. How then can a reader comprehend all that an author is saying? More specifically, how can a reader go about reading an essay critically?

8   It helps to know what different kinds of writing have in common. Whether business letter, lab report, journal entry, news story, poem, or essay, all focus on a subject, address a reader, and have a point. And, too, all have a purpose and a style; they are written for specific reasons and in a certain way. These shared elements are perhaps more familiar as questions used to spark ideas for writing, the familiar journalistic *who? what? where? when? how? why?*

9   Yet these questions can be equally useful for reading. To whom is an essay addressed? What is the writer's main point? How is the piece organized? Why is it structured that way? Where and when does the action take place? Many, many more inquiries can be spun off those six simple words, and they are useful tools for exploring an essay. The kind of analysis they lead to not only contributes to the pleasure you derive from an essay, it makes you more aware of how to address similar concerns in your own writing. No one ever learned to write only by reading, but good writers are also good readers.

Detecting the Thesis

10   In most of the reading we do, we are looking for information. The election coverage reported in the newspaper, the syllabus for a course, a set of directions all exemplify this kind of reading, but reading for information and reading for comprehension are as different as a vitamin pill and a five-course dinner. To understand not only what a writer is saying but its implications and also why that writer might have chosen to say it that way isn't easy.

11   The title of an essay is a good place to start, for most titles tip you off not only about the subject of the piece but also of the author's stand. You don't need to turn to the essay titled "Sweatin' for Nothin' " to figure out the essay may be about exercising and that the author doesn't see much point to it. Other essays, such as "Left Sink," just imply a subject and raise your curiosity. What about a left sink? What does it mean? Still other titles tip you off to the author's tone, the writer's attitude toward the subject: "Honking

Tonking" is an entertaining but still informative account of the author's incurable fondness for country-western music; "Spinsterhood Is Powerful" is one writer's opinion of the unsung joys of being female and unmarried.

12   Knowing or at least having a hint about the subject is the first step to discovering an essay's thesis, the assertion the author is making about the subject. The first paragraph or set of paragraphs that act as an introduction will also help you form a tentative thesis. Sometimes the writer will place the thesis in the first paragraph or introduction. In this essay, for example, the thesis appears in the last sentence of paragraph 6: "Reading critically with pen or pencil in hand, will give you a fuller appreciation of what you read and a better understanding of how to write." But sometimes a bare-bones version of the thesis will appear in the title. If you see it, you should mark it. If you don't see a thesis, you should still jot down a tentative version of your own so that you have a focus for what is to follow, an idea that you can test other ideas against.

13   The obvious comparison here is your own writing. Many writers start with a general idea that then gets refined into a thesis as they write. Once that thesis is clear, then the writer must decide where to place it for the greatest effect. Some opt for the introduction, others choose the conclusion, and still others decide on a more subtle solution by weaving bits and pieces of the thesis into the essay as a whole.

14   If you are reading the essay, this last choice can give you a challenge. You must create the thesis by identifying key sentences and then mentally composing a statement that covers those ideas, a process that often takes more than one reading but is made easier if you underline the important sentences.

15   Sometimes writers set traps, making it easy to mistake a fact for a thesis. If you keep in mind that a thesis is both a sentence and an assertion—a value judgment—those traps can be avoided. "The average American watches a lot of TV" states a fact most readers would shrug off with a "So what?" On the other hand, "Television rots the minds of its viewers" takes a stand that will probably raise hackles and a "Hey, wait a minute!"

16   When you read an essay that has a thesis that you must put together from several sentences, you may well find that someone else who reads the essay may come up with a different thesis statement. And you both may be right. What's happening here? If

you think about how slippery words are and the different experiences that different readers bring to an essay, you can begin to see why there's more than one "correct" thesis.

17   If you were to give the same essay to ten critical readers, you might find that their versions of the thesis differ but overlap. Their readings would probably cluster around two or three central ideas. If an eleventh person read the essay and came up with a thesis that contradicted the ten other readings, that version would probably be off base. Perhaps that was the reader who almost drowned and can't take the sun.

18   For instance, Tania Nyman's "I Have a Gun" (pages 58–61) tells of the author's fear of urban violence and her ambivalent feelings about owning a handgun. After reading the essay, you may decide that Nyman's subject is handguns and that she is asserting that they are a necessary precaution in an urban environment. Another reader might focus on fear of violence as the subject and come up with a thesis that deciding to buy a handgun has made clear that most urban residents, black and white together, are bound by a net of fear. Both readings would be "correct" in that you can find adequate textual support for both versions of the thesis. Yet a reading that proposed "Everyone should buy handguns" won't work because little if any evidence in the text supports that conclusion.

Recognizing Patterns of Development

19   Once you've nailed down a thesis, go a step further to examine how that thesis is developed. Writers depend on various patterns of thought that are almost innate. To tell a joke is to *narrate*, to convey what a party was like is to *describe* and to use *examples*; to jot down a grocery list is to *divide and classify;* to figure out which car to buy is to *compare and contrast* (if you think of your old car as a peach or a lemon, you are drawing an *analogy*); to give directions is to use *process*; to consider how to improve your tennis game is to weigh *cause and effect;* to explain how you feel is to *define*. Narration, description, example, division and classification, comparison and contrast, analogy, process, cause and effect, and definition are the natural modes of thinking that writers rely upon.

20   Used singly and in combinations, these modes provide the structure of the essay, the means by which the author conveys the major point, the thesis. The qualification *in combinations* is an important

one, for rarely does an essay rely solely on one pattern of development. So far, for instance, the essay you are now reading has used definition (paragraph 5), cause and effect (paragraph 7), process (paragraph 4), and description (paragraph 5), and will use analogy (paragraph 32), and, most of all, example (virtually every paragraph). The other essays that you will read in this book also employ more than one mode, but each has been placed in a category according to the primary means of development. In fact, the whole textbook can be thought of as organized by division and classification: the essays are first divided into primary purpose—to explain or to argue—and then classified according to primary mode.

21   When you are writing, however, these modes provide ways to think about your topic as well as ways to organize your essay. With practice, they become as much second nature as shifting gears in a manual-transmission car. At first you might be a bit tentative about knowing when to shift from first to second, but with time you don't even think about it. Similarly, you might wonder if your point is clear without an example; in time, you automatically supply it.

Identifying the Purpose

22   Why would you want to tell a joke, describe a party, jot down a grocery list, compare one car to another, give directions, analyze a tennis stroke, define a feeling? That *why* is your purpose: to entertain, to inform, to persuade, to vent your feelings.

23   In writing, as in speech, your purpose determines the relationship among your subject, yourself, and your reader. Most of the writing you will be doing in college, for instance, is intended to inform. For that reason, most of the essays included in this book are expository; their purpose is to explain a subject, to inform the reader. In most of your other courses, you will find that your reading fits into this category, one occupied by stacks of textbooks. As for your writing, when you write a lab or book report, a précis, or an essay exam, you focus on your subject so that you explain it to your readers. How you feel about what was at the opposite end of the microscope or the article you are abstracting is not pertinent to your purpose; nor are you trying to persuade your reader that the essay you are writing a précis of is the best you have ever read.

24   As for the essay exam, the only persuading you are trying to do is to convince your reader that you know what you are writing about—again, the focus is on your subject. Think of textbooks, news articles, business letters, manuals, how-to books, and you will find that as you read, you are not very conscious of the writer or the style. What you are dealing with is expository writing.

25   If you do find yourself responding to the writer's personal reaction to a subject, you are probably reading a journal or diary entry, a personal letter, an opinion piece in the newspaper, or a meditative essay. In this kind of writing, the focus is on the writer. If, for example, your teacher asks you to keep a journal in which you respond to what you read, your responses may range from fury over an opinion you disagree with to mild musings on what you think about the author's subject. What is important is what you feel, and your writing expresses those feelings by communicating them clearly to your reader.

26   Conveying what you feel about a subject and persuading your reader to share your opinion, however, are two different aims. Consider the difference between a letter to the editor and an editorial, both on the 55 mph speed limit. The letter to the editor may rage against the idiots who came up with the idea and describe how stupid it is to be required to drive 55 for 150 back-country Montana miles when there isn't another car on the road. The editorial, however, considers the larger context for the law—the lives saved, the accidents avoided—and concludes that what is a minor inconvenience for some makes roads safer for many. While the writer of the letter may feel better for having let off some steam, no minds will have been changed. In fact, probably the only readers who finished that letter were those who agreed to begin with. The editorial writer, however, is careful to address a multiple audience of readers who agree, who disagree, and who have no opinion. The author's intent is to change minds, and the argument's appeal rests primarily on reason, not emotion.

27   That is also your goal when you are given a writing assignment that asks you to take a stand and defend it. You must know your audience and rely on authority, on reason, and to a lesser extent on emotion to win over those readers. Blatant persuasion hawks products on television commercials, sells political candidates, and begs you to support various causes, the more subtle variety appears in college catalogs, public debates, and the editorial pages.

All ask you to consider a certain stand, adopt a given opinion, or take an action: the writer focuses primarily on the reader.

28   Recognizing valid evidence, separating emotional appeals from appeals to reason, and spotting logical fallacies can protect you in a world of contradictory claims and high-powered propaganda. In the newspapers, on the television set, in the halls of Congress, and in your living room, issues are debated and opinions voiced. Sorting through them takes the kind of concentrated thought that reading and writing argumentative essays requires. Whether the argument is blatant or subtle, being able to recognize the techniques at work, the purpose, and the intended audience helps you evaluate assertions and illuminate their validity, whether debating a point in class or at home or reading or writing an essay for a course.

Refining the Purpose

29   Just as few essays depend solely on one pattern of organization, few depend on only one purpose, so that more often than not the reader, like the writer, will have to work at determining the primary purpose behind a piece. An effective description of an unusual scene such as a giant feedlot, for example, will not only explain what it looks, smells, and sounds like but also convey how the author feels about it and perhaps imply a need for change. While basically expository, such an essay also incorporates self-expression and persuasion. And other motives and audiences lie beneath the surface. A student, for instance, may write a paper for the simple reason that it is assigned or to get a good grade; but successful essays go beyond those immediate goals to change both reader and writer. The author learns from the act of writing because it forces the writer to examine the subject closely, to explore it, and to communicate something of interest about it. So, too, the reader learns from a good essay, perhaps finding a fresh perspective on a familiar topic or discovering information about the unfamiliar. Both reader and writer work to create meaning out of what is on the page. The result is not just sweat and knowledge, but pleasure. Good prose delights.

30   And as all who write can attest, meaning can be elusive. Knowing what one wants to write and having a fair idea of how it should be organized still does not necessarily help shape individual sentences so that they convey the desired tone. That requires draft after draft.

31   Hemingway rewrote the last page of *A Farewell to Arms* 39 times, and Katherine Anne Porter spent 20 years writing and rewriting *Ship of Fools*. Writing nonfiction doesn't make the process any easier. Wayne Booth, a distinguished essayist and scholar, speaks for most writers: "I revise many, many times, as many times as deadlines allow for. And I always feel that I would have profited from further revision." Poet, novelist, essayist, journalist, student, or professional, all continue in the tradition expressed in the eighteenth century by a fellow writer, Samuel Johnson, who said: "What is written without effort is in general read without pleasure." Pleasurable reading derives from a pleasing writing style, and though some writers strive for elegance as well as clarity, most readers will happily settle for clarity.

Writing—the Challenge

32   Far from following a recipe, writing an essay is like driving a car while at the same time trying to impress the passengers, read a road map, recognize occasional familiar landmarks, follow scrawled and muttered directions, and watch for and listen to all the quirks of the car. You know vaguely where you are going and how you want to get there, but the rest is risk and adventure. With work and a number of dry runs, you can smooth out the trip so that the passengers fully appreciate the pleasure of the drive and the satisfaction of reaching the destination. That is the challenge the writer faces, a challenge that demands critical reading as well as effective writing.

Pointers for Reading

1. **Settle in.** Gather up a good dictionary and whatever you like to write with, and then find a comfortable place to read.
2. **Think about the title.** What sort of expectations do you have about what will follow? Can you identify the subject? A thesis? Can you tell anything about the writer's tone?
3. **Look for a specific focus.** Where is the essay going? What appears to be its thesis? At what point does the introduction end and the body of the essay begin? What questions do you have about the essay so far? Is the essay directed at you? If not, who is the intended audience?
4. **Look for a predominant pattern of organization.** What are the most

important ideas in the body of the essay? Note the modes the writer uses to develop those ideas. Note those you disagree with or question.

5. **Identify the conclusion.** Where does the conclusion begin? How does it end the essay? What effect does it have on you?

6. **Evaluate the essay.** Did the essay answer the questions you had about it? How effective was the support for the main ideas? Did the writer's choice of words fit the audience? What effect did the essay have on you? Why?

Pointers for Writing

1. **Settle in.** Get hold of whatever you find comfortable to write with— computer, pen, pencil, legal pad, note paper, notebook—and settle into wherever you like to write. Start by jotting down words that represent a general idea of your subject. As words cross your mind, write them down so that at this point you have a vague focus.

2. **Focus.** Try writing right away and quickly, just getting ideas down on paper without worrying about organization or punctuation or whether what you write is "right." If you run out of steam, pause and read over what you have written and then summarize it in one sentence. Then start up again, writing as quickly as you can. At some point, you will have written your way into a tentative thesis that will help you focus as you revise what you have written.

3. **Reread.** Go over what you have written, looking for sentences that state an opinion. Mark them in some way (a highlighter is useful). These sentences can become topic sentences that lead off paragraphs and therefore help you organize your ideas.

4. **Organize what you have.** Go through what you have written, asking yourself questions: What would make a good introduction? A good conclusion? What order best suits what's in between? What examples do I have? Where would they work best?

5. **Think about your purpose.** As you reread what you've written, think about the kind of effect you want to have on your readers. Are you explaining something to them? Arguing a cause? Telling them how you feel? Entertaining them? Some combination of purposes?

6. **Think about your readers.** What do they know about your subject? Your answer to this question may make you cut out some information; and what they *don't* know will guide you to what you need to include. Do they have a bias for or against what you have to say? Your answer here will tell you if you need to account for those biases and suggest how you might do that.

7. **Revise.** You've probably been revising all along, but at this point you

can revise more thoroughly and deeply. You know your purpose, audience, and thesis—all of which will help you organize your paper more effectively.

8. **Proofread.** Now look for surface errors, checking for spelling and punctuation. If you're using a word-processing program, run your text through the spelling checker. As for punctuation, if you have access to a grammar checker on your word-processor, try it. You may find it useful, but probably a handbook of grammar and usage will be much more helpful. When using a handbook, you can find answers to your questions quickly if you look up the key word in the index.

Description

Description turns up in various guises in all types of prose, for it is the basic device a writer uses to convey sense impressions. For that reason, it is as essential to **objective**[1] writing as it is to **subjective** prose, and of course to everything in between. A quick sketch of a family gathering that you might include in a letter to a friend draws upon the same skills as a complex report on the effectiveness of a new product. Both rely on the ability to observe, to select the most important details, to create a coherent sequence for those details, and then to convey the result by appealing to the reader's senses. To describe something, then, is to re-create it in such a way that it becomes alive again, so that the reader can see and understand it. Prose that depends heavily on description invites the reader to share the writer's initial sense of vividness and perception.

The role description plays in writing will vary. Personal narratives depend heavily on description to being scenes and actions to life, to depict an outdoor wedding, for instance, or to convey what it feels like to have a toothache. Other types of **expository** essays use description in a less obvious role, perhaps to clarify a step in a process or make vivid an example. And **persuasion** often gets its punch from description, for it enables the reader to see the prisoner on death row or the crime that led to the death sentence. In each of the essays that follow, however, description dominates the structure. The essays' general subjects are familiar—a place, a person, a frog—but by selecting details, each author tailors description uniquely.

1. Words printed in boldface are defined under "useful terms" at the end of each introductory section.

AUDIENCE AND PURPOSE   Most writers start with a general sense of purpose and audience. Akers, for instance, assumes her reader is familiar with bathrooms and frogs, but she goes on to tell the tale of this particular bathroom and the frog she names Left Sink. J. Merrill-Foster, however, writes to an audience that may know little of the details of the subject—old age—and that leads the author to heap detail upon detail, to contrast past with present, and to make the reader see and feel what it is to be old. Because the audience is somewhat distant from that topic, Merrill-Foster keeps the readers on the outside, looking in.

Sue Hubbell, on the other hand, wants her readers right beside her. Although most people can identify with the idea of a farm, Hubbell creates a relationship with her audience that is intimate, describing her setting so that she places the reader in it to see with her eyes and share her thoughts. But placing the reader on the scene is a more difficult task if the scene is not part of the reader's world, and that is the problem Mario Suarez faces when he writes of "El Hoyo," a Chicano neighborhood in Tucson. To make the unfamiliar familiar, he must choose his details carefully, present them in a memorable sequence, and use what his readers know as points of comparison.

All of the writers in this chapter inform their readers, but self-expression and persuasion also enter in. The reader shares the quiet pleasure that Hubbell feels and recognizes Guarino's and Merrill-Foster's sense of admiration and Suarez's fondness for their subjects. So, too, the reader senses an argumentative edge behind Merrill-Foster's brief character sketch of an old woman.

SENSORY DETAIL   No matter what the purpose or audience, descriptive essays are characterized by their use of detail, particularly detail that appeals to the senses. Ellery Akers' account of "a small green tree frog, no bigger than a penny" whose "round, salmon-colored toes stuck out like tiny soupspoons" allows us to see what she sees, and it is vision that description appeals to most frequently. But vision rarely stands alone. Sue Hubbell's "swift, showy river to the north and a small creek to the south, its run broken by waterfalls" evokes our sense of hearing as well. Hearing also brings Akers' description to life as a place so dry that "when buckeye leaves hissed in the wind they sounded like rattlesnakes." Appeals such as these to the senses not only help the reader fix the picture in time and space but bring the scene to life so that the reader can hear, see, smell, touch, and taste it.

DICTION   The words a writer chooses determine whether the description is more objective or subjective, whether its tone is factual or impressionistic. Although total objectivity is impossible, description that leans toward the objective is called for when the writer wants to focus on subject as opposed to emotional effect, on what something *is* rather than how it felt. Compare, for example, two descriptions by J. Merrill-Foster, both on the same subject, an 85-year-old woman:

> She is frightened and distressed by letters from retired military men. They write that unless she sends $35 by return mail, the Russians will land in Oregon and take over America. The arrival of the daily mail looms large in her day. Once, every few weeks, it contains a personal letter. The rest is appeals and ads. She reads every item.
>
> I watch the woman—my mother—walking carefully down the frozen, snow-filed driveway to the mail box. She is a photograph in black and white, which only loving memory tints with stippled life and color.

The first description reports the unnamed woman's feelings and the facts that give rise to them, and then generalizes on the importance of the daily mail, noting what it contains and the attention the woman gives it. The second description uses first person and identifies the woman as the author's mother, the words *I* and *mother* forming an emotional bond between reader and writer, overlaying with feeling the picture of the woman walking to the mailbox. What then follows is the author's direct and personal comment, phrased as **metaphor** and signifying the mother's loss of power, energy, life. On finishing the first passage, the reader understands the role an everyday event—the arrival of the mail—plays in the life of an old woman; on finishing the second, the reader knows and feels how old age has diminished a once vital person.

COMPARISON   Comparisons also enrich description. Like details, they vitalize, and they can produce an arresting image, explain the unfamiliar, make a connection with the reader's own experience, or reinforce the major point in the essay. That reinforcement is what Akers is after when she describes the two frogs that live in the bathroom:

> Even before I turned on the water in the right-hand basin, I noticed a second frog, and when I stepped back to look at both of them in their respective sinks, I started to laugh: They reminded me of a couple of sober, philosophical old monks peering out of their cells.

Metaphor caps Suarez's essay as he stretches it to its limit with a closing **analogy**, comparing El Hoyo's Chicanos to the local dish capirotada.

THESIS AND ORGANIZATION   All the details, all the comparisons are presented according to a pattern so that they add up to a single dominant impression. In descriptive essays, this single dominant impression may be implicit or explicit, and it stands as the thesis. An explicit **thesis** jumps off the page at you and is usually stated openly in one or two easily identifiable sentences. An implicit thesis, however, is more subtle. As reader, you come to understand what the thesis is even though you can't identify any sentence that states it. If that process of deduction seems mysterious, think of reading a description of the ultimate pizza, a description that details its aroma, taste, texture. After reading about that pizza you would probably think to yourself, "Wow, that's a really good pizza." And that's an implied thesis.

Whether implicit or explicit, the thesis is what the writer builds the essay upon. The writer must select the most important details, build sentences and paragraphs around them, and then sequence the paragraphs so that everything not only contributes to but also helps create the thesis. In description, paragraphs can be arranged by **patterns of organization**, such as process and definition, and according to spatial, temporal, or dramatic relationships. Like Kristy Guarino, the writer can describe a scene so that the reader moves from one place to another, from the time of Guarino's first run-in with Ruthie in the Alibi Lounge to her full acknowledgment of her in the Port of Call. Guarino also takes the reader from one point in time to another, using chronology to guide the essay's organization. Hubbell, Suarez, and Merrill-Foster, however, organize their paragraphs according to a dramatic order, moving from the physical to the emotional.

USEFUL TERMS
Allusion   An indirect reference to a real or fictitious person, place, or thing.
Analogy   *Analogy* examines a subject by comparing it point by point to something seemingly unlike but more commonplace and less complex than the subject. An analogy is also an extended *metaphor*.
Exposition   Writing that explains, also called *expository writing*.
Metaphor   An implied but direct comparison in which the primary term is made more vivid by associating it with a quite dissimilar term. "Life is a roller coaster" is a metaphor.

Objective prose   Writing that is impersonal.

Patterns of organization   Paragraphs and essays are usually organized according to the patterns illustrated in this book: *description, narration, example, division and classification, comparison, process, cause and effect,* and *definition.*

Persuasion   Writing that argues a point, that attempts to persuade the reader that the writer's stand is the correct one.

Sentence fragment   An incomplete sentence, one that is missing a subject or a main verb.

Subjective prose   Writing that is personal.

Thesis   A one-sentence statement or summary of the basic arguable point of the essay.

Tone   A writer's attitude toward the subject and the audience.

Topic sentence   A statement of the topic of a paragraph that contains an arguable point that is supported by the rest of the paragraph.

IDEAS FOR WRITING   To sharpen your sense of detail, consider writing a journal entry that describes someone or some place you know well or have a strong feeling about. Write without stopping for five minutes and then use a highlighter as you look over your entry, marking any word that makes a value judgment, such *as beautiful, strong, tall,* and the like. Then revise your entry by deleting the value words and substituting details.

■ POINTERS FOR USING DESCRIPTION

Exploring the Topic

1. **What distinguishes your topic?** What characteristics, features, or actions stand out about your subject? Which are most important? Least important?
2. **What senses can you appeal to?** What can you emphasize about your subject that would appeal to sight? Smell? Touch? Taste? Motion?
3. **What concrete details can you use?** What abstract words do you associate with each of the features or events you want to emphasize? How can you make those abstractions concrete?
4. **How can you vary your narrative?** Where might you use quotations? Where might you use dialogue?
5. **What can your audience identify with?** What comparisons can you use? What similes, metaphors, allusions come to mind?

6. **What order should you use?** Is your description best sequenced by time? Place? Dramatic order?
7. **What is your tentative thesis?** What is the dominant impression you want to create? Do you want it to be implicit? Explicit?
8. **What is your relationship to your subject?** Given your tentative thesis, how objective or subjective should you be? Do you want to be part of the action or removed? What personal pronoun should you use?

Drafting the Paper

1. **Know your reader.** If you are writing about a familiar object, ask yourself what your reader might not know about it. If you are writing about an unfamiliar subject, ask yourself what your reader does know that you can use for comparison.
2. **Know your purpose.** If you are writing to inform, make sure you are presenting new information and in enough detail to bring your subject to life. If you are writing to persuade, make sure your details add up so that the reader is moved to adopt your conviction. Keep in mind that your reader may not share your values and indeed may even hold opposite ones.
3. **Pile on sensory detail.** Don't settle for vague adjectives such as "tall"; replace them with sharper details such as "6 feet 7 inches." Emphasize important details by appealing to the senses.
4. **Show, don't tell.** Avoid abstract terms (*funny, beautiful*) in favor of concrete details, quotations, dialogue.
5. **Use comparisons.** Make your description vivid with an occasional metaphor or simile. If you are writing about something quite unfamiliar, use literal comparison to make your description clear.
6. **Arrange your details to create a single dominant impression.** If you are writing descriptive paragraphs, check the order of your sentences to make sure they follow each other logically and support the impression you wish to create. If you are writing a descriptive essay, check for the same points. Is your topic sentence or thesis implicit or explicit? For a descriptive essay, reexamine your first paragraph. Does it establish the scene? The tone?

here I Live

Sue Hubbell

This essay appeared as the foreword to Sue Hubbell's book A Country Year: Living the Questions *(HarperCollins, 1987), an account of her year on her farm, raising bees and gathering honey. The questions she explores in that book are those mentioned at the end of the essay. A self-taught naturalist, Hubbell has an acute eye for detail.*

WHAT TO LOOK FOR *Sentence variety gives prose a change of pace, but often students are afraid to write a long sentence for fear of making mistakes. Next time you draft an essay, try at least one sentence that is considerably longer than your others. Look, for example, how Hubbell controls the list she gives in her last paragraph by stringing together clauses beginning with* that.

KEY WORDS AND PHRASES
marginal (2)   *peninsula (3)*

1   There are three big windows that go from floor to ceiling on the south side of my cabin. I like to sit in the brown leather chair in the twilight of winter evenings and watch birds at the feeder that stretches across them. The windows were a gift from my husband before he left the last time. He had come and gone before, and we were not sure that this would be the last time, although I suspected that it was.

2   I have lived here in the Ozark Mountains of southern Missouri for twelve years now, and for most of that time I have been alone. I have learned to run a business that we started together, a commercial beekeeping and honey-producing operation, a shaky, marginal sort of affair that never quite leaves me free of money worries but which allows me to live in these hills that I love.

3   My share of the Ozarks is unusual and striking. My farm lies two hundred and fifty feet above a swift, showy river to the north and a small creek to the south, its run broken by waterfalls. Creek and river join just to the east, so I live on a peninsula of land. The back fifty acres are covered with second-growth timber, and I take my

firewood there. Last summer when I was cutting firewood, I came across a magnificent black walnut, tall and straight, with no jutting branches to mar its value as a timber tree. I don't expect to sell it, although even a single walnut so straight and unblemished would fetch a good price, but I cut some trees near it to give it room. The botanic name for black walnut is *Juglans nigra*—"Black Nut Tree of God," a suitable name for a tree of such dignity, and I wanted to give it space.

4   Over the past twelve years I have learned that a tree needs space to grow, that coyotes sing down by the creek in January, that I can drive a nail into oak only when it is green, that bees know more about making honey than I do, that love can become sadness, and that there are more questions than answers.

Thesis and Organization

1. *Setting* is a term that includes time, place, and objects. Given that definition, what is the setting in paragraph 1?
2. What else do you learn about the setting in paragraph 2?
3. Paragraph 3 begins with a topic sentence. List the details that support the idea that the particular setting is "unusual and striking."
4. Given the setting in paragraphs 1–3 and the topic sentence you would provide for paragraph 4, what is the essay's thesis?

Technique and Style

1. Hubbell often uses an adjective that she then fleshes out with details. Cite one or two examples. Are the details sufficient? How or how not?
2. What emotion does the essay convey? Is the author sad, happy, resigned, triumphant, or what?
3. What do the thesis and tone lead you to expect in the pages that followed this foreword? Would you like to read on? Why or why not?
4. Draw a map of the farm based on the description in paragraph 3. How precise is the description?

Suggestions for Writing

Using Hubbell's essay as a close model, write your own "Where I Live." Describe where you usually sit or spend most of your time, what you see from that perspective, the immediate area around your house or apartment, the length of time you've lived there, and then list selectively what you've learned.

A Confederacy of Friends

Kristy Guarino

The title of the essay is an allusion to A Confederacy of Dunces, *a novel by John Kennedy Toole set in New Orleans. New Orleans is also where tourists flock to the French Quarter—also known as the "Vieux Carré" or old square, formed by streets named Decatur, Canal, Rampart, and Esplanade—wander around Jackson Square, and drink hurricanes at Pat O'Brien's bar. The Quarter is also the setting for Kristy Guarino's description of a well-known local character. As you might suspect from reading the essay, Kristy Guarino is a native New Orleanian who knows the French Quarter well. She is also a former "drop-in drop-out" student going for a record two-years straight enrollment at the University of New Orleans. She is currently a junior, as she puts it, "majoring in majoring."*

WHAT TO LOOK FOR *You'll find that the essay reads as though the writer is talking to you, an effect achieved at the expense of a few rules of formal written English. The principle that allows a writer to break rules is one of appropriateness. A formal essay that described this person would be more of a case history than a portrait of a person. Be on the lookout for fragments, slang, and unusual punctuation.*

KEY WORDS AND PHRASES

TKE, ATO (3)	riled (3)
routinely (5)	disoriented (7)
mischievous (22)	acknowledge (23)

1   "Get off my sidewalk," she mutters, as someone passes her, slouched curbside against a stop sign on Bourbon and Dumaine. Her head hangs as though she hasn't the strength or need to lift it. Hidden beneath a dingy pile of polyester, she drags her fingertips across the leather of her face, which she shifts slowly, side-to-side, as her lips scrunch roundabout as if she's talking to someone. But no one is there.

2   She gets up, staggering. Then stands—and stands tall (though she barely measures five feet in height). Better move, . . . or she'll move you.

3   I should know. Pushed me clear off a bar stool once. Cursed me too. I was sitting in the Alibi Lounge on Iberville, drinking with some friends. Wasn't the usual food and beverage crowd; too early in the evening, I guess. Mostly college frats—spread out wall-to-wall, wearing tee-shirts advertising TKE's Carnival Cruise Night, ATO's Beach Blanket Bonsai Bash (whatever that might be). A rowdy bunch; chanting fight songs between funnelling beers and shooting vodka slammers; slapping high-fives for any reason what-soever; paying no mind to the hunched-over pile of polyester lurking in the back of the club. But they managed to get her riled up as well. While forcing her way to the bar, she stumbled over, jabbed me in the side with her elbow, and told me to get the hell away. I did. No problem. I didn't mind standing. Anyway, my friends got a laugh out of it, saying, "That's Ruthie for ya'."

4   They were right. That is Ruthie.

5   But no one in the French Quarter remembers when she first appeared, and yet no one can imagine the streets and bars of the Vieux Carré without her. Like a doctor on rounds, Ruthie, "The Duck Lady," routinely curses and knocks her way about—somehow capturing the hearts of many locals, making herself as much a landmark as Jackson Square and Pat O'Brien's.

6   Rumors make up Ruthie's past. Tales of wealth and eccentricity spread throughout the Quarter. How she comes from money; how her family owned prime real estate on Bourbon Street, right across from Lafitte's Blacksmith Shop. Supposedly, when her parents died and the property was sold, Ruthie inherited a fortune, and now she parades about the streets doing whatever she pleases.

7   And parade she does. All over. From Esplanade to Canal. From Decatur to Rampart. Aimlessly going to who-knows-where or why. These outings only fuel up rumors of mental illness, leading some people to believe she's sick and disoriented. Warren, a bartender at Lafitte's, remembers Ruthie having a "half-wit" brother, but says "It's anybody's guess. Even though everyone may know of Ruthie, no one person knows too much about her."

8   And some prefer not to. Like Warren. "I don't know if she's rich, mental, or what. And I could care less. To me, she's just a disgusting old drunkard."

9   Others dismiss the rumors entirely. One local guy doesn't even worry about it; he enjoys believing she has just "sprung out the

concrete." Although Ruthie's past remains a mystery, everyone does know how she earned her trademark name.

10   For years, Ruthie would dress in a battered wedding gown and floppy hat and go roller skating along the streets of the Quarter with a duck training her. Locals joke that "wherever Ruthie went, that duck was sure to go." And go it did—everywhere from mass at St. Louis Cathedral to the corner grocery. The clerk at Grandad's General Store remembers Ruthie coming in—especially when the duck would "squirt all over the place." Wasn't one particular duck, though. Seems Ruthie had a number of them over time; and often, when one died, she'd skate around with it cradled in her arms. People must have complained, because the police finally forced her to get rid of them. That didn't stop her. She still carries a duck—a stuffed one. But a duck no less.

11   Now, Ruthie, "The Duck Lady," celebrates celebrity status. *Gambit* and WGNO television featured her in articles and specials centering on New Orleans. Her image, captured on film, canvas, and postcards, represents the French Quarter.

12   Which is sometimes hard to understand—considering how much she likes her Budweiser. But, like a celebrity, Ruthie gets catered to, watched over, and even forgiven. Merchants and vendors sneak food out to her, bartenders and waiters hand over spare change. She rarely pays for a thing. Paul, manager of Lafitte's, believes that "if we lose Ruthie, we lose the Quarter. She's the cornerstone." And he watches out for her. When she's had too much to drink (which is most of the time), he'll get someone to walk her home. She lives only a few bocks from Lafitte's, right off Esplanade, on Dauphine. But he won't chance her safety. "Means too much to us. If anybody would try to hurt her, the whole Quarter would come out of the woodwork."

13   Except Warren. Unlike Paul, he won't let her in the bar. "No way." But if Paul is tending bar, he doesn't mind. He can handle her. "She was in here the other day, kicking some tourists. I just raised my voice, told her to sit her ass down and behave. She listens. I think I'm the only bartender here she hasn't slugged." The majority of locals, like Paul, put up with her. "No one wants to break her spirit," Paul says. "That's just Ruthie."

14   And he's right. That is Ruthie—at least sometimes.

15   I should know. Saw it with my own eyes. I was sitting in Port of Call, drinking with some friends. Was the usual local crowd, with a

few tourists sipping on monsoons, paying no mind to the lady sitting at the bar. Why should they mind? Nothing strange about her. Dressed neatly in a black lace gown that draped to the ground, she was covered by a red, tapered peacoat with a shiny, red floppy hat. Pinned at the flap with a black carnation.

16   "It can't be her." I kept repeating. My friends got a laugh out of it, saying, "Well, it is Sunday."

17   I didn't buy it. *"Can't be her—her clothes match."* And she just sat, drinking her Budweiser, bothering no one.

18   I kept watching her. I was amazed and confused at the same time. Then, from the back of the bar, a loud voice started singing along with the jukebox: "I'm just a gigolo, and everywhere I go. . . ."

19   The lady at the bar just lowered her head as the voice grew louder and more off-key with every note being sung.

20   "Miss Ruthie," the voice hollered, as a man swayed over to the lady. Placing his arm around her, he asked, "What's the matter? You like my singin', don't you?"

21   Eagerly, I watched. It was Ruthie. I just knew she was gonna sock him in the jaw. But she didn't.

22   Instead, she looked at the bartender, flashing a grin so hard and wide her rosy cheeks almost slammed her eyes shut. That's when I saw her. For the first time, I was really seeing Ruthie; seeing the sparkle in her eyes; seeing her as many locals must—like a child. A kid at heart and at play. Both mischievous and innocent at the same time. That's Ruthie.

23   Before I left Port of Call, I sent her down a Budweiser. She didn't acknowledge me. I didn't expect her to, and I didn't care. I just wanted to join in on the confederacy of friends she has here in the Quarter.

Thesis and Organization

1. What information is supplied by the introduction, paragraphs 1–4?
2. What connects paragraphs 5–8? 9–14? 15–22?
3. Which details most effectively create the picture of Ruthie?
4. Guarino uses a framing device to begin and end her essay. Summarize it.
5. Like many essays that describe people, this one shows rather than tells. One example of that technique is Guarino's use of an implied thesis. State that thesis in your own words.

Technique and Style

1. What does the author's interaction with Ruthie lend to the essay?
2. Paragraphs 3, 7–10, 12, 13, and 17–20 use dialogue. How many different people are quoted? What reasons can you think of for using that many?
3. The pace and tone of the essay are affected by the intentional use of fragment. Choose one and convert it into a full sentence. What is gained or lost?
4. What reasons can you think of for delaying the information about Ruthie's nickname?
5. Guarino depends heavily on details of the local setting. How necessary do you find the references to street names, people, and places? In what ways do they add to or detract from the essay?

Suggestions for Writing

Almost every neighborhood, family, school, or business has at least one "character." Think of one you know and write down what that person looks like as well as any distinctive dress, statements, and behavior. Think, too, of the setting the person is in and how it contrasts or serve as a backdrop. Also note how other people react to the person, and try to record a range of responses. When you write your draft, consider how conversational you want to be and whether or not dialogue would add to the essay.

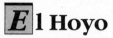l Hoyo

Mario Suarez

In "El Hoyo," Mario Suarez faces a problem common to many writers: how to describe something so that readers who have little knowledge of a subject will nonetheless be able to see and understand it. Suarez's problem is double, for most of his readers will not only be unfamiliar with barrios but also with Latino culture. The neighborhood Suarez describes existed in 1947, but since then many similar ones have sprung up all over the United States. The essay was originally published in the Arizona Quarterly *(1947).*

WHAT TO LOOK FOR   *Repetition of a word or phrase can be very effective if used intentionally, lending emphasis to a paragraph. When you read Suarez's second paragraph, read it out loud so you can more clearly hear the repetition.*

KEY WORDS AND PHRASES
adobe (1)	*chavalos (1)*
solace (2)	*crusaded (2)*
boleros (3)	*conquistador (3)*
panocha (4)	

1   From the center of downtown Tucson the ground slopes gently away to Main Street, drops a few feet, and then rolls to the banks of the Santa Cruz River. Here lies the section of the city known as El Hoyo. Why it is called El Hoyo is not very clear. In no sense is it a hole as its name would imply; it is simply the river's immediate valley. Its inhabitants are chicanos who raise hell on Saturday night and listen to Padre Estanislao on Sunday morning. While the term chicano is the short way of saying Mexicano, it is not restricted to the paisanos who came from old Mexico with the territory or the last famine to work for the railroad, labor, sing, and go on relief. Chicano is the easy way of referring to everybody. Pablo Gutíerrez married the Chinese grocer's daughter and now runs a meat department; his sons are chicanos. So are the sons of Killer Jones who threw a fight in Harlem and fled to El Hoyo to marry

Cristina Mendez. And so are all of them. However, it is doubtful that all these spiritual sons of Mexico live in El Hoyo because they love each other—many fight and bicker constantly. It is doubtful they live in El Hoyo because of its scenic beauty—it is everything but beautiful. Its houses are simple affairs of unplastered adobe, wood, and abandoned car parts. Its narrow streets are mostly clearings which have, in time, acquired names. Except for some tall trees which nobody has ever cared to identify, nurse, or destroy, the main things known to grow in the general area are weeds, garbage piles, dark-eyed chavalos, and dogs. And it is doubtful that the chicanos live in El Hoyo because it is safe—many times the Santa Cruz has risen and inundated the area.

2   In other respects living in El Hoyo has its advantages. If one is born with weakness for acquiring bills, El Hoyo is where the collectors are less likely to find you. If one has acquired the habit of listening to Octavio Perea's Mexican Hour in the wee hours of the morning with the radio on at full blast, El Hoyo is where you are less likely to be reported to the authorities. Besides, Perea is very popular and sooner or later to everyone "Smoke in the Eyes" is dedicated between the pinto beans and white flour commercials. If one, for any reason whatever, comes on an extended period of hard times, where, if not in El Hoyo, are the neighbors more willing to offer solace? When Teofila Malacara's house burned to the ground with all her belongings and two children, a benevolent gentleman carried through the gesture that made tolerable her burden. He made a list of 500 names and solicited from each a dollar. At the end of a month he turned over to the tearful but grateful señora $100 in cold cash and then accompanied her on a short vacation. When the new manager of a local store decided that no more chicanas were to work behind the counters, it was the chicanos of El Hoyo who, on taking their individually small but collectively great buying power elsewhere, drove the manager out and the girls returned to their jobs. When the Mexican Army was en route to Baja California and the chicanos found out that the enlisted men ate only at infrequent intervals, it was El Hoyo's chicanos who crusaded across town with pots of beans and trays of tortillas to meet the train. When someone gets married, celebrating is not restricted to the immediate friends of the couple. Everybody is invited. Anything calls for a celebration and a celebration calls for anything. On Memorial Day there are no less than half a dozen

good fights at the Riverside Dance Hall. On Mexican Independence Day more than one flag is sworn allegiance to amid cheers for the queen.

3   And El Hoyo is something more. It is this something more which brought Felipe Suarez back from the wars after having killed a score of Vietnamese with his body resembling a patchwork quilt to marry Julia Armijo. It brought Joe Zepeda, a gunner, . . . back to compose boleros. He has a metal plate for a skull. Perhaps El Hoyo is proof that those people exist, and perhaps exist best, who have as yet failed to observe the more popular modes of human conduct. Perhaps the humble appearance of El Hoyo justifies the indifferent shrug of those made aware of its existence. Perhaps El Hoyo's simplicity motivates an occasional chicano to move away from its narrow streets, babbling comadres and shrieking children to deny the bloodwell from which he springs and to claim the blood of a conquistador while his hair is straight and his face beardless. Yet El Hoyo is not an outpost of a few families against the world. It fights for no causes except those which soothe its immediate angers. It laughs and cries with the same amount of passion in times of plenty and of want.

4   Perhaps El Hoyo, its inhabitants, and its essence can best be explained by telling a bit about a dish called capirotada. Its origin is uncertain. But, according to the time and the circumstance, it is made of old, new or hard bread. It is softened with water and then cooked with peanuts, raisins, onions, cheese, and panocha. It is fired with sherry wine. Then it is served hot, cold, or just "on the weather" as they say in El Hoyo. The Sermeños like it one way, the Garcias another, and the Ortegas still another. While it might differ greatly from one home to another, nevertheless it is still capirotada. And so it is with El Hoyo's chicanos. While being divided from within and from without, like the capirotada, they remain chicanos.

Thesis and Organization

1. Examine the essay using the standard journalistic questions. Which paragraph describes *where* El Hoyo is? What paragraphs describe *who* lives there? What paragraph or paragraphs describe *how* they live? *Why* they live there?

2. All of the questions above lead to a larger one: *What* is El Hoyo? Given the people and place, and how and why they live there, what statement is the author making about El Hoyo?
3. The essay ends with an analogy, and toward the end of paragraph 4, Suarez spells out some details of the analogy. What other characteristics of capirotada correspond to those of chicanos? Where in the essay do you find evidence for your opinion?
4. How would you describe the movement in the essay? Does it move from the general to the particular? From the particular to the general? What reasons can you give for the author's choice of direction?
5. In one sentence, state Suarez's opinion of El Hoyo.

Technique and Style

1. The introductory paragraph achieves coherence and cohesion through the author's use of subtle unifying phrases. Trace Suarez's use of "it is doubtful." How often does the phrase occur? Rewrite the sentences to avoid using the phrase. What is lost? Gained?
2. What key words are repeated in paragraph 2? Why does he repeat them?
3. Paragraph 2 gives many examples of the advantages of living in El Hoyo. List the examples in the order in which they appear. The first two can be grouped together under the idea of El Hoyo as a sanctuary, a place where people aren't bothered. What other groupings does the list of examples suggest? What principle appears to have guided the ordering of the examples?
4. Why might the author have chosen not to use either first or second person? What is gained by using "one?"

Suggestions for Writing

If you live in an ethnic neighborhood, you can adopt the essay as a close model. If you do not, however, you can still use the essay as a general model by choosing a topic that combines people and place, such as a characteristic family ritual at Christmas or Hanukkah or Thanksgiving, or a representative time at the university student center or neighborhood restaurant.

F rightened by Loss

J. Merrill-Foster

By combining the objective with the subjective, the particular with the general, and the past with the present, the author sets out a compelling picture of old age. The essay was published in the New York Times *in 1988.*

WHAT TO LOOK FOR *Metaphor can lend vividness and emphasis to your writing. Note, for example, how Merrill-Foster's concluding metaphor wraps up the whole essay, allowing the reader to see the difference between past and present.*

KEY WORDS AND PHRASES

traceries (1)	*importuned (2)*
civility (13)	*jousting (17)*
stippled (18)	

1   Her walk is slow, hesitant, leaning slightly forward from the waist. Her hands, swollen and misshapen with arthritis, have traceries of blue veins across the back. They are never still.

2   She often interrupts to ask what we are talking about. The telephone seems to confuse her; she thinks the ringing is on the television. She calls us to report that she has lost her Christmas card list. It turns up on her desk, hidden under a pile of appeals. She is on every mailing list there is, and is constantly importuned to "Save the whales" and "Stop the Japanese slaughter of dolphins."

3   She is frightened and distressed by letters from retired military men. They write that unless she sends $35 by return mail, the Russians will land in Oregon and take over America. The arrival of the daily mail looms large in her day. Once, every few weeks, it contains a personal letter. The rest is appeals and ads. She reads every item.

4   Her checkbook is a constant puzzle of missing entries and double deposits of retirement checks. She goes out to do an errand and cannot find the place—a place she's frequented for years. She telephones to say the furnace door has exploded open; the kindly

repair man arrives at 10 P.M. to check and assure her that all is well. She tells you about it, not because there is anything needing to be done. She tells you in order to make you understand that life is out of control—that there is a conspiracy of inanimate objects afoot.

5   Often, if you suggest this or that solution, she is annoyed. She wasn't asking for a solution. She was merely reporting disaster. She sits down to read and falls asleep.

6   America's life style prepares us well for our first day at school, for adolescence, for college, for matrimony, for parenthood, for middle age, for retirement. But it prepares us not at all for old age. Busy and active until her seventy-eighth year, the woman, now 85, is frightened by her own loss of power.

7   "Why am I so tired all the time?" she asks.

8   "I couldn't figure out how to turn on the dashboard lights."

9   "I look at the snow and wonder how I'll live through the winter."

10   "I think I must light the wood stove. I'm so cold."

11   I do not see the woman as she is today. I look at her familiar face and see her on a stage, floating up a flight of stairs in *Arsenic and Old Lace,* with that skilled power in her knees that made her seem to glide form one step to another. I hear her speak and remember her light but lovely contralto singing Katisha in *The Mikado.*

12   I watch her sleeping in her chair, her head on her chest, and remember her pacing up and down an English classroom, reading aloud from Beowulf, bringing to life the monster Grendel for a class of 16-year-olds. I remember late winter afternoons, fortified with hot cocoa, sitting on the floor at her feet, listening to "The Ballad of the White Horse," *Don Quixote* and *King Lear.*

13   I remember her as a young widow, coming home from school and pulling three children through the snow on a sled. I remember always the summer jobs when school was let out, selling life insurance or encyclopedias, or studying remedial reading at New York University. I remember her as a bride the second time, and the second time a widow. Hers was the home the family came to, a place of books, a big, old house where civility was spoken.

14   There is some rage in aging—a disbelief that one's life has rounded its last curve and this stretch of road leads to death. She has always been a woman of strong faith, and it seems that faith at last has failed her. She quotes Claudius in *Hamlet:*

15   "My words fly up, my thoughts remain below;

16   Words without thoughts never to heaven go."

17   Widowed, alone, children and grandchildren flung wide from California to New England, she fills her days with little things. Socializing fatigues her. She withdraws from the intense conversational jousting that used to delight her.

18   I watch the woman—my mother—walking carefully down the frozen, snow-filled driveway to the mail box. She is a photograph in black and white, which only loving memory tints with stippled life and color.

Thesis and Organization

1. Paragraph 1 describes the woman physically, and paragraphs 2–5 describe her psychologically, both leading up to the concluding sentence of paragraph 6. What details in paragraphs 1–5 relate to the idea of being "frightened by her own loss of power"?

2. Test out the assertions in the first two sentences of paragraph 6. To what extent do they hold true in the experience of you and your family? Are the assertions valid?

3. Paragraphs 7–10 use quotations from the present to illustrate the generalization that ends paragraph 6 and to set up the shift to the past that takes place in paragraphs 11–13, while paragraphs 14–18 return to the present. Do you find the essay's chronology effective or ineffective? How so?

4. How would you characterize the author's feelings for the old woman? What evidence can you cite to support your ideas?

5. Where in the essay do you find the author generalizing upon old age? What generalization is being made about the author's mother? About old age? Putting the two generalizations together, how would you express the thesis of the essay?

Technique and Style

1. The author alludes to a play and an operetta (11) and to an epic, a poem, a novel, and a play (12). What do these allusions imply about the author's mother? What do they contribute to her characterization—the person she was then and the person she is now?

2. In a standard dictionary, look up *pity* and *empathy*. Which does the author feel for the old woman? Which does the writer evoke in you? Cite examples to support your opinion.

3. You will note that throughout the essay the author never refers to the old woman by name. What is the effect of using a pronoun instead? What effect is achieved by holding off identifying her as "my mother"?

4. Examine paragraph 13 for details. What do they imply about the author's mother? How do those characteristics compare with those you can deduce from paragraphs 7–10? What does this contrast achieve?

5. The essay concludes with a metaphor. Rephrase the metaphor into your own words and explain how that statement supports the thesis of the essay.

Suggestions for Writing

Think of someone you know who typifies a certain age, occupation, or region. In a character sketch, describe that person so that you report the qualities that make up the individual and also generalize about the larger category that the person represents. Rely on quotation as well as description to create the overall impression you wish to make.

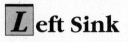eft Sink

Ellery Akers

A writer and naturalist who lives in San Francisco, Ellery Akers is also a poet. Knocking on the Earth, *her first book of poems, was published in 1989 by Wesleyan University Press. As you read the essay, you'll discover her prose reflects a number of characteristics of poetry—imagery, concise language, and an acute eye for detail. You'll also see that the line between description and narration is a fine one. The essay won the 1990 Sierra Club Award for nature-writing and was published the same year in* Sierra. *While the essay is longer than most in this book, you'll find its length is deceptive. You'll read it quickly.*

WHAT TO LOOK FOR   Detail *is what stands out about Akers' essay. Many writers, for instance, would simply write "The frog was small." Akers, however, takes that word* small *and gives it substance, "no bigger than a penny, and his round, salmon-colored toes stuck out like tiny soupspoons." Remember as you write that one person's idea of a general term, such as* small, *may not be the same as another's, so it's best instead to use details to show just what you mean.*

KEY WORDS AND PHRASES
porcelain (1)	*looming (4)*
chaparral (6)	*seep (7)*
algae (7)	*staccato (8)*
hibernation (10)	*respective (11)*
Buddha (12)	*geometrical (15)*
terrarium (16)	*repertoire (17)*
abyss (18)	*skittish (20)*
Quasimodo (20)	*pupating (25)*
curdled (37)	*towhees (39)*

1   The first time I saw Left Sink I was brushing my teeth and almost spit on him. I wasn't expecting to find a frog in a Park Service bathroom, but there he was, hopping out of the drain and squatting on the porcelain as casually as if he were sitting beside a pond.

2   He was a small green tree frog, no bigger than a penny, and his round, salmon-colored toes stuck out like tiny soupspoons. For a few minutes I stared into his gold eyes, each pupil floating in the middle like a dark seed.

3   I was so close I could see his throat pulse, but I was probably too close, for he looked at me fearfully and leaped onto the silver "C" of the cold-water faucet.

4   Then he must have thought better of it, for he jumped down again, and sat, hunched over, by the soap. He kept making nervous little hops toward the safety of the drain, but my looming face was obviously in the way, so I ducked below the basin for a moment, and when I looked again he was descending into the hole, head first.

5   Feeling I'd disturbed his evening hunt, I decided to make amends. I grubbed around the floor for a dead moth, found one (though it was a little dried up), and offered it to the hole. The wing slanted into the drain, but nothing happened. I thought perhaps he'd hopped back down into the pipe. Trying to find something a little more appealing, I picked around the window sills until I discovered a really decent-looking moth, pushed it up to the drain, and waited. After a few minutes, I got discouraged and walked away. When I turned back to sneak one last look, I found both moths had vanished.

6   The next day was so hot I forgot Left sink completely. It is always hot in the California chaparral in September, especially in the Gabilan Mountains. I spent the afternoon in the shade, lying on the cool pebbles of a dry wash and looking over my field notes. I had been camping for weeks, studying birds, and by now I had gotten used to the feeling of expectation in the landscape.

7   Everything seemed to be waiting for rain. The streambeds were dry, the fields were dry, and when the buckeye leaves hissed in the wind they sounded like rattlesnakes. Ravens flew overhead, croaking, their wings flapping loudly in the air, and the rocks baked. Once in a while a few thirsty finches fluttered up to a seep in a cliff and sipped from a damp clump of algae.

8   I leaned against the cool flank of a boulder and fanned myself with my hat. From far away I could hear the staccato drill of a Nuttall's woodpecker.

9   All the animals had some way of coping with the heat. The wrentits could last for several weeks without drinking. The deer

found beds of shade and waited patiently until evening. Even the trees adapted. Though I couldn't see it, I knew that somewhere beneath my boots, 100 feet down, the root of a digger pine was twisting along a crevice in the bedrock, reaching far below the surface to tap into the permanent water.

10   And the frogs—the normal ones—were sleeping away the summer and fall, huddled in some moist spot in the ground in a kind of hot-weather hibernation.

11   That night, when I went back to the bathroom, I discovered Left Sink had a neighbor. Even before I turned on the water in the right-hand basin, I noticed a second frog, and when I stepped back to look at both of them in their respective sinks, I started to laugh: They reminded me of a couple of sober, philosophical old monks peering out of their cells.

12   Overhead was a third frog, puffy and well-fed, squatting on top of the fluorescent lights, surrounded by tattered moths. Light Buddha, I would call him.

13   In the world of the bathroom the light shelf was a delicatessen of the highest order. Light Buddha sat there night after glorious night, lazily snapping up moths as they fluttered past. The other two frogs seemed content to stake out the sinks, which weren't quite as dependable a food source, though they weren't bad. Almost every night I found a damp moth thrashing around in one of the basins, one little flopping death after another, leaving a trail of scales behind.

14   Right Sink was extremely shy, and spent most of his time crouched far back in the pipe. Usually I saw his gold eyes shining in the darkness, but that was all. Left Sink was more of an adventurer, and explored the whole bathroom, darting behind the mirror, splatting onto the porcelain, hopping on the window sills, leaping on the toilet, and climbing the slippery painted walls toe pad by toe pad.

15   From time to time I was tempted to pick him up as he was climbing. But I didn't think it would be fair; I knew this geometrical universe, and he didn't. Besides, there was no place for him to hide on those smoothe, painted bricks, so I let him be.

16   I was amazed at how few people noticed Left Sink, even when he was sitting on top of the faucet. Kids saw him right away, though, and I worried sometimes that one night a little girl would pop him into a jar and take him home to some confining terrarium.

17   Also, he stood out. Even though tree frogs can change color in ten minutes, there was nothing in Left Sink's repertoire that could possibly match white paint; the best he could do was a sickly pink.

18   I could always tell if he had just emerged from the drain because he would still be a murky gray-green. As the evening wore on he got paler and paler. Once I couldn't find him for half an hour. Finally I caught sight of him over my head. Plopped on a narrow ledge, he looked like a pale pebble in all that metal and paint. I climbed onto the toilet for a better look. To my horror he began hopping along the ledge, which was no wider than half an inch. It was a ten-foot fall to the floor—for a frog that small, an abyss. He bounded past me, his grainy throat quivering.

19   He headed toward a swarm of moths and flies that circled the fluorescent lights. A fly drifted down from the glare; Left sink, his pink mouth flashing, snapped it up.

20   I was never quite sure just how skittish he really was. Sometimes he tolerated my watching him, sometimes he didn't. I got in the habit of sidling up to the plumbing, bent over so as not to be seen, and I must have looked pretty peculiar. One night a woman came into the bathroom and caught me hunched over like Quasimodo, staring intently at the drains, my hands full of dead moths.

21   "Left Sink! Right Sink!" I was saying. "Got a little treat for you guys!"

22   The woman bolted out the door.

23   For the next few weeks I checked on the frogs every morning and evening. Sometimes when I saw Left Sink skidding down a length of plastic, unable to hold on in spite of his adhesive toe pads, I worried. I couldn't help thinking there was something unnatural about a frog in a bathroom.

24   Of course, I knew there were a few oddballs that *had* managed to live with us in our artificial world, but they were mostly insects. One year in school I had learned about the larvae of petroleum flies: They lived in the gunk of oil fields, so numerous at times that, according to my textbook, they imparted "a shimmering effect to the surface of the oil." Their world was oil; if you deprived them of it, took them out and cleaned them off, they'd curl up and die in less than a day.

25   In that same class I'd learned that furniture beetles live in our table legs, and occasionally, in wooden spoons; drugstore beetles

float happily in bottles of belladonna, mating, pupating, dying. We have cheese mites in our cheese, and flour mites in our flour.

26   As far as I knew no one had ever done any research on frogs and plumbing. Luckily, I always carried a trunkful of books and field guides in my car, and one night I flipped through every book I had to see if I could find any instances where humans and animals—wild ones—had actually gotten along. Arthur Cleveland Bent said that wrens nested in old clothes in barns, and swallows on moving trains. Edwin Way Teale said he had once read about a pigeon using rubber bands and paper clips in her nest on a window ledge off Times Square. One year, he wrote, a thrush spent the entire winter in a florist's shop on Madison Avenue, flitted about between the iced gladiolas and roses, and flew away in spring.

27   But no one mentioned anything about frogs.

28   Actually, considering the drought, Left Sink had a pretty good set-up. It was already October and still no rain. Once in a while a few drops would plop into the dirt and gravel, and I would catch a whiff of wet dust, soaked cheat grass, and buckwheat. But that was all.

29   All the other frogs were holed up in the dirt, huddled in a moist crack or an abandoned gopher hole, waiting for the first rains of winter to wake them up. There were probably a few hiding in the field next to Left Sink's bathroom, their eyelids closed, their toes pulled under them to conserve moisture, unmoving, barely breathing, their heartbeats almost completely stilled. If I dug them up they would look like small stones.

30   One night just before I was about to leave, I had a nightmare. It was a dream I had had many times, a dream of a city so polluted the air rose in black plumes above the granite and cement. I was at the entrance of a tunnel. Inside I could hear a whoosh of air: Millions of butterflies were flashing in the dark, thousands of ducks, eagles, sparrows, their wings making a vast rustling as they flew off and vanished.

31   I heard a low shuffling. After a while I realized it was the sound of feet: the slow trudge of bears, the pad of badgers, the pattering of foxes, the rasp of a hundred million beetles, rabbits, ants, mice. I looked around, panicked, to see if any animals were left. There were still cockroaches scuttling over the window sills. There were pigeons, flies, starlings. I named them over and over in a kind of

chant: the adaptable, the drab, the ones who could live with us, who had always lived with us.

32   A fox coughed close to my camp in the middle of the nightmare and woke me up. I unzipped the tent and looked out at the stars: Rigel, Algol, clear, cold, and changeless. A golden-crowned sparrow chirped from a nearby branch, then sputtered off into silence. For a while I tried to stay awake, but soon drifted off.

33   The next morning huge bluish clouds rolled across the sky. A couple of ravens sailed past the cliff in front of me. One of them jackknifed its wings, plummeted straight down, and then, at the last minute, unfolded them and flapped away. It was still early, but when I reached the bathroom it had already been cleaned. It reeked of ammonia, and a mop and bucket leaned against the door.

34   I rinsed off my face, brushed my hair, and looked sleepily into the drains. As usual, Right Sink was huddled far back into the dark pipe; he retreated still further when I bent over.

35   Left Sink, however, was gone. I wondered if he had slipped behind the mirror, or had come up in the world and was squatting above with Light Buddha. The shelf was empty. I looked on the window sill—not there either.

36   It was not until I opened the door to the toilet that I found him. There, in the center of the ammonia-filled bowl, his green bloated body turning gray, was Left Sink, splayed out in the milky liquid, dead. Floating in front of him was a dead damselfly. I suppose he must have jumped in after his prey, convinced he was at the edge of a strange-looking pond, his toe pads gripping the cold, perfectly smooth surface of the porcelain.

37   His skin looked curdled, and it occurred to me he might have been there all morning waiting to die. Then I remembered that frogs breathe through their skin; it must have been a hard, stinging death, but a quick one.

38   I flushed him down, wishing I could think of something to say as he made his way through the pipes and rolled out to the septic tank, some acknowledgment of the link between my kind and his, but I couldn't think of anything except that I would miss him, which was true.

39   When I opened the door a couple of nervous towhees blundered into the bushes. It was beginning to rain.

Thesis and Organization

1. The story of Left Sink unfolds slowly. Which paragraphs provide the introduction? What reasons can you give for your choice?
2. An essay of this length tends to group paragraphs around a topic sentence or main idea rather than have a topic sentence for each paragraph. What groupings can you identify? What ideas tie those paragraphs together?
3. Paragraphs 30 and 31 stand out because they strike a very different note from the rest of the essay. What function do they serve?
4. Akers says "there was something unnatural about a frog in a bathroom" (23). What does she imply in that paragraph and elsewhere about the relationship between humans and nature?
5. Many essays have an explicit thesis, one that you can spot in a complete sentence. Others, however, have an implied thesis, one that the writer suggests and the reader must deduce. That is the case with Akers' essay. What do you find to be its thesis?

Technique and Style

1. What does Akers think and feel about Left Sink? what details can you find to support your opinion?
2. What details can you find that lead to the conclusion that Akers is a naturalist?
3. Unlike many more formal essays, Akers uses lots of short paragraphs. Look up types of paragraphs in your handbook. What justification can you find for short paragraphs?
4. Akers' choice of verbs helps create the fast pace of the essay and its readability. Find a sentence that uses unusual verbs and rewrite it, substituting other verbs in their place. What is gained? Lost?
5. At various places in the essay, Akers refers to rain or the lack of it. What does that contribute to the essay?

Suggestions for Writing

Day-to-day life is apt to be full of contrasts, though not usually so striking as a frog in a bathroom. See how many contrasts you can spot in the course of a day when you're looking for them—a fully dressed person at a beach, a baby at a horror film, a nervous person in a library, a person studying in the middle of a busy cafeteria. Jot down what you see and then choose from your notes to work up the contrast into a descriptive essay. Use details to give your adjectives substance.

Narration

Whether prompted by the child's "Tell me a story" or the adult's "What happened?" narration supplies much of our entertainment and information. But anyone who has asked "What happened?" only to be overwhelmed with every detail knows that telling everything can blunt the point and bore the listener. To use narration effectively takes more than telling a story; it calls for compressing and reshaping experience so that the listener or reader relives it with you and is left with a particular point. Shaping narrative draws upon some of the same skills used in description: keen observation, careful selection of details, and coherent sequencing. But with a narrative you must go a step further: you must present a **conflict** and its resolution. A story with no point is a shaggy-dog story; one with no conflict is no kind of story at all.

Often the narrative and the subject are the same: if you are writing about what happened to you when lightning struck your house, what happened is the subject of your narrative. Frequently, however, a writer chooses narrative to introduce or to conclude an essay or perhaps to do both, which sets up a narrative framework. Or perhaps you would opt for narrative to emphasize a particular point. An essay that explains the dangers of toxic waste may be made more effective if it starts with a brief narrative of what happens at a place where pollution threatens the area and its residents, such as Los Angeles and its smog. So, too, a paper on the same subject that argues for stricter federal and state controls may end by predicting what might happen without tougher regulation. The essays in this chapter, however, rely on narration for their primary structure. All present conflicts, build to a point, and spring from personal experience, from the something that happened.

Audience and Purpose   Sandra Cisneros writes about a friend in Sarajevo, Bosnia, at a time when the city has been under heavy mortar fire and shelling. And even though the plight of Sarajevo was in the news, her readers do not necessarily know much about the city. Cisneros must therefore fill in a good deal of information about the kind of life she led there in 1983 and what's going on ten years later. Although her essay is directed to the general reader, it is also an open letter to everyone in positions of power.

"Living an Adventurous Life" and "I Have a Gun" are written for an audience composed of specific and general readers. Some, like Nancy Mairs, know the difficulty of trying to lead a life of adventure within circumstances that forge a new definition of *adventurous,* but other readers need to know more about the difficulties she faces. So too in "I Have a Gun," some readers feel the same mixture of shame and fear as the author; others may not know the shame but know too well the atmosphere of violent crime. The narratives of Calandra and Soto, however, focus more squarely on the general reader.

WHO, WHAT, WHERE, WHEN, HOW, WHY   Most narratives set out these elements (*who, what,* etc.) early in the story. In "Angels on a Pin," Calandra establishes them within the first two paragraphs; Mairs and Cisneros do the same in their essays. From that point on, however, the essays focus on what happened: Cisneros seeks help, Calandra's student seeks answers, Mairs seeks adventure; Cisneros fails, the student and Mairs succeed.

CONFLICT   Narratives begin at a certain time, establish the nature of the conflict, and move toward a point that resolves the conflict. But conflict can be many-layered. In "Angels on a Pin," the conflict is not only between the instructor and the student but also between the student and the educational system. "Who Wants Stories Now" uses the literal conflict of the war in Bosnia to depict two personal conflicts, that of Cisneros's friend Jasna who struggles to survive and of Cisneros herself who tries to help her. On a broader scale, the conflict is between the vulnerable and the unfeeling. some essays, such as "The Pie" and "I Have a Gun," suggest internal conflict as well.

POINT OF VIEW   By deciding who tells the story and from what perspective, the author selects a **point of view** that controls how the story is told and how the reader responds to it. Third-person pronouns serve to distance the reader from the story, and the word *I* usually enlists the reader's identification. Note, though, that a story can be written in the first person yet have a narrator somewhat removed from the action. "Angels on a Pin" is written as a first-person narrative, but the narrator, though part of the action is more observer than actor. In "Living an Adventurous Life" and "I Have a Gun," the line between action and narrator disappears. The narrator and action are one.

Within a narrative's chronology, the sequence of events can be shaped to emphasize different elements. "The Pie" not only emphasizes *what* happens but *where:* the market, the front yard, the curb, under the house. So, too, "I Have a Gun" stresses setting and atmosphere. Sometimes chronology is disrupted, as in "I Have a Gun," where the author uses flashbacks. In all the essays, the events, both in their chronology and in the principle behind their presentation, lead the reader to the author's point. In "Living an Adventurous Life," the author's point is easy to identify, but in the other essays, it is more subtle. Soto, in "The Pie," is content to hint at his thesis, leaving the reader to deduce what it is. Calandra, Nyman, and Cisneros are more overt. Like Soto, they reserve their points for the last paragraphs.

USEFUL TERMS

Conflict   An element essential to narrative. Conflict involves pitting one force against another.

Connotation   The meanings associated with and suggested by a word that add to its literal, explicit definition.

Denotation   The literal, dictionary meaning of a word.

Narrative   A narrative tells a story, emphasizing what happened.

Point of view   In essays, point of view usually refers to the writer's use of personal pronouns. These pronouns control the perspective from which the work is written. For example, if the writer uses *I* or *we* (first person pronouns), the essay will have a somewhat subjective tone because the reader will tend to identify with the writer. If the writer depends primarily on *he, she, it,* or *they* (third person pronouns), the essay will have a somewhat objective tone because the reader will be distanced from the writer. Opting for *you* (second person) can be a bit tricky in that the *you* can be you the reader, quite particular, or you a member of a larger group, fairly general. In both cases, *you* brings the reader into the text.

IDEAS FOR WRITING   Use your journal to write a narrative, perhaps the story of something that happened to you recently or something you know that happened to someone else. Try to write without stopping, piling in as much information as possible. After you've finished, let what you have written cool for a bit and then go back to it. At the end of your narrative, write what you find is the conflict. Then in one sentence write out the point of the narrative, your thesis. What you have now can be the basis for an essay. Having your conflict and thesis clearly stated will help you shape your narrative effectively. You can also decide whether the thesis is best implied or stated explicitly.

▪ POINTERS FOR USING NARRATION

Exploring the Topic

1. **What point do you want to make?** What is the subject of your narrative? What assertion do you want your narrative to make about the subject? Is your primary purpose to inform, to persuade, or to entertain?
2. **What happened?** What are the events involved in the narrative? When does the action start? Stop? Which events are crucial?
3. **Why and how did it happen?** What caused the events? How did it cause them?
4. **Who or what was involved?** What does the reader need to know about the characters? What do the characters look like? Talk like? How do they think? How do others respond to them?
5. **What is the setting for your story?** What does the reader need to know about the setting? What features are particularly noteworthy? How can they best be described?
6. **When did the story occur?** What tense will be most effective in relating the narrative?
7. **What was the sequence of events?** What happened when? Within that chronology, what is most important: time, place, attitude, what?
8. **What conflicts were involved?** What levels of conflict exist? Is there any internal conflict?
9. **What is the relationship between the narrator and the action?** Is the narrator a participant or an observer? What is the attitude of the narrator toward the story? What feelings should the narrator evoke from the reader? What should be the attitude of the reader toward the narrative? What can be gained by using first person? Second person? Third person?

Drafting the Paper

1. **Know your reader.** Try to second-guess your reader's initial attitude toward your narrative so if that attitude is not what you want it to be, you can choose your details to elicit the desired reaction. A reader can be

easily bored, so keep your details to the point and your action moving. Play on similar experiences your reader may have had or on information you can assume is widely known.

2. **Know your purpose.** If you are writing to inform, make sure you provide enough information to carry your point. If you are writing to persuade, work on your persona so that the reader will be favorably inclined to adopt your viewpoint. If you are writing to entertain, keep your tone in mind. A humorous piece, for instance, can and probably will vary from chuckle to guffaw to belly laugh. Make sure you're getting the right kind of laugh in the right place.

3. **Establish the setting and time of the action.** Use descriptive details to make the setting vivid and be concrete. Keep in mind the reaction you want to get from your reader, and choose your details accordingly. If, for instance, you are writing a narrative that depicts your first experience with fear, describe the setting in such a way that you prepare the reader for that emotion. If the time the story took place is important, bring it out early.

4. **Set out the characters.** When you introduce a character, immediately identify the person with a short phrase such as "Anne, my sister." If a character doesn't enter the narrative until midpoint or so, make sure the reader is prepared for the entrance so that the character doesn't appear to be plopped in. If characterization is important to the narrative, use a variety of techniques to portray the character but make sure whatever you use is consistent with the impression you want to create. You can depict a person directly—through appearance, dialogue, and actions—as well as indirectly— through what others say and think and how they act toward the person.

5. **Clarify the action.** Narration is set within strict time limits. Make sure the time frame of your story is set out clearly. Within that time limit, much more action occurred than you will want to use in your narrative. Pick only the high points so that every action directly supports the point you want to make. Feel free to tinker with the action, sacrificing a bit of reality for the sake of your point.

6. **Sharpen the plot.** Conflict is essential to narration, so be sure your lines of conflict are clearly drawn. Keeping conflict in mind, review the action you have decided to include so that the plot and action support each other.

7. **Determine the principle behind the sequence of events.** Given the action and plot you have worked out, determine what principle should guide the reader through the events. Perhaps time is the element you want to stress, perhaps place, perhaps gradual change. No matter what you choose, make sure that the sequence has dramatic tension so that it builds to the point you want to make.

8. **Choose an appropriate point of view.** Your choice of grammatical point of view will depend on what attitude you wish to take toward your narrative. If you can make your point more effectively by distancing yourself from the story, you will want to use the indefinite pronouns as-

sociated with an objective point of view. If you want to get a little closer, use a limited omniscient point of view. On the other hand, if you can make your point most effectively by being in the story, use first person. Then decide whether you want to be *I* the narrator or *I* the narrator and character. You should shape your persona to elicit the desired reaction from your audience.

9. **Make a point.** The action of the narration should lead to a conclusion, an implicit or explicit point that serves as the thesis of the piece. If explicit, the thesis can appear in a single sentence or it can be inferred from several sentences. Ask yourself if everything in the narrative leads up to this conclusion and if the conclusion resolves the conflict.

Living an Adventurous Life

Nancy Mairs

Adventure and adventurer evoke images of heroic feats, exotic places, and daring people, but Nancy Mairs makes us reconsider our ideas and give new meaning to what it takes to be heroic and daring. The essay first appeared in 1985 in Kaleidoscope, *a journal published by United Cerebral Palsy and Services for the Handicapped. The piece was reprinted in the* Utne Reader *in 1990.*

WHAT TO LOOK FOR   *One way to make connections between your own experience and the experience of the reader is to use allusions. You'll see that's what Mairs does in her third paragraph so that her reader can better understand her adventuring.*

KEY WORDS AND PHRASES
multiple sclerosis (1)   *minutiae (2)*
refine (5)   *bettas (5)*

1   Nearly ten years ago, I was told that I had a brain tumor, and this experience changed my attitude about adventure forever. I thought that I was going to die and that all my adventures were over. I did not have a brain tumor, it turned out, but rather multiple sclerosis, which meant that, although they were not over, the nature of my adventures would have to change.

2   Each morning that I wake up, that I get out of bed, is a fresh event, something that I might not have had. Each gesture that I make carries the weight of uncertainty, demands significant attention: buttoning my shirt, changing a light bulb, walking down stairs. I might not be able to do it this time. Inevitably the minutiae of my life have had to assume dramatic proportions. If I could not delight in them, they would likely drown me in rage or in self-pity.

3   I admire the grand adventures of others. I read about them with zest. With Peter Matthiessen I have trekked across the Himalayas to the Crystal Mountain. One blistering July I moved with John McPhee to Eagle, Alaska, above the Arctic Circle. I have trudged with Annie Dillard up, down, into, and across Tinker Creek in all

seasons. David Bain has accompanied me along 110 miles of Philippine coast, and Ed Abbey has paddled me down the Colorado River. I've ridden on the back of Robert Pirsig's motorcycle, climbed 95 feet to George Dyson's tree house, and grown coffee in Kenya with Isak Dinensen. I relish the adventures of these rugged and courageous figures, who can strike out on difficult trips—2 miles, 250 miles, 3000 miles—ready to endure cold, fatigue, human and natural hostility—indeed not just to endure but to celebrate.

4   But as for me, I can no longer walk very far from the armchair in which I read. I'll never make it to Tibet. Maybe not even to Albuquerque. Some days I don't even make it to the backyard. And yet I'm unwilling to forgo the adventurous life: the difficulty of it, even the pain, the suspense and fear, and the sudden brief lift of spirit that graces a hard journey. If I am to have it too, then I must change the terms by which it is lived. And so I do.

5   I refine *adventure,* make it smaller and smaller. And now, whether I am feeding fish flakes to my bettas or crawling across the dining room helping my cat Burton look for his blind snake, lying wide-eyed in the dark battling yet another bout of depression, cooking a chicken, gathering flowers from the garden at the farm, meeting a friend for lunch, I am always having the adventures that are mine to have.

Thesis and Organization

1. How does paragraph 1 answer the old questions of *who, where, what, when, how,* and *why?*
2. Reread paragraph 2. Which sentence functions as the paragraph's topic sentence? What reasons can you find for its placement?
3. Paragraphs 3 and 4 use comparison and contrast. Trace what is being compared. What is the point of the comparison?
4. How has Mairs "refined" adventure? Why is *refine* an appropriate word?
5. Consider the last sentence of the essay together with its title. What is the thesis?

Technique and Style

1. Try to separate your later impressions of the essay from your first response to its title. Given that title, what expectations did you have of the essay? To what extent were they fulfilled? How or how not?

2. What is the central conflict of the essay? What sort of person is Mairs? Given that impression and the conflict, what is the tone of the essay?

3. *Denotation* refers to the literal meaning of a word, what you wold find in a dictionary. *Connotation* takes in the emotional aspect of a word, the associations it has built up over the years. What associations do you ordinarily have with the word *adventure?* To what extent does Mairs play on the connotation of the word in her essay?

4. Paragraph 3 uses allusion, referring to adventurers and the places they have explored. Assuming you may not be familiar with all the names Mairs mentions, how effective or ineffective is her use of allusion?

5. Good writing depends in part on the writer's use of details. To what extent does Mairs use detail? What effect does it have?

Suggestions for Writing

Think of a physical challenge you have had. Perhaps it involved a sport, an illness, an accident, a dare, a catastrophe. Think about the challenge in terms of a conflict. The external conflict is the most obvious, but internal conflict was probably involved as well. Think also about what details are the most significant ones.

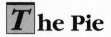he Pie

Gary Soto

Local News, Gary Soto's *latest book, was published in 1993, one of many Soto has written. Born in Los Angeles, Soto is best known for his poetry and his books for young children, but the essay that follows also shows how effectively he writes prose aimed at an adult audience. It was first published in his collection* A Summer Life *(1990). Though the essay is hardly "poetic" in the stereotypical sense, you'll find he uses a number of techniques that also characterize his poetry: precise diction, strong verbs, and imagery that appeals to the senses.*

WHAT TO LOOK FOR   *The most frequent verb that is apt to appear in unedited writing is the verb* to be, *often in the simple form* is. *Soto shows how to avoid that trap by using action verbs that convey far more precisely exactly what he is describing.*

KEY WORDS AND PHRASES
proximity (2)   discus (3)
falling from grace (4)   taut (7)

1   I knew enough about hell to stop me from stealing. I was holy in almost every bone. Some days I recognized the shadows of angels flopping on the backyard grass, and other days I heard faraway messages in the plumbing that howled underneath the house when I crawled there looking for something to do.

2   But boredom made me sin. Once, at the German Market, I stood before a rack of pies, my sweet tooth gleaming and the juice of guilt wetting my underarms. I gazed at the nine kinds of pie, pecan and apple being my favorites, although cherry looked good, and my dear, fat-faced chocolate was always a good bet. I nearly wept trying to decide which to steal and, forgetting the flowery dust priests give off, the shadow of angels and the proximity of God howling in the plumbing underneath the house, sneaked a pie behind my coffee-lid frisbee and walked to the door, grinning to the bald grocer whose forehead shone with a window of light.

3   "No one saw," I muttered to myself, the pie like a discus in my hand, and hurried across the street, where I sat on someone's

lawn. The sun wavered between the branches of a yellowish sycamore. A squirrel nailed itself high on the trunk, where it forked into two large bark-scabbed limbs. Just as I was going to work my cleanest finger into the pie, a neighbor came out to the porch for his mail. He looked at me, and I got up and headed for home. I raced on skinny legs to my block, but slowed to a quick walk when I couldn't wait any longer. I held the pie to my nose and breathed in its sweetness. I licked some of the crust and closed my eyes as I took a small bite.

4   In my front yard, I leaned against a car fender and panicked about stealing the apple pie. I knew an apple got Eve in deep trouble with snakes because Sister Marie had shown us a film about Adam and Eve being cast into the desert, and what scared me more than falling from grace was being thirsty for the rest of my life. But even that didn't stop me from clawing a chunk from the pie tin and pushing it into the cavern of my mouth. The slop was sweet and gold-colored in the afternoon sun. I laid more pieces on my tongue, wet finger-dripping pieces, until I was finished and felt like crying because it was about the best thing I had ever tasted. I realized right there and then, in my sixth year, in my tiny body of two hundred bones and three or four sins, that the best things in life came stolen. I wiped my sticky fingers on the grass and rolled my tongue over the corners of my mouth. A burp perfumed the air.

5   I felt bad not sharing with Cross-Eyed Johnny, a neighbor kid. He stood over my shoulder and asked, "Can I have some?" Crust fell from my mouth, and my teeth were bathed with the jam-like filling. Tears blurred my eyes as I remembered the grocer's forehead. I remembered the other pies on the rack, the warm air of the fan above the door and the car that honked as I crossed the street without looking.

6   "Get away," I had answered Cross-Eyed Johnny. He watched my fingers greedily push big chunks of pie down my throat. He swallowed and said in a whisper, "Your hands are dirty," then returned home to climb his roof and sit watching me eat the pie by myself. After a while, he jumped off and hobbled away because the fall had hurt him.

7   I sat on the curb. The pie tin glared at me and rolled away when the wind picked up. My face was sticky with guilt. A car honked, and the driver knew. Mrs. Hancock stood on her lawn, hands on hip, and she knew. My mom, peeling a mountain of potatoes at the Redi-Spud factory, knew. I got to my feet, stomach

taut, mouth tired of chewing, and flung my frisbee across the street, its shadow like the shadow of an angel fleeing bad deeds. I retrieved it, jogging slowly. I flung it again until I was bored and thirsty.

8   I returned home to drink water and help my sister glue bottle caps onto cardboard, a project for summer school. But the bottle caps bored me, and the water soon filled me up more than the pie. With the kitchen stifling with heat and lunatic flies, I decided to crawl underneath our house and lie in the cool shadows listening to the howling sound of plumbing. Was it God? Was it Father, speaking from death, or Uncle with his last shiny dime? I listened, ear pressed to a cold pipe, and heard a howl like the sea. I lay until I was cold and then crawled back to the light, rising from one knee, then another, to dust off my pants and squint in the harsh light. I looked and saw the glare of a pie tin on a hot day. I knew sin was what you take and didn't give back.

Thesis and Organization

1. What does the first paragraph lead you to expect in the rest of the essay?
2. The time sequence traces Soto's guilt. What stages can you identify?
3. How would you describe the nature of the conflict in the essay?
4. What emotions does Soto feel in the course of his narrative?
5. What does Soto learn?

Technique and Style

1. Soto relates his narrative from the perspective of his 6-year-old self. What is the first clue about his age?
2. Reread paragraph 4. What images appeal to what senses?
3. Paragraphs 5 and 6 bring in Cross-Eyed Johnny. What does that incident add to the narrative?
4. What other titles can you think of for the essay? What is gained? Lost?
5. Choose two sentences from paragraph 3 and rewrite them, using different verbs. Which versions do you prefer and why?

Suggestions for Writing

Being embarrassed, feeling guilty, running risks, getting caught (or "getting away with it") are common to us all. Recall a time when you lived through one of those experiences and use your memory of it as the basis of a narrative. Like Soto, you will want to describe not only what you did but also how it made you feel. If the idea for such an essay seems too personal, relate the tale of someone else's experience.

Who Wants Stories Now?

Sandra Cisneros

*Author of two collections of short stories—*The House on Mango Street *(1991) and* Woman Hollering Creek (1991)—*Sandra Cisneros lives in San Antonio, Texas. The following essay is adapted from a speech she gave there for the International Women's Day Rally, March 7, 1993. In a recent interview, she spoke of herself as a "translator" whose writing enables her to "cross bridges from [her] community into the community of power." The communities she speaks of in this essay are multiple: her own, Hispanic and American; her friend Jasna's, who lives in Sarajevo in the midst of the Bosnia war; and that of those who have political power. Cisneros's narrative traces her friendship with Jasna in the form of an open letter, a letter addressed to multiple readers. Her most recent book is a reissue of her earlier work,* My Wicked, Wicked Ways *(1992), a collection of poems.*

WHAT TO LOOK FOR *Oddly enough, good short sentences are hard to write, for paring them down until they pack power takes a lot of rewriting. As you read Cisneros's essay, notice how often she uses short sentences, even fragments, and try to account for the effect they have.*

KEY WORDS AND PHRASES

Yugoslavia (1)	*partisans (1)*
Tito (1)	*begonias (4)*
piñata (5)	*kaffa (5)*
minarets (5)	*Serbo-Croatian (6)*
Buddhist (13)	

1   Nema. It means, "There isn't any." And it was the first word I learned when I crossed the border into Yugoslavia in 1983. Nema. Toothpaste? Nema. Toilet paper? Nema. Coffee? Nema. Chocolate? Nema. But, yes, plenty of roses when I was there, plenty of war memorials to fallen partisans and mountains screaming Tito in stone.

2   It's true. I lived there on that street with that man Salem, the printer, in the house that used to be the grocery. That was the summer I spent being a wife. I washed shirts by hand; with a broom and bucket of suds I scrubbed the tiles of the garden each

morning from all the pigeon droppings that fell from the flock that lived on the roof of the garden shed. It was summer. Everything was blossoming. Our dog Lea had 14 puppies. The children in the neighborhood came in and out of the garden gate. The garden was filled with walnuts and fruit and roses with flowers so heavy they dropped.

3   And you lived across from me, Jasna. In the house that was once your mother's, and before her, her mother's.

4   I have your recipes for fry bread, for your famous fruit bread, "It always turns out good," you said. You were filled with potted begonias and recipes and sewing, and did all the amazing domestic stuff I can't do. You were difficult. You smoked too much and were terribly moody. On the afternoon I met you on the wooden bench outside the summer kitchen of our garden, you looked at me as if you'd always known me, and I looked at you as if I'd always known you. Of that we were convinced.

5   After I met you, I was always at your house, with its thick stone walls and deep-set windows, its dust, its forever need of repair, helping you fold the wash or talking with you while you ironed or whitewashing the walls. It was your grandmother's house, the place where you married and divorced a husband, where I made you a piñata and we celebrated your birthday and joked it was the only piñata to be had in all of Yugoslavia. Remember the afternoons of kaffa, roasted in the garden, served in thimble-sized cups, the Turkish way? Remember the minarets and the sad call to prayer like a flag of black silk fluttering in the air?

6   You would come to the U.S. and begin translating my stories into Serbo-Croatian. We were just getting the stories published in Sarajevo when the war ruined everything. Who wants stories now? There is no shortage of stories when there is no heat or bread or water or electricity. Nema, nema, nema.

7   Jasna, it's 10 years since that summer. I haven't heard from you since last summer. When there was still time, you didn't leave. Now I hear you won't leave. Your mother sick, too frail no doubt to travel, your sister never strong enough to even make a decision. I imagine it's you who is taking care of them. I'm certain of this.

8   I've talked to your other sister in Slovenia. I've talked to your brother in Germany. We light our candles and are sick with worry. I dream of you, Jasna. You are not dead. Not yet. I can say this with certainty because I know you too well, and if you died, you'd come and tell me.

9   Mr. President of the United States, leaders of every country across the globe, all you politicians, all you deciding the fates of nations, your excellencies of power, I mean you listening to me and not listening, Dear To Whom It may Concern, I've had it with the lot of you, all of you. This is real. I'm not making this story up. A woman is there. She's my friend, take my word for it.

10   She's in there. Get her out, I tell you. Get them out. They're in that city, that country, that region, that mouth of hell, that house on fire, get her out of there, I demand you.

11   I demand you march, take a plane, better take a tank. Take some of these blankets I have, my beautiful new home, my silk suits, my warm stockings, my full belly, my refrigerator with things to eat, my supermarket, my spring weather, my electricity, my clean water, my pickup truck, my U.S. dollars, my trees and flowers and nights soundless and whole.

12   I demand you go right in there, I demand you give me a sword mightier than this useless pen of mind, I demand you arrive in Sarajevo. I'll take you to her house. I am afraid, but I'll take you.

13   About words. I know what my demands mean. I know about words. There is no shortage of words in Sarajevo. I am a writer, I am a woman. I am a human being. In other wars I remember watching Buddhist priests set themselves on fire, begging for no less than what I ask for, and what good did it come to?

14   A woman I know is in there. In that country. A woman I love as any woman would love a woman. That woman, hermana de mi corazón, sister of my heart. I know this woman. And I am in San Antonio, and the days and the hours and the months pass and the newspapers cry: Something must be done! Somebody, someone, help this somebody!

15   And I *hear* that somebody. And I *know* that somebody. And I *love* that somebody. And I don't know what to do. I don't know what to do.

Thesis and Organization

1. The essay begins by quickly establishing *who, what, when, why,* and *how.* Which paragraphs carry what information?
2. Add up the number of times Cisneros refers to war, directly and indirectly. What do the frequent allusions add to the essay? What do they help explain?
3. The essay is obviously very emotional, and Cisneros draws upon a

number of techniques to convey her emotion—repetition, word choice, short sentences, direct address. Choose an example that you find particularly effective and explain how it achieves its effect.

4. You can argue that the essay is about war or helplessness or friendship or the facelessness of suffering. Explain what you believe to be the essay's subject.

5. Given that subject, what is Cisneros's thesis?

Technique and Style

1. At times Cisneros's tone seems pleading, angry, nostalgic, bitter, despairing. Consider the essay as a whole and explain what you interpret as her primary tone.

2. Use a handbook of grammar and usage to look up sentence fragments. To what extent does the explanation account for the fragments in paragraph 14?

3. Cisneros frequently uses repetition, as in paragraphs 1 and 15. Rewrite one example without the repetition. What is gained? Lost?

4. Where in the essay does Cisneros address someone or some people directly? How effective do you find her form, that of an open letter?

5. Paragraph 13 refers to Cisneros's profession. What point is she making in that paragraph?

Suggestions for Writing

Think of a problem that worries you. Perhaps, like Cisneros, you have a friend or relative caught in a terrible situation, or perhaps you are angry about a particular issue (voter apathy, high tuition, censorship, violence on television) or an attitude (racism, sexism, snobbism). Pick something you're upset about and write an open letter about it. Like Cisneros, you might want to first explain your connection and then call for action. If that idea doesn't appeal, then write an essay that tells the story of your friendship with someone. Like Cisneros, use details to convey just what the friendship consists of.

I Have a Gun

Tania Nyman

Sometimes being able to defend yourself can be as frightening as being defenseless, a paradox sharply felt by Tania Nyman, who wrote this essay her sophomore year at the University of New Orleans. At the time, 1989, New Orleans was fast becoming the murder capital of the United States, a fact that the editors of the local newspaper, the Times-Picayune, *were well aware of. Urban violence makes many people feel the way Tania Nyman does, which is one reason the* Times-Picayune *published her essay as an opinion piece.*

WHAT TO LOOK FOR *Pace, the speed at which the story unfolds, is crucial to the impact of a narrative, and one way to quicken the pace is to use present tense. Notice how Nyman relies on the present tense to make her story immediate.*

KEY WORDS AND PHRASES
immune (4)   scenario (17)
nonchalantly (19)   confrontation (21)

1   I have a gun, a .38 caliber that holds five bullets. It is black with a brown handle and it stays by my bed.

2   I don't want a gun. I don't even like guns. But it seems I need one.

3   I've always believed in gun control, and the funny thing is I still do. But my gun is loaded next to my bed.

4   It wasn't ignorance of crime statistics that previously kept me from owning a gun. Nor was it the belief that I was immune to violence.

5   I thought that because I didn't believe in violence, that because I wasn't violent, I wouldn't be touched by violence. I believed that my belief in the best of human nature could make it real.

6   I want to believe in a world where people do not need to protect themselves from one another. But I have a gun, and it stays by my bed.

7   I should carry the gun from my house to my car, but I don't. What the gun is capable of, what the gun is for, still frightens me more than what it is supposed to prevent.

8   If I carry my gun and I am attacked, I must use it. I cannot shoot to injure. I must shoot to kill.

9   I have confronted an attacker not in reality but in my imagination. The man is walking down the street. To prove I am not paranoid, I lock my car and walk to my door with my house key ready.

10   Before I reach the steps, I think I hear a voice. "Money." Before I open the door I hear a voice. "Money." I turn to see the man with the gun.

11   He is frightened. I am frightened. I am frightened that I will scare him and he will shoot. I am frightened that I will give him my money and he will shoot.

12   I am frightened, but I am angry. I am angry because there is a gun pointed at me by someone I've never met and never hurt.

13   There is something that bothers me about this robbery I have created in my head. It is something that makes me uncomfortable with myself. It is something I don't want to admit, something I almost intentionally omitted because I am ashamed.

14   I guess I understand why I imagine being robbed by a man. They're physically more intimidating and I've never heard of anyone being robbed by a woman, though I'm sure it happens. but I'm being robbed by a man.

15   But why is he a black man? Why is he a black man with a worn T-shirt and glassy eyes? Why do I not imagine being robbed by a white man?

16   I am standing in a gas station on Claiborne and Jackson waiting to pay the cashier when a black man walks up behind me. I do not turn around. I stare in front of me waiting to pay. I try not to admit that I am nervous because a black man has walked up behind me in a gas station in a bad neighborhood and he does not have a car.

17   There is another scenario I imagine. I am walking to my door with my gun in my hand and I hear the voice. The man mustn't have seen my gun. I get angry because I am threatened, because someone is endangering my life for the money in my pocket.

18   I turn and without really thinking, angry and frightened, I shoot. I kill a man for $50. Or it could be $100. It does not matter that he was trying to rob me. A man has died for money. Not my money or his money, just money. Who put the price on his life, he or I?

19   I remember driving one night with my friend in her parents' car. We stop at a red light at Carollton and Tulane and a black man is

crossing the street in front of us. My friend quickly but nonchalantly locks the doors with the power lock.

20   I am disgusted that she sees the man as a reminder to lock her doors. I wonder if he noticed the two girls nonchalantly lock their doors. I wonder how it feels to have people lock their doors at the sight of you.

21   I imagine again a confrontation in front of my house. I have my gun when the man asks for money. I am angry and scared, but I do not use the gun. I am afraid of what may happen to me if I don't use it, but I am more afraid of killing another human being, more afraid of trying to live with the guilt of murdering another person. I bet my life that he will take my money and leave, and I hope I win.

22   I am in a gas station on St. Charles and South Carollton near my house and there is a black man waiting to pay the cashier. I walk up behind him to wait in line and he jumps and turns around.

23   When he sees me, he relaxes and says I scared him because of the way things have gotten in this neighborhood.

24   "Sorry," I say and smile. I realize I am not the only one who is frightened.

Thesis and Organization

1. Like the Cisneros essay, the paragraphs here conform to newspaper columns. If you were reparagraphing for a regular page, what paragraphs would you use to make up an introduction? What reasons do you have for your decision?
2. List the three imaginary incidents. What do they have in common? How are they different?
3. List the real incidents. What do they have in common? How are they different?
4. What is the point of the last narrative?
5. What is the author's attitude toward violence? Toward having a gun? Toward race? Combine your answers into a thesis statement.

Technique and Style

1. How would you describe the *I* in this essay? Is this the kind of person you would like to know? Why or why not?
2. The author uses repetition intentionally. Find an example and describe its effect.

3. What effects are achieved by mixing real and imagined situations?

4. How would you describe the various conflicts in the narrative? Which is the most important and why?

5. The author depends heavily on the first-person singular, *I*. Explain whether or not she overuses the pronoun.

Suggestions for Writing

Think of a time when your action or actions contradicted your values. Perhaps you were forced to lie to protect a friend, perhaps you kept silent at a time when you should have spoken up, or perhaps pressure from others pushed you into doing something you knew you shouldn't do. What were your values? What situation or action conflicted with those values? Perhaps you will want to develop how the conflict made you feel, how it affected others, and how you either resolved the conflict or learned to live with it.

Angels on a Pin

Alexander Calandra

"Angels on a Pin" was first published in the Saturday Review *in 1968 in the wake of the United States' push to surpass Russia's strides in scientific technology, strides that led to Sputnik, the first artificial earth satellite. Sputnik was launched in 1957. Now, some 35 years later, we no longer have "Sputnik-panicked classrooms," but we are still trying to come to terms with our educational system.*

WHAT TO LOOK FOR   *More often than not when you write a narrative, you find yourself at the center of it. But that may not be where you want to be. Calandra, for example, could have told the story of the student from the point of view of the teacher. Instead, he tells it from his own perspective, that of an impartial observer. When you write a narrative, ask yourself what point of view would be most effective.*

KEY WORDS AND PHRASES
colleague (1)   barometer (2)
conventional (13)   pedantic (13)
scholasticism (13)   lark (13)

1   Some time ago, I received a call from a colleague who asked if I would be the referee on the grading of an examination question. He was about to give a student a zero for his answer to a physics question, while the student claimed he should receive a perfect score and would if the system were not set up against the student. The instructor and the student agreed to submit this to an impartial arbiter, and I was selected.

2   I went to my colleague's office and read the examination question: "Show how it is possible to determine the height of a tall building with the aid of a barometer."

3   The student had answered: "Take the barometer to the top of the building, attach a long rope to it, lower the barometer to the street, and then bring it up, measuring the length of the rope. The length of the rope is the height of the building."

4   I pointed out that the student really had a strong case for full

credit, since he had answered the question completely and correctly. On the other hand, if full credit were given, it could well contribute to a high grade for the student in his physics course. A high grade is supposed to certify competence in physics, but the answer did not confirm this. I suggested that the student have another try at answering the question. I was not surprised that my colleague agree, but I was surprised that the student did.

5   I gave the student six minutes to answer the question, with the warning that his answer should show some knowledge of physics. At the end of five minutes, he had not written anything. I asked if he wished to give up, but he said no. He had many answers to this problem; he was just thinking of the best one. I excused myself for interrupting him, and asked him to please go on. In the next minute, he dashed off his answer which read:

6   "Take the barometer to the top of the building and lean over the edge of the roof. Drop the barometer, timing its fall with a stopwatch. Then, using the formula $S = 1/2at^2$, calculate the height of the building."

7   At this point, I asked my colleague if *he* would give up. He conceded, and I gave the student almost full credit.

8   In leaving my colleague's office, I recalled that the student had said he had other answers to the problem, so I asked him what they were. "Oh, yes," said the student. "There are many ways of getting the height of a tall building with the aid of a barometer. For example, you could take the barometer out on a sunny day and measure the height of the barometer, the length of its shadow, and the length of the shadow of the building, and by the use of a simple proportion, determine the height of the building."

9   "Fine," I said. "And the others?"

10   "Yes," said the student. "There is a very basic measurement method that you will like. In this method, you take the barometer and begin to walk up the stairs. As you climb the stairs, you mark off the length of the barometer along the wall. You then count the number of marks, and this will give you the height of the building in barometer units. A very direct method.

11   "Of course, if you want a more sophisticated method, you can tie the barometer to the end of a string, swing it as a pendulum, and determine the value of g at the street level and at the top of the building. From the difference between the two values of g, the height of the building can, in principle, be calculated."

12   Finally he concluded, there are many other ways of solving the problem. "Probably the best," he said, "is to take the barometer to the basement and knock on the superintendent's door. When the superintendent answers, you speak to him as follows: 'Mr. Superintendent, here I have a fine barometer. If you will tell me the height of this building, I will give you this barometer.' "

13   At this point, I asked the student if he really did not know the conventional answer to this question. He admitted that he did, but said that he was fed up with high school and college instructors trying to teach him how to think, to use the "scientific method," and to explore the deep inner logic of the subject in a pedantic way, as is often done in the new mathematics, rather than teaching him the structure of the subject. With this in mind, he decided to revive scholasticism as an academic lark to challenge the Sputnik-panicked classrooms of America.

Thesis and Organization

1. In a narrow sense, the essay focuses on the question, "What is the correct answer to the examination question?" But paragraphs 8–13 take up a broader point, and there the essay concentrates on the question, "What is the purpose of education?" How do the three participants answer this question?
2. At first, the conflict arises between the instructor and the student. What larger conflict is involved in their dispute? What paragraph serves as a transition between the smaller and larger conflicts?
3. Does the author intend the essay primarily to inform, persuade, or entertain? What evidence can you cite to support your view?
4. The subject of the essay is education. What statement is the author making about education? Where in the essay does he put forth his assertion? Is the essay's thesis expressed in one of Calandra's sentences? Which one? Or do you find that the thesis is composed of several ideas? Where are they expressed?
5. What principle guides the order in which the paragraphs are presented? What words or phrases does the author use to bring out that principle?

Technique and Style

1. To show how "to determine the height of a tall building with the aid of a barometer," the student depends on process analysis. How many

processes does he provide in answer to the examination question? Why might the student have saved his "best" answer for last?

2. In every example the student gives, the barometer plays a role that belies its most important function. What roles does it play? How do these roles subvert the instructor's questions?

3. What is the relationship of the narrator to the story? What is the narrator's point of view? Given the information in paragraph 4, what impression of the narrator is conveyed to the reader? Does the narrator take sides? What evidence can you find to support your opinion?

4. Use your library to find out about *scholasticism* (13) and the allusion to "angels on a pin." How does the author's choice of title relate to his thesis?

Suggestions for Writing

Recall an incident in which you were the victim of education. Perhaps a teacher falsely accused you of cheating or plagiarizing or of receiving help on a paper. Perhaps you did something to embarrass the teacher or vice versa. Perhaps you were not allowed to make up a test when you had a doctor's excuse for missing it. Perhaps a teacher lost your paper and gave you a zero for it. On the other hand, perhaps one of these instances or something similar happened to a friend. Make up what you cannot remember and embroider the details to suit your purpose.

Example

A ny time you encounter *for instance, such as,* or *for example,* you know what will follow: an **example** that explains and supports the generalization. Used with general statements, examples fill in the gaps. If you write "Many people believe most crime is violent and that crime is increasing" and then only support the statement by citing statistics to show the rate of crime peaked in the seventies but then ceased to rise in the eighties and actually fell in the nineties, you would have disproved your second assertion, but the first would still be up in the air. Readers also need to know what evidence supports your claim that crime, to many people, means violent crime. An example, then, is an illustration that clarifies or develops a point, and for the essay it is the most basic building block of all. Example pins down generalizations, supporting them with specifics.

To use examples well, you first need to know when to use them, then what ones to select, and finally, how to incorporate them. If you read actively, responding to the words on the page as you would to a person talking to you, odds are you will spot where examples are needed. On reading the sentence above about crime, you might think to yourself, "Hey, wait a minute! How about that violent crime statement?" Often it helps to read your own work belligerently, ready to shoot down any generalization with a "Says who?" The response to "Says who" will vary according to your audience. A sociology paper will call for statistics; a personal narrative will draw on your own experience. Other good sources are the experience of others and that of authorities. The skill here is to match the example not only to the generalization it supports but to the readers to whom it is addressed.

Example   **67**

After you have found good examples, you need to sequence them logically, while at the same time you avoid overusing terms such as "for example." Where you use multiple examples, you can use **transitions** that signal addition (*and, again, besides, moreover, next, finally,* etc.); where you use examples that compare, opt for transitions that indicate a turn (*but, yet, however, instead, in contrast,* etc.). And you can usually find a key word in the last part of a sentence that you can repeat or refer to to introduce the new example. Used often, appropriately, and smoothly, examples enlarge meaning by weaving the particular into the general.

AUDIENCE AND PURPOSE   Analyzing the audience helps a writer select examples. Molly Ivins, for instance, can assume her readers are generally familiar with country-western music but not that they share her appreciation of it, an appreciation built on a liking for the bizarre. To make her point she therefore piles on examples of musicians, titles, lyrics. So too Michael Barlow can assume his readers know about fitness clubs and exercise machines, so he can use that knowledge to build his case for the futility of it all.

But Barlow's readers may include some fitness fans who may take exception to his point. He is therefore careful to coat his argument with a humorous tone so as not to give too much offense. Brent Staples also treads carefully. In writing about the black male "monster role," he assumes that his readers are generally uninformed about his point. Although much has been made of the "monster" because of "America's fascination with the angry black man," the impact of that kind of media coverage has received far less attention. Staples must inform his readers without necessarily blaming them for their ignorance. So, too, Michiko Kakutani takes our culture to task for our seeming obsession with the O. J. Simpson case, which he does by placing it in a wider cultural context.

Anna Quindlen has a similar problem. Her general subject is abortion, an issue on which almost everyone has a strongly held opinion. To communicate her ideas, she must be sensitive to those views and try to avoid alienating those whose views represent opposing sides of the issue.

TYPES OF EXAMPLES   Examples generally fall into two types, extended and multiple. An essay that rests its assertion on only one example is relatively rare, but Michael Barlow's use of extended example is more typical. He relies on his personal experience and uses his pet hamster Mimi as an extended example representing the futility of running around in an exercise wheel, and then cites multiple examples to show how humans behave in a similar fashion. Multiple examples add clarity, support, and emphasis, and thus are the most frequent type found in essays. A writer who builds example on example provides a firm foundation for generalizations.

Whether you are looking for multiple or extended examples, you can draw them from sources close to you, from your own experience, and the experiences of others, which is what Barlow does in his essay; or like Kakutani and Staples you can opt for outside sources, from books, magazines, interviews, reports, and so on. Or you can quote people, which is Anna Quindlen's technique.

No matter what the source, however, the example should be representative and fitting. Quindlen, for example, gives meaning to a recent Supreme Court ruling by giving it a face, an example drawn from the experience of a "frightened 15-year-old." Drawing upon her own general experience, common to us all, as an adolescent "private as a safe-deposit box" and her recent conversation with the woman who runs the abortion clinic in Duluth, Quindlen cites examples to support her point about the complexity of a Supreme Court ruling.

DETAILS   In presenting an example, the writer uses many of the same techniques that come into play in description. Descriptive details enter into Molly Ivins "Honky Tonking" with her claim that

> Women in country music are either saints or sluts, but they're mostly sluts. She's either a "good-hearted woman" or a "honky-tonk angel." There are more hard-hearted women in country music ("I Gave Her a Ring, She Gave Me the Finger") despicable bimbos ("Ruuuby, Don't Take Your Love to Town"), and heartless gold diggers ("Satin Sheets to Lie On, Satin Pillow to Cry On") than scholars can count.

But Molly Ivins can count and does.

On a more serious subject, Anna Quindlen uses details to make an abstract decision into a concrete reality. To illustrate the effect of the law requiring that parents grant permission for an abortion, Quindlen cites two detailed examples: "The best case is the daughter who decides, with supportive parents, whether to end a pregnancy or have a

Example   **69**

baby. The worst case . . . is Becky Bell, a 17-year-old Indianapolis girl who died after an illegal abortion. She could not bear to tell her parents she was pregnant."

THESIS AND ORGANIZATION   Whether the essay is developed by multiple examples or a single extended example, it has a major assertion. Often, as in the case of "Honky Tonking," "Sweatin' for Nothin," "Why We Still Can't Stop Watching," "When Only Monsters are Real," and "Mom, Dad and Abortion," the major assertion comes from the ideas contained in several key sentences. Note, however, that in all those essays the titles announce the subject in such a way that the reader's interest is apt to be aroused. An essay's title, together with its organization, paves the way for the thesis.

Although all the essays that follow have a thesis developed by examples, the examples themselves often cross over into other categories. The example that opens Barlow's essay is both an example and a narrative, or put more precisely, it is a narrative that functions as an example. So, too, descriptions, causal relationships, comparisons, processes, and the like can serve as examples. As you read the essays that follow, be on the lookout for the kinds of examples that writers use, but keep in mind that it is the example, not the type, that counts.

USEFUL TERMS
Example   An illustration that supports an assertion by providing evidence, showing how the assertion applies in particular instances.
Irony   A statement or action in which the intended meaning or occurrence is the opposite of the surface one.
Transition   A word, phrase, sentence, or paragraph that carries the reader smoothly from point A to point B. Some transitions, such as time markers (*first, next,* and the like) are obvious; others are more subtle, such as a repeated word or phrase or a synonym for a key term. Transitions provide coherence and improve readability.

IDEAS FOR WRITING   Flip through one of your earlier papers or a journal entry, looking for examples. What kind do you use the most, extended or multiple? What sources do you draw your examples from?

Select one paragraph and rewrite it, changing the examples to ones from different sources.

■ POINTERS FOR USING EXAMPLE

Exploring the Topic

1. **What examples can you think of to illustrate your topic?** Are all of them from your own experience? What examples can you find from other sources?
2. **Check to see that your examples are both pertinent and representative.** Do they fit? Do they illustrate?
3. **Which examples lend themselves to extended treatment?** Which are relatively unimportant?
4. **How familiar is your audience with each of your examples?**
5. **Which examples best lend themselves to your topic?** In what order would they best be presented?
6. **What point do you want to make?** Do your examples all support that point? do they lead the reader to your major assertion?
7. **What is your purpose behind your point?** Is your primary aim to express your own feelings, to inform, to persuade, to entertain?

Drafting the Paper

1. **Know your reader.** Figure out where your reader may stand in relation to your topic and thesis. It may be that your audience knows little about your subject or that the reader simply hasn't thought much about it; on the other hand, maybe the reader knows a great deal and holds a definite opinion. Once you have made an informed guess about your audience's attitude toward your topic and thesis, reexamine your examples in the light of that information. Some may have to be explained in greater detail than others, and the more familiar ones will need to be presented in a new or different light. Use the techniques you would employ in writing descriptive papers.
2. **Know your purpose.** Self-expressive papers are often difficult to write because you are so close to being your own audience. If you are writing with this aim in mind, try making yourself conscious of the personality you project as a writer. Jot down the characteristics you wish to convey about yourself and refer to this list as you revise your paper. While this is a highly self-conscious way to revise, when it is done well, the result appears natural. You will also need to double-check your examples, making sure that you present them in sufficient detail to communicate fully to

Example **71**

your audience. That warning serves as well for informative and persuasive papers. Again, use description to make your examples hit the mark: use sensory detail, compare the unfamiliar to the familiar, be concrete. If you are writing a persuasive paper, use these techniques to develop your emotional appeal.

3. **Consider extended example.** If an essay rests on one example, that illustration must be chosen and developed with great care. Make sure your example is representative of its class and that you provide all relevant information. Make as many unobtrusive connections as you can between your example and the class it represents. During revision, you may want to eliminate some of these references, but at first it's best to have too many. If you are writing a persuasive paper, you don't want to be found guilty of a logical fallacy.

4. **Consider multiple examples.** Most essays rely on multiple examples to support their points; nevertheless, some will be more developed than others. Figure out which examples are particularly striking and develop them, reserving the others for mere mention. Show how your examples fit your point and stress what is noteworthy about them. To lend breadth and credibility to your point consider citing statistics, quotations, authorities, and the experience of others as well as your own experience. Comment on what you take from other sources in order to make it more your own.

5. **Arrange your examples effectively.** The most frequent pattern of organization moves from the less dramatic, less important to the most, but examples can also be arranged chronologically or in terms of frequency (from the least frequent to the most). Like the essay itself, each paragraph should be developed around a central assertion, either stated or understood. In longer papers, groups of paragraphs will form a paragraph block in support of a unifying statement. These statements guide the reader through your examples and save the paper from turning into a mere list.

6. **Make a point.** Examples so obviously need to lead up to something that it's not hard to make a point in this kind of paper. The only real pitfall is that your point may not be an assertion. Test your thesis by asking whether your point carries any information. If it does, it's an assertion. Say you come up with, "We live in a world of time-saving technology." You can think of lots of examples and even narrow down the "we" to "anyone who cooks today." The setting is obviously the kitchen, but is the revised thesis an assertion? Given the information test, it fails. Your audience already knows what you are supposedly informing them about. But if you revise and come up with "Electronic gizmos have turned the kitchen into a laboratory," you've given the topic a fresher look, one that does contain information.

*H*onky Tonking

Molly Ivins

Molly Ivins isn't ashamed to admit she loves country music, and she isn't ashamed to write about it in her typical style, a cross between Deep Texan and Standard American English. A confessed member of what she terms the "arthur bidness," she is a regular contributor to several newspapers and various magazines such as Atlantic, Texas Monthly, The Washington Journalism Review, Mother Jones, *and* The Progressive. *This essay was first published in* Ms. *in September, 1988, and then reprinted in her first collection of essays,* Molly Ivins Can't Say That, Can She?, *published in 1991. Molly Ivins continues to be outrageous, and country music continues to attract more fans and more amazing song titles.*

WHAT TO LOOK FOR   *Not many writers can match Molly Ivins for range of diction, so as you read the essay be aware of the different types of diction she uses—colloquial, slang, conversational, formal, academic.*

KEY WORDS AND PHRASES

Dave Brubeck (2)	*deconstructive criticism (10)*
Edith Piaf (2)	*mandatory (11)*
Earnest Tubb (2)	*dudgeon (12)*
cosmopolite (2)	*futile (12)*
folkies (3)	*expenditure (12)*
Bull Connor (3)	*passé (12)*
masochism (5)	*stupefying (12)*
despicable (5)	*Ludwig van Beethoven (13)*
anthems (6)	*Earl Scruggs (13)*
parody (6)	*neoconservative (13)*
redeeming (7)	*relativism (13)*
genre (7)	*abandonment (13)*
Moral Majority (8)	*absolute (13)*
Pat Robertson (8)	*morality (13)*
Tech (9)	*The Three Musketeers (13)*
elitists (10)	*menace (13)*
monetary policy (10)	*Dante (13)*

1   I can remember being embarrassed about liking country-western music, but I can't remember when I quit. It was a long time before they put Willie Nelson on the cover of *Newsweek*. Since there's a country song about everything important in life, there's one about this too—"I Was Country, When Country Wasn't Cool."

2   Being hopelessly uncool is the least of the sins of country music. Back when I went to college, listening to Dave Brubeck and Edith Piaf was a fundamental prerequisite for sophistication, on a par with losing your virginity. Knowing a lot of Ernest Tubb songs didn't do squat for the reputation of the aspiring cosmopolite.

3   Country music was also politically incorrect. The folkies were on the right side of issues: Bob Dylan and Joan Baez sang at civil rights rallies; it seemed more than likely that Bull Connor listened to country.

4   The Beatles, Janis Joplin, the Jefferson Airplane, the Doors—everybody anybody listened to in the 1960s was against the Vietnam War. From the country side, Merle Haggard contributed "I'm Proud to Be an Okie from Muskogee." (Hippies quickly turned "Okie" into a longhair anthem and Kinky Friedman contributed a version entitled "I Am Just an Asshole from El Paso.")

5   And to be a feminist country music fan is an exercise in cultural masochism. There you are trying to uphold the personhood of the female sex, while listening to "She Got the Gold Mine, I Got the Shaft" or "Don't the Girls All Get Prettier at Closing Time." Women in country music are either saints or sluts, but they're mostly sluts. She's either a "good-hearted woman" or a "honky-tonk angel." There are more hard-hearted women in country music ("I Gave Her a Ring, She Gave Me the Finger"), despicable bimbos ("Ruuuby, Don't Take Your Love to Town"), and heartless gold diggers ("Satin Sheets to Lie On, Satin Pillow to Cry On") than the scholars can count. Even the great women country singers aren't much help. The immortal Patsy Cline was mostly lovesick for some worthless heel ("I Fall to Pieces") and Tammy Wynette's greatest contribution was to advise us "Stand by Your Man." (Tammy has stood by several of them.)

6   Not until the great Loretta Lynn, who is also musically lovelorn with great frequency but shows more spunk about it, did we hear some country songs that can be considered feminist. "Don't Come Home A-Drinkin' with Lovin' on Your Mind" is one of Loretta's

better ass-kickin' anthems. The high-spirited spoof "Put Another Log on the Fire" is a classic parody of sexism: "Now, don't I let you wash the car on Sunday?/Don't I warn you when you're gettin' fat?/Ain't I gonna take you fishin' with me someday?/Well, a man can't love a woman more than that." Evidence of the impact of the Women's Movement on country music can be found in the hit song "If I Said You Had a Beautiful Body, Would You Hold It Against Me?"

7   But this is fairly limited evidence of redeeming social value in the genre. So what do we see in it? For one thing, how can you not love a tradition that produces such songs as "You Done Stompt on my Heart, an' Squished That Sucker Flat"? (Featuring the refrain "Sweetheart, you just sorta/ stompt on my aorta.") Or "Everything You Touch Turns to Dirt." Many cultures have popular song forms that reflect the people's concerns. In Latin cultures the *corridos,* written by immortal poets such as Garcia Lorca, give voice to the yearnings of the voiceless. In our culture, "Take This Job and Shove It" serves much the same function.

8   If you want to take the pulse of the people in this country, listen to country-western music. I first knew a mighty religious wave was gathering when I heard ditties like "Drop-kick Me, Jesus, Through the Goalposts of Life." I also knew the Moral Majority was past its prime and Pat Robertson would go nowhere when I heard "I Wrote a Hot Check to Jesus" on country radio, followed by "Would Jesus Wear a Rolex on His Television Show?"

9   Contrary to popular opinion, it is not easy to write country songs: many try and fail. One guy who never made it is Robin Dorsey from Matador, Texas. He went to Tech and had a girlfriend from Muleshoe about whom he wrote the love song "Her Teeth Was Stained but Her Heart Was Pure." She took offense and quit him over it, which caused him to write the tragedy-love song "I Don't Know Whether to Commit Suicide Tonight or Go Bowlin'."

10   Country music is easily parodied and much despised by intellectuals, but like soap operas, it is much more like real life than your elitists will admit. What do most people truly care about? International arms control? Monetary policy? Deconstructive criticism? Hell, no. What they care about most is love ("We Used to Kiss Each Other on the Lips, but Now it's All Over"). Betrayal ("Your Cheatin' Heart"). Revenge ("I'm Gonna Hire a Wino to Decorate Our Home"; "Who's Sorry Now?"). Death ("Wreck on the

Highway"). Booze ("Four on the Floor and a Fifth under the Seat"; "She's Actin' Single, I'm Drinkin' doubles"). Money ("If You've Got the Money, Honey, I've Got the Time"). Loneliness ("Hello, Walls"). Tragedy-love songs ("She Used My Tears to Wash her Socks"; "My Bride's Wedding Dress Was Wash-and-Ware").

11 Now here we're talking major themes. In a song called "You Never Even Called Me by My Name," which author Steve Goodman labeled "the perfect country-western song," momma, trucks, trains, and prison are also suggested as mandatory country-western themes.

12 In this country we waste an enormous amount of time and energy disapproving of one another in three categories where only personal taste matters: hair, sports, and music. We need not review the family trauma, high dudgeon, tsk-tsking, and lawsuits caused over the years by hair and how people wear it. Consider the equally futile expenditure of energy in condemning other people's sports. And in music, good Lord, the zeal put into denouncing rock, sneering at opera, finding classical a bore, jazz passé, bluegrass fit only for snuff-dippers—why, it's stupefying. It's incomprehensible.

13 I am open to the argument that Ludwig van Beethoven has contributed more great music to the world than has Earl Scruggs. But there is a tiresome neoconservative argument these days that holds relativism responsible for all the evil in the modern world. These folks denounce the abandonment of absolute standards in everything—morality, taste, the postal service. As though the fact that people enjoy reading *The Three Musketeers* were a menace to Dante. I have felt the sting of their snotty scorn, the lash of their haughty sneers, and what I have to say is "You Are Just Another Sticky Wheel on the Grocery Cart of Life."

Thesis and Organization

1. What idea about country music does Ivins set out in her introduction, paragraphs 1 and 2?
2. Paragraphs 3–5 group together to support the idea that country music is "politically incorrect," an idea that Ivins develops using multiple examples. Choose one of those examples that you are familiar with and explain in greater detail how it does or does not support her assertion.
3. Ivins maintains that "If you want to take the pulse of the people in this country, listen to country-western music." She then uses paragraphs 8–11 to support that idea. What other examples can you think of?

4. The essay is a bit more subtle than it may first appear in that it covers a number of subjects: why Molly Ivins likes country music, attitudes toward country music, and snobbism are a few of those subjects. What else does she touch on? What is her main subject? What reasons do you have for your choice?

5. Given Ivins' point in her introduction, her assertions in paragraphs 3 and 8, and her conclusion in paragraphs 12 and 13, what is her thesis? Summarize your idea in one sentence.

Technique and Style

1. Using the WHAT TO LOOK FOR as a starting point, see how many types of diction you can find. Explain how that range of diction affects you as a reader.

2. At various points in the essay, Ivins is funny, scornful, serious, and annoyed. What other emotions come through? How would you characterize Ivins' tone?

3. Ivins begins with her personal experience, but by the end of the essay she has moved to more general statements about American culture and tastes. Explain how you would categorize the essay—as personal, general, or somewhere in between.

4. What reasons can you think of for including paragraph 9? What, if anything, does it add to the essay?

5. Think about the examples of country music singers, titles, and lyrics that Ivins cites. Given those examples, how would you define country music?

Suggestions for Writing

Consider another category of popular music—rap, rock 'n roll, blues, heavy metal, New Age, and the like. Choosing a type of music that you both like and know about, examine it as though it were a window into our culture. What do you see? What does it say about our concerns? Why do some people not like it? If music doesn't seem to be a worthwhile subject, then consider kinds of television shows, films, or books.

S weatin' for Nothin'

Michael Barlow

Unlike many students at the University of New Orleans, Michael Barlow went straight on to college after graduating from high school. As his essay implies, he is not a fitness freak, although he is engaged in a number of college activities. An education major concentrating in teaching English at the secondary level, he may soon turn up in the classroom on the other side of the desk. No matter what he does, he will try not to emulate Mimi.

WHAT TO LOOK FOR *Starting and ending an essay are often the most difficult parts of writing. One technique that works well is the one Barlow uses. You'll see that he sets up a framework by first setting out the image of the hamster in the cage and then, in his conclusion, returning to it. The effect is a sense of closure. You can use the same technique by ending your essay with a reference to an idea you bring out in your introduction.*

KEY WORDS AND PHRASES

entropy (3)	cams (9)
incandescent (4)	turbines (9)
amorphous (5)	pony wheel (10)
gratuitous (9)	wattage (10)
narcissism (9)	

1   During spring break, I visited my family in Fort Worth. It was a pleasant visit, but my how things have changed. My mother has purchased a stairmaster and joined a fitness club. My father now jogs at 6:00 every morning, and my sister is contemplating aerobics as one of her first electives when she goes off to college this August. This was not the group of people I last saw in January. These were not the laid-back complacent folks I've known so well. This was not *my* family.

2   One night around 2 A.M., after partying with some friends from high school, I was lying in bed watching Mimi, my pet hamster, crank out revolutions on an exercise wheel. I should have gone to sleep but I was captivated. The creaking of the wheel made me think of the strenuous exercise that seems to have plagued every-

one at 301 Lake Country Drive. What was it? What was going on? So I asked myself whether or not Mimi knew that sprinting in a metal cylinder wouldn't get her out of the cage. She probably didn't know—her brain is smaller than a kernel of corn.

3   But what about humans? What about my family? I see millions of Americans, like my family, in Spandex outfits and gel-cushioned shoes trying to get out of their cages. Something is wrong with the fitness mania that has swept the Western World, and from watching Mimi I know what it is. Entropy.

4   Entropy is the measure of the amount of energy unavailable for useful work in a system—metaphorically speaking, it is a measure of waste. In our throwaway society, we waste energy at a maddening pace. Coal is lit to make a fire, which produces a lot of carbon dioxide, while heating a small amount of water to make steam, which produces electricity, which lights an incandescent bulb in a room in a house where nobody's home. Basic waste.

5   Exercise mania has crippled our culture. It is no coincidence that we are running out of cheap and available energy while at the same time polluting the air, land, and sea with our waste. According to the laws of physics, entropy diminishes in a closed system, meaning that eventually everything will be reduced to an amorphous, undifferentiated blob. The universe is a closed system. There are some parallels to a hamster cage, and Mimi creates entropy at a noisy rate.

6   What did we do for exercise in those past centuries when people did not act like captive hamsters? If a person chopped down wood or ran a long way, it was because he or she needed fuel or wanted to get somewhere. Now we do such things to fit into new pants or to develop our biceps. We have treadmills, rowing machines, stairmasters, stationary bikes, Nordic Tracks, butt busters, and wall climbers, and we labor at them while going nowhere. Absolutely nowhere! We do work that is beyond useless; we do work that take energy and casts it to the wind like lint. And we don't even enjoy the work. Look at people in a health club. See anybody smiling?

7   There is nothing magical about fitness machines. We can get the exact same result by climbing up stairs in our homes or offices. Take a look at any set of stairs in any building. Anybody in Spandex headed up or down? No. People ride elevators all day, then drive to their fitness centers where they pay to walk up steps.

8   When I was looking at Mimi, I was thinking of Richard Simmons, the King of Entropy, who wants everybody to exercise all the time and has made insane amounts of money saying so. Simmons says that he has raised his metabolism so high that he can eat more without gaining weight. Working out to pig out—an entropy double whammy.

9   I have a solution for such gratuitous narcissism and I think Simmons might find a tearful video in it. Let people on the machines create useable energy as they burn off their flabby thighs and excess baggage. Hook up engines and cams and drive shafts that will rotate turbines and generate electricity. Let exercisers light the health club itself. Let them air condition it. Let the clubs store excess energy and sell it to nearby shop owners at low rates.

10   Better yet, create health clubs whose sole purpose is the generation of energy. Pipe the energy into housing projects. Have energy nights where singles get together to pedal, chat, and swap phone numbers. Build a giant pony wheel that operates a flour mill, a rock crusher, a draw bridge, a BMW repair shop. Have the poles protrude from the wheel with spots for a couple hundred joggers to push the wheel around. Install magazine racks on the poles. Have calorie collections and wattage wars. Make it "cool" to sweat for the betterment of mankind, not just for yourself.

11   We cannot afford much more entropy. If we forget that, we might as well be rodents in cages, running into the night. Just like Mimi.

Thesis and Organization

1. The essay is organized around the idea of problem and solution. In your own words, what does Barlow describe as the problem?
2. Paragraphs 5–7 give examples of kinds of exercise. What distinctions does Barlow draw among them?
3. The solution appears in paragraphs 9–10 and is a humorous one. Summarize it.
4. In your own words, state the serious point made in the last paragraph.
5. What do you find to be the main subject of the essay? Exercise? Fads? Waste? Entropy? American culture? What reasons can you find for your choice?

Technique and Style

1. Look up *analogy* in an unabridged dictionary and in the "Glossary of Usage." What analogy does Barlow draw? What does the analogy contribute to the essay?
2. Paragraph 4 defines *entropy*. How necessary is that definition? What does it add to the essay?
3. What does the essay gain with the example of Richard Simmons?
4. Imagine you are one of the people filling up the fitness club. Would you be offended by this essay? Why or why not?
5. The person behind the words always comes through in an essay, sometimes more clearly than others. Explain why you would or would not want Michael Barlow as a classmate or friend.

Suggestions for Writing

Try your own hand at a problem-solution essay, giving detailed examples of both the problem and the solution. Like Barlow, you may want your tone to be humorous, sugar-coating a serious point. As for the problem, you're apt to be surrounded with choices—getting enough hours into the day, scraping tuition together, keeping up with schoolwork, deciding in which pleasure to indulge, sorting out family loyalties. Illustrate the problem by using examples. You may find examples for the solution harder to come by, in which case, like Barlow, you may want to propose something fantastic.

Why We Still Can't Stop Watching

Michiko Kakutani

Many of us watched the arrest and subsequent news coverage and trial of O. J. Simpson with the same mixture of "ghoulish" horror and fascination that Michiko Kakutani notes in her essay. A book reviewer and media critic for The New York Times, *Kakutani wrote her essay at the height of that initial news coverage, right after the chase and arrest of Simpson. Kakutani analyzes the public's fascination with Simpson, using him as an extended example of our culture's continuing admiration of the outlaw. As Kakutani develops her analysis, she uses multiple examples from our history and popular culture to support her point. The essay was published on July 3, 1994, two weeks after Simpson's arrest.*

WHAT TO LOOK FOR *Kakutani uses many examples throughout her essay, many of which will be familiar to the reader. Notice which names are explained and which are not, and also look out for how Kakutani identifies those that may be unfamiliar. Did she choose the right ones to identify?*

KEY WORDS AND PHRASES
cinema verité (2)	*sanctimonious (6)*
chastised (2)	*envoys (6)*
voyeurism (2)	*totalitarian (9)*
phalanx (3)	

1   Just what has made the O.J. Simpson story fascinating enough to dominate news coverage and talk show (and living room) conversations for days?

2   Certainly there is something a little ghoulish about the whole spectacle: 95 million Americans watching the 90-minute car chase to see if the whole awful story would end in further violence, a car crash perhaps or a cinema verité gunshot; and on Thursday, an estimated one in four households tuning into the first day of the preliminary hearings, as though a new murder mystery miniseries had debuted. Many of those who watched last week's installment—

concerning the bloody murder scene and efforts on the part of Mr. Simpson's defense team to suppress evidence they say was improperly gathered by the police—chastised themselves for their voyeurism, even as they continued to channel surf avidly from network to network.

3   What the Simpson story possesses is a raw narrative appeal that uncannily taps into the collective unconscious, combining the most sensationalistic aspects of a variety of literary genres, from Greek tragedy to the gothic romance to the true-crime thriller. Much has already been made of Mr. Simpson's celebrity and our fascination with the fall of a famous man, but if the old O.J., the one we thought we knew from the football field and the Hertz commercials, appeared to personify one version of the American dream—the poor kid from the ghetto who reinvented himself as a genial spokesman for corporate America—the new O.J., the one we saw in the white Bronco, being chased by a phalanx of police cars and helicopters, seems to embody another potent American myth, that of the outlaw, the renegade in flight from the law. Perhaps this is one reason why people stood on overpasses in L.A., shouting "Go, Juice, Go," and why vendors selling T-shirts (reading "Pray for O.J." and "Turn the Juice Loose") continue to do brisk business, even in the face of disturbing revelations about Mr. Simpson's history of spousal abuse.

4   No doubt most of these supporters believe or hope that he is innocent; no doubt many have not even allowed the fact of the brutal murders—which he may or may not have committed—to fully sink in. Others do not seem to even want to address the question of guilt. Indeed, the presumption of innocence Mr. Simpson enjoys in our legal and civic tradition wars with our romantic impulse to believe the worst, to seek Mr. Hyde in Dr. Jekyll, the monster within the gentleman.

5   From the start, there has been a bizarre circus atmosphere surrounding the case, heightened by the defense and prosecution's theatrics and the news media's raucous coverage. Helping to blur the lines between reality and fiction, many commentators have come up with movie analogies to try to describe the Simpson phenomenon, including "The Fugitive," which recounted the story of a man wrongly accused of killing his wife; "Thelma and Louise," which ended with its two heroines driving off a cliff, as they're pursued by the police; "Dog Day Afternoon," which depicted a lik-

able bank robber's hapless efforts to pull off a heist, and "The Sugarland Express," which chronicled a young fugitive couple's flight from the law.

6   These movies, like "Butch Cassidy and the Sundance Kid" and "Bonnie and Clyde," reinforce the myth of the outsider, the people on the fringes who somehow find themselves beyond the law. What's more, they help nurture a reflex reaction—to root against the sanctimonious envoys of officialdom (be they humorless police officers or stuffy government bureaucrats), and to root for the beleagured hero, regardless of whether he's committed a harmless prank or a savage crime.

7   Evil, of course, has always exerted a powerful fascination. Satan remains the most compelling character in "Paradise Lost," just as Darth Vader dominates "Star Wars" and Hannibal Lecter commandeers "The Silence of the Lambs." Members of the Romantic movement embraced man's darker impulses as a source of energy and freedom, while Dostoevsky frequently used the criminal as a mirror of man's conflicted nature. Today it is serial killers (until the advent of the Simpson case, anyway) who have cornered the market on public attention, generating grisly T-shirts, trading cards and comic books of their own.

8   Actually, the ordinary, non-political criminal, especially when gifted with intelligence and talent, has long exerted a bizarre hold on the literary imagination. André Gide, Jean Cocteau, Paul Claudel and Jean-Paul Sartre helped win a presidential pardon for Jean Genet, who had been jailed for theft and prostitution, while Norman Mailer helped win parole for the writer Jack Henry Abbott, who subsequently killed a waiter in Manhattan's East Village six weeks after being released from prison.

9   In his famous 1957 essay, "The White Negro," Mr. Mailer equated violence with virility and creativity: "One is Hip or one is Square," he wrote. "One is a rebel or one conforms, one is a frontiersman in the Wild West of American night life, or else a Square cell, trapped in the totalitarian tissues of American society, doomed willy-nilly to conform if one is to succeed."

10   Such arguments, clearly, are well rooted in this country's pioneer tradition, which has fed the American impulse to romanticize outlaws, vigilantes and gangsters. The anti-authoritarian legacy of the Revolutionary War, after all, was galvanized by the frontier ex-

perience—which gave us folk heroes like Jesse James and Billy the Kid, and which suggested, as the historian Richard Slotkin has observed, that redemption could be found in violence, that the violent man of action was superior to the plodding machinery of the law.

11   All of which perhaps helps to explain how a woman in front of the Los Angeles courthouse could stand before a CNBC camera and make the astonishing statement: "Guilty or not, we love you O.J."

Thesis and Organization

1. Kakutani introduces her essay with a one-sentence paragraph that is a question. What advantages and disadvantages can you think of for opening the essay in that manner?
2. Paragraph 2 provides the immediate context for the analysis that follows in paragraphs 3–10. Explain why paragraph 2 is or is not essential.
3. List the examples Kakutani uses in paragraphs 3–10. What examples can be grouped together to illustrate larger points? What are those points?
4. Consider what Kakutani says about the public's fascination with O.J. Simpson together with Kakutani's other examples and the points they illustrate. What is the essay's thesis?
5. Paragraph 11 concludes the essay with an example. How does it relate to Kakutani's thesis?

Technique and Style

1. Look up *paradox* in the "Glossary of Terms." What paradoxes do you find in the essay? What do they add?
2. Based upon the examples that Kakutani uses, how would you describe the essay's audience? What (if anything) can you deduce about the audience's age, educational level, habits, gender, race, and the like?
3. Choose one of Kakutani's paragraphs to explain how she uses a topic sentence and how she supports it.
4. Long sentences can be very effective as long as they guide the reader through the ideas clearly. The second sentence in paragraph 3 is a case in point and a length most writers would not attempt. Try your own hand at a similar sentence, using the parts of speech and punctuation of Kakutani's sentence to help you.
5. Look at the list of examples you drew up and label the fields they

came from. What are they? What examples from other fields can you think of?

Suggestions for Writing

Think about the kinds of shows that you see on television—sit-coms, family shows, talk shows, contests, "Sixty Minutes" kinds of programs, cartoons—to discover why people might watch them. Choose one type and analyze it in terms of its appeal, citing multiple examples of shows you have seen or know about. If you prefer, choose a magazine you're familiar with and look at the advertisements, finding one kind of product that appears in a number of ads. Depending upon the magazine, you might find lots of cosmetics ads or advertisements for cars or kinds of drinks. Using one category, select an advertisement that you can analyze in terms of its appeal, what the advertising agency is trying to sell you that is embodied in the product. When you write your essay, you can use one ad as your extended example and the others in the same category as multiple examples. No matter what assignment you choose, remember that you need to show why your examples are examples of a larger point or else you end up with a list instead of support for your thesis.

$\boxed{W}$hen Only Monsters Are Real

Brent Staples

Now on the editorial staff of the New York Times, *Brent Staples has had a long and distinguished career in journalism. Throughout that career, he has been particularly sensitive to the relationship between the media and Afro-Americans, between the reporting of the black experience and its reality. The essay that follows appeared in the* New York Times *in November 1993. It was originally subtitled "'The Black Experience' And Kody Scott."*

WHAT TO LOOK FOR   *Odd as it may sound, verbs have moods, and, as you might expect, their moods reveal the attitude of the writer. Most of the time when you write, you use the indicative mood, one that states a fact or asks a question—as in "I am reading this paragraph." Now and then you'll use the subjunctive to state possibility, desire, contradiction, or uncertainty, as in a sentence built around* if: *"If I read the essay, I might enjoy it." The imperative mood—one that states a command or request—doesn't occur as often but can be very useful. Consider (an imperative) how much mileage Staples gets out of it in his essay.*

KEY WORDS AND PHRASES

Phillips Exeter (1)	*denounced (5)*
stereotypical (2)	*torso (6)*
Harlem (2)	*inevitable (6)*
embark (3)	*inferno (6)*
perverse (3)	*equivalent (6)*
romanticism (3)	*Grosse Pointe (6)*
swaggering (3)	*estranged (7)*
Rodney King (4)	*Richard Wright (9)*
Reginald Denny (4)	*abject (9)*
illuminating (5)	*valid (10)*
machete (5)	*bias (10)*
primary (5)	

1   Never forget Edmund Perry, the black Phillips Exeter graduate who seemed destined for Wall Street or Congress until he was shot to death trying to rob an undercover cop.

2   Edmund Perry did not come from the stereotypical underclass

family. His mother was a teacher and president of the P.T.A. His older brother attended an Ivy League college. Growing up in Harlem, Edmund had been a bright Bible school student who quizzed the minister about God. But when he arrived at Exeter, Edmund shed his middle-classness and donned the mask of the angry urban thug. He played the role so well that other black students were encouraged to be like him. And playing tough ended his life.

3   Like many before and after him, Edmund succumbed to the American fascination with angry black men. The Cosby family notwithstanding, black prep school boys who study the classics and live within the law have found only marginal acceptance in American cultural reality. The culture's taste runs heavily to black Frankensteins. Lacking a visible alternative, black boys rush to the monster role. And when the news, entertainment and publishing industries embark on a "black story," they often focus, with a kind of perverse romanticism, on the swaggering urban criminal.

4   Consider the L.A. riots. When the press shifted its eye from the central characters, Rodney King and Reginald Denny, L.A.'s gangsters got more attention than people like Congresswoman Maxine Waters, or the prosperous blacks of Baldwin Hills. The most enduring figure to emerge was Monster Kody Scott, a murderous person and member of one of L.A.'s most brutal street gangs. Monster is now an inmate at Pelican Bay State Prison, a high-security fortress in northern California. He became a celebrity when interviewed on "60 Minutes."

5   Kody Scott's memoir, "Monster: The Autobiography of an L.A. Gangmember," is the subject of an illuminating article in the December *Atlantic Monthly*. The book describes how Monster shot a dozen rivals and how one was dismembered with a machete. He has never been convicted of murder but has spent half his life in jail for assault and other crimes. Early publicity from the publisher, Grove/Atlantic, characterized Monster as "a primary voice of the black experience." After being denounced by Leonce Gaiter in *Buzz* magazine, Grove/Atlantic amended the phrase to "a primary voice coming out of the black underclass." But even that's too simple.

6   Kody—photographed in dark glasses, machine pistol in hand, his mammoth torso bare—presents himself as the inevitable product of the urban inferno. "To be in a gang in South Central when I joined," he writes, "is the equivalent of growing up in Grosse Pointe, Michigan, and going to college: everyone does it."

7   But Kody's criminalization was less inevitable than he lets on. The singer Ray Charles was his godfather. Kody's mother, though estranged from her husband, was a diligent homemaker and homeowner. Kody's brother Kevin is an actor living in Burbank. His brother Kim joined the Air Force. A third brother, Kerwin, works at the 32nd Street Market in South Central. His sister, Kendis, is studying data processing. Certainly the lure of the streets was strong. But Kody Scott had choices. He chose to become Monster.

8   In *The Atlantic Monthly*, Mark Horowitz writes: "Apart from a few brief mentions Kevin, Kim, Kendis and Kerwin are nowhere to be found in 'Monster.' There's no childhood, and very little about Kody's mother. They don't fit Monster's version."

9   In spirit, Monster's version of himself is pretty much the same as Richard Wright's portrayal of Bigger Thomas, the twisted, Frankenstinian character in the novel "Native Son." Bigger rapes and murders, we're told, because he can't help it; abject poverty pushed him to it. Bigger—the soulless beast, empty of humanity—is the sort of person many Americans reflexively think of when they seek to define "the black experience." But there is no *one* black experience.

10   The black middle class is larger than ever, but the black prep school boy has yet to become a valid literary type. Morgan Entrekin, Grove/Atlantic's publisher, agrees that the bias is unfortunate. A book about the black middle class is scheduled for next year, but Grove/Atlantic worries that people will ignore it. Put me down for a dozen copies, Mr. Entrekin. Deliver me from Biggers and Monsters and Frankensteins.

Thesis and Organization

1. Staples opens his essay with the example of Edmund Perry, paragraphs 1–3. What is the point of that example?

2. The essay shifts from Edmund Perry to the Los Angeles riots, then to Kody Scott. What connection links these people and events?

3. Paragraph 5 discusses the publicity for Kody Scott's book. What does Staples object to?

4. Staples' essay touches on a number of subjects: America's "fascination" with "black Frankensteins" (3), the media's "perverse romanticism" (3), the media's coverage of blacks (3–5, 10), and the black middleclass

(10). Which is his main subject? What reasons can you supply for your choice?

5. Given that subject, what is Staples' thesis?

Technique and Style

1. What connection can you discover between the introduction (1–3) and the conclusion (10)?
2. Look up *irony* in an unabridged dictionary. What examples of it can you find in Staples' essay?
3. Paragraph 9 alludes to two literary figures, Bigger Thomas and Frankenstein. What do these allusions add to the essay?
4. Explain whether Staples' use of the imperative makes the essay more formal or more informal.
5. Staples uses Kody Scott as the extended example in the essay (4–9). In what ways does that example support the thesis?

Suggestions for Writing

The line between being an individual and being an outlaw is a fine one that is sometimes hard to draw. Think of a person you know or have read about who walks that line. Perhaps one of your high school classmates fits the category, or a big name in music, films, or sports. Write an essay describing that person, giving ample examples to prove your point. Or, if you prefer, think of someone who projects a distinct "image." As you draft your essay, use examples to describe the image and explain what it means to you. Perhaps it's an image you despise or admire.

Mom, Dad and Abortion

Anna Quindlen

Anna Quindlen's column, "Public & Private," appeared regularly in the New York Times. *Since then, Quindlen has retired from her position at the* Times *so that she can work full time on her fiction. Her column's title is a particularly appropriate one for an essay about a pregnant minor's right to privacy, the issue she considers in the essay that follows. It was published in 1990.*

WHAT TO LOOK FOR   *Many argumentative essays take one side and argue it, often drawing upon one counterargument to refute. Quindlen, however, takes a different approach that you may find easier to work with. As you read her essay, notice how she stakes out both sides to an argument and then proposes a middle ground, her own.*

KEY WORDS AND PHRASES
succor (8)   *mandate (19)*
inhibit (18)   *persona (22)*
facilitate (18)

1   Once I got a fortune cookie that said: to remember is to understand. I have never forgotten it.

2   A good judge remembers what it was like to be a lawyer. A good editor remembers what it was like to be a reporter.

3   A good parent remembers what it was like to be a child.

4   I remember adolescence, the years of having the impulse control of a mousetrap, of being as private as a safe-deposit box. If my mother said "How are you?" she was prying.

5   And I've remembered it more keenly since the Supreme Court ruled that the states may require a pregnant minor to inform her parents before having an abortion.

6   This is one of the most difficult of many difficult issues within the abortion debate. As good parents, we remember being teenagers, thinking that parents and sex existed in parallel universes.

7   But as good parents, it also seems reasonable to wonder why a

girl who cannot go on a school field trip without our knowledge can end a pregnancy without it.

8   The Supreme Court found succor in a Minnesota law that provides for something called "judicial bypass." If you are 15 and want to have an abortion but cannot tell your parents—for the law provides that both must be informed, not simply one—you can tell it to the judge. You come to the clinic, have an exam and counseling. Then you go to the courthouse, meet with a public defender and go to the judge's chambers, to be questioned about your condition, your family, your plans for the future.

9   If the judge agrees, you can have the abortion.

10   The Court did not find this an undue burden for a frightened 15-year-old.

11   Tina Welsh, who runs the only abortion clinic in Duluth, remembers the first girl she took to the courthouse when the law went into effect. The young woman did not want to notify her father; he was in jail for having sex with her sister. Ms. Welsh remembers taking girls up in the freight elevator because they had neighbors and relations working in the courthouse. You can just hear it:

12   "Hi, sweetheart, how are you? What brings you here?"

13   So much for the right to privacy.

14   But Ms. Welsh best remembers the young woman who asked, "How long will the jury be out?" She thought she was going on trial for the right to have an abortion.

15   Much of this debate centers, like the first sentence of *Anna Karenina,* on happy families, and unhappy ones. Abortion rights activists say parental notification assumes a world of dutiful daughters and supportive parents, instead of one riven by alcoholism, incest and abuse. Those opposed to abortion say it is unthinkable that a minor child should have such a procedure without her parents' knowledge.

16   But I remember something between the poles of cruelty and communication. I remember girls who wanted their parents to have certain illusions about them. Not girls who feared beatings, or were pregnant by their mother's boyfriend. Just girls who wanted to remain good girls in the minds that mattered to them the most.

17   Ms. Welsh remembers one mother who refused to let her husband know their daughter was having an abortion. "Twenty-five years ago," the woman said, "we made a promise to one another. I

would never have to clean a fish, and he would never have to know if his daughter was pregnant."

18   If parental notification laws are really designed to inhibit abortion—and I suspect they are—Ms. Welsh's experience suggests they are not terribly successful. Not one teenager who came to the Duluth clinic changed her mind, even in the face of public defenders and judicial questioning. If the point is to facilitate family communication, that's been something of a failure, too. In the five years the Minnesota law was in effect, 7000 minors had abortions. Half of those teenagers chose to face a stranger in his chambers rather than tell both parents.

19   But perhaps there is another purpose to all this. If adolescents want their parents to have illusions about them, parents need those illusions badly. These laws provide them. They mandate communication. If she has nothing to tell you, then it must mean nothing is wrong.

20   Ah, yes—I remember that.

21   These are difficult questions because they involve not-quite adults facing adult decisions. The best case is the daughter who decides, with supportive parents, whether to end a pregnancy or have a baby. The worst case is the girl who must notify the parent who impregnated her. Or the worst case is Becky Bell, a 17-year-old Indianapolis girl who died after an illegal abortion. She could not bear to tell her parents she was pregnant.

22   In the middle are girls who have been told by the Supreme Court that they must trade. They can keep a good-girl persona at home, but in exchange they must surrender some of their privacy and dignity. That is what adults want, and that is what we will have. We will take our illusions. The teenagers will take the freight elevator.

Thesis and Organization

1. What is the connection between the fortune cookie and the Supreme Court decision?
2. Which paragraphs explain the Supreme Court decision?
3. What paragraphs deal with examples of its effect?
4. What is Quindlen's opinion of the ruling?
5. Considering the ruling, the examples Quindlen provides, and her opinion, what do find to be the essay's thesis?

Technique and Style

1. How would you describe Quindlen's tone? Is she angry? Calm? Emotional? Logical? Sad? Distressed? What?
2. Now and then, Quindlen sets off a personal comment in a separate paragraph. Do you think this technique strengthens or weakens the essay? Explain.
3. Reread Quindlen's description of adolescence (4). What metaphors can you substitute for the ones she uses? Which do you like best and why?
4. The two sentences of paragraph 2 and the one in paragraph 3 together illustrate the technique of parallelism. Rewrite the sentences so that the parallelism is destroyed. What is lost? Gained?
5. One of the techniques Quindlen uses is to set out two opposing views and then find a middle ground. What examples can you find of this technique? What does it contribute to her tone? Her persona?

Suggestions for Writing

In a way, you can characterize Quindlen's essay as a thinking through of a compromise, which in that case was one reached by the Supreme Court. Think about the compromises in your own life, the times when you or your family found a middle ground. Think too about the compromises that exist in our culture, say the balance between rights and responsibilities, freedom and constraint, individual and group liberty.

Division
and Classification

*T*he next time you shop in a supermarket or clean out a closet, think about how you are doing it and you will understand the workings of **division** and **classification.** "How often do I wear those shoes?" and "I never did like that sweater" imply that dividing items according to how frequently you wear them would be a good principle for sorting out your bedroom closet. Supermarkets, however, do the sorting for you. Goods are divided according to shared characteristics— all dairy products in one section, meat in another, and so on—and then items are placed into those categories. The process looks easy, but if you have ever tried to find soy sauce, you know the pitfalls: Is it with the spices? Sauces? Gourmet foods? Health foods?

To divide a subject and then classify examples into the categories or classes that resulted from division calls for the ability to examine a subject from several angles, work out the ways in which it can be divided, and then discern similarities and differences among the examples you want to classify. A huge topic such as *animals* invites a long list of ways they can be divided: wild animals, work animals, pets; ones that swim, run, crawl; ones you have owned, seen, or read about. These groups imply principles for division—by degree of domesticity, by manner of locomotion, by degree of familiarity. Division and classification often help define each other in that having divided your subjects, you may find that once you start classifying, you have to stop and redefine your principle of division. If your division of animals is based on locomotion, for instance, where do you put the flying squirrel?

Division and classification is often used at the level of the paragraph. If your essay argues that a particular television commercial for toilet cleaner insults women, you might want to introduce the essay by enumerating other advertisements in that category—household products—that also insult women's intelligence.

From Julius Caesar's "Gaul is divided into three parts" to a 10-year-old's "animal, vegetable, or mineral," classification and division has had a long and useful history. And, of course, it has a useful present as well. You will see that in each of the essays in this chapter, the system of division and classification supports a thesis, though the essays use their theses for different purposes: to entertain, to explain, to argue.

AUDIENCE AND PURPOSE   Knowing who your readers are and what effect you want to have on them will help you devise your system of classification and sharpen your thesis. If your audience is quite specific, Laurel Dewey's essay, "Gads! It's Garlic," should be a useful model, for it is aimed at a specific audience, those who are interested in the positive effects of herbs but whose noses wrinkle at the mention of garlic. Beginning with her audience's negative associations, she moves quickly to the many good uses to which garlic can be put, categorizing them according to the herb's different effects. Dewey informs her readers. In writing about the significance of garlic, however, she also argues that it has definite positive qualities and therefore should be taken seriously.

To explain, however, is the more obvious use of division and classification. Richard Brookhiser informs his readers. In writing about intense people, he must define exactly what *intense* means and uses a variety of techniques to do so, thus mingling definition into division and classification. Writers who address a more general audience also need to know their audiences. In Russell Baker's "The Plot Against People," for example, his reader is the average human whose car breaks down, whose keys get lost, and whose flashlight rarely works. Baker proposes a theory that makes sense out of this chaos; he divides objects into three categories: "those that don't work, those that break down, and those that get lost." The principle behind Baker's sorting of inanimate objects is the method each uses to achieve its aim: "to resist man and ultimately to defeat him." Furnaces, pliers, barometers, keys, and various other objects are classified according to their method of waging war. Ostensibly, Baker is writing to inform; but because the reader readily recognizes the absurdity of Baker's system and his ironic tone, his true purpose is to entertain. That, too, is the main purpose behind the essay by James and Sammons, though James has an informative aim as well.

DIVISION   Some writers, such as Dewey, leap right into their system of classification, but others begin with division. Brookhiser, for example, first divides the intense from the non-intense and then goes on to fill each category with examples. James, however, focuses primarily on division, trying to find the line between good-natured and dangerous "hassling." Along the way, she discovers that the line is not so easy to draw.

SYSTEM OF CLASSIFICATION   To work effectively, a system of classification must be complete and logical. The system that governs how goods are arranged in a supermarket needs to be broad enough to cover everything a supermarket might sell, and it needs to make sense. Can openers should be with kitchen implements, not with vegetables; cans of peas should be with other canned goods, not with milk. Richard Brookhiser, for instance, after dividing the intense from the non-intense, then piles up examples of well-known people in each category. At the same time, he is careful to show that the quality of intensity is not linked to other categories, such as good and evil, nor is it to be confused with being busy. His categories are cleanly divided.

More likely, however, you will find some overlap among classes. This overlap can be accounted for by explaining it or by adjusting the system of division. Russell Baker, for example, writes of a world of willful inanimate objects and places women's purses in the category of "things that get lost." He notes that although the purse "does have some inherent capacity for breaking down, [it] hardly ever does; it almost invariably chooses to get lost."

Baker's categories exemplify a complete system, though it is humorously exaggerated. Just about all inanimate objects one might care about do have a habit of breaking down, getting lost, or not working. Baker pokes fun at the logic of his system, pointing out that furnaces break down with some frequency, but will never get lost. And just in case the reader may think that breaking down and not working are similar, Baker goes to some trouble to show the difference: the things we expect to work, do, but then break down; the things we expect not to work, don't, except perhaps the first time.

EXAMPLE   Examples are essential to classification, usually in the form of multiple illustrations. To differentiate the intense from the non-intense, Brookhiser draws first upon an example from his own experience, and then, when that doesn't work, moves on to public figures, starting with the most public—the President and the First Lady. Since those examples ring a bell he continues with presidents, goes on to other political figures, and then to celebrities and even to a saint. All of Caryn James's examples, however, are taken from her personal experience, beginning with the story of her encounter with a man "visibly affected by some chemical or other" and ending with a "cheerful version of an oldies song."

THESIS AND ORGANIZATION   Essays structured by division and classification are usually organized simply and have a clear-cut thesis. All the essays use a straightforward pattern of organization. "The New York Walk: Survival of the Fiercest" takes some liberties in that James weaves narrative, description, and example in and out of the essay along with division and classification. "Felines of the Interior Guard," "Gads! It's Garlic," "Intense!" and "The Plot Against People" follow the classic method of development for division and classification essays, with the body of the paper devoted to developing the various categories involved in the author's system of classification. Two of these essays also have the most easily spotted kind of thesis, one that is made up of various explicit statements contained in the essay.

USEFUL TERMS
Classification   You would use classification to examine a class of things according to shared characteristics, grouping the things according to a similar feature.
Division   The process of separating, usually associated with classification. First a subject is divided into groups, then examples can be sorted out—classified—into the groups or categories.

IDEAS FOR WRITING   For practice in your journal or for a rough draft of an essay, draw up two columns. Label the first one with any positive characteristic that occurs to you—good, exciting, loyal, friendly, beautiful—anything. Then label the next column with the opposite word—evil, dull, unreliable, hostile, ugly. To practice simple division, think of examples you can plug in to illustrate your opposite qualities. To go a step further and work up a system of classification, choose the characteristic you find easiest to work with and think about various categories it can be broken into. For evil, you might think of different kinds of evil people or acts, such as social, political, religious, artistic, athletic, and so on.

▨ POINTERS FOR USING DIVISION AND CLASSIFICATION

Exploring the Topic

1. **How can your topic be divided?** What divisions can apply? Of those you list, which one is the best suited?
2. **What examples can you think of?** What characteristics do your examples have in common? Which do you have the most to say about?
3. **Are your categories for classification appropriate?** Are the categories parallel? Do they overlap? Do you need to make any adjustments?
4. **Do your examples fit your categories?** Are you sure the examples have enough in common? Are they obvious? Which are not?
5. **What is your principle for classification?** Have you applied it consistently to each category?
6. **Are your categories complete?** Do they cover the topic? Do they contain enough examples?
7. **How can your categories be sequenced?** From simple to complex? Least to most important? Less to most effective?
8. **What is your point?** What assertion are you making? Does your system of classification support it? Are your examples appropriate?
9. **What is your purpose?** Are you primarily making your point to express your feelings, to inform, to persuade, to entertain?

Drafting the Paper

1. **Know your reader.** Where does your reader fit in relation to your system of classification? Is the reader part of it? If so, how? If the reader is not part of your system, is he or she on your side, say a fellow student looking at teachers? What does your audience know about your topic? About your system of classification? What does the reader not know? Your audience might be biased toward or against your subject and classification system. How can you best foster or combat the bias?
2. **Know your purpose.** If your primary purpose is to express your feelings, make sure that you are not just writing to yourself and that you are not treading on the toes of your audience. Similarly, if you are writing to persuade, make sure you are not convincing only yourself. Check to see

that you are using material that may convince someone who disagrees with you—or at the least is either sitting on the fence or hasn't given the matter much thought. Writing to inform is probably the easiest here, for though your subject may be familiar, your system of classification is probably new. On the other hand, writing to entertain is difficult and will require a deft use of persona.

3. **Set up your system of classification early in the paper.** You may find that a definition is in order or that some background information is necessary, but make your system clear and bring it out early.

4. **Explain the principle behind the system.** To give your system credibility, you need to provide an explanation for the means of selection you chose. The explanation can be brief, a phrase or two, but it should be there.

5. **Select appropriate examples.** Perhaps you can best illustrate a class by one extended example, or maybe it would be better to pile on examples. If your examples are apt to be unfamiliar to your audience, make sure you give enough detail so that they are explained by their contexts.

6. **Make a point.** Remember that what you have to say about your subject is infinitely more interesting than the subject itself. So, too, your major assertion is more important than your system of classification; it is what your system of classification adds up to. It's easy, in writing this kind of paper, to mistake the means for the end, so make sure that you use classification to support an overall assertion.

*F*elines of the Interior Guard

Jim Sammons

Having spent 26 years as a Washington state trooper, Jim Sammons decided to retire from the force and return to college. When he's not studying civil engineering and surveying at Renton Technical College in Renton, Washington, where he is now in his second year, he lives with his wife and the Interior Guard on a ranch in Idaho. Even after six years in the Marine Corps and service in Vietnam, Sammons was only somewhat prepared for the feline invasions and manuevers he describes in his essay.

WHAT TO LOOK FOR   Wordplay *is a term used when the author is obviously having fun with words. Often that fun takes the form of puns, twisted clichés, and language that emphasizes metaphor. Sammons, for example, takes the ordinary term "one or two" and changes it to "one or three," a verbal bit of slapstick. As you read his essay, see what other forms of wordplay you can find.*

KEY WORDS AND PHRASES

troika (1)	*clemency (5)*
on the lam (5)	*Sergeant Murphy (6)*
bivouac (5)	

1   I've always had a cat or three around my house. My troika, as I refer to them, has evolved into a loose-knit Interior Guard unit whose function is to patrol my home and take charge of my most comfortable piece of furniture—the couch. I never thought I'd have to defend my couch from those cats' well-organized efforts, but given the nature of my felines, I do.

2   General Schwartskoff, the first-born cat, is the commander of the guard. He is a natural leader. While a bit of a sourpuss much of the time, he is a large, but not fat, pompous, black cat. With his ego leading the way, he swaggers into the kitchen, inspecting behind the pantry door for friend or foe. Inspection completed, he rapidly marches across the floor to his food dish bunkered between the refrigerator and the far wall. Once there, he loudly be-

gins crunching down his dry rations as if arming a weapon. Should another cat approach, the General hunches his shoulders, partially turns, and hisses a warning.

3   Colonel North, our second cat, is usually the recipient of this warning. The Colonel is a yellow, tiger-striped feline who is as mischievous as he looks. He has a catch-me-if-you-can attitude. Colonel North is the officer of the day, every day. He will begin a skirmish by scratching the furniture. Then, when he hears me approach, he runs for cover under the kitchen table, denying me the opportunity of tossing him outside. If I try capturing him, he often pretends to dash for the kitchen door, then escapes using the chair as cover. The Colonel is a sharp-looking, well-groomed, tidy-to-the-extreme cat who will stand his ground unless caught off-guard while coughing up hair balls. That's when he's easiest to take prisoner. Colonel North will not be intimidated by General Schwartskoff.

4   The Colonel will stand his ground and fight as he did the other day during a skirmish over some loose kitty-candy that had spilled onto the pantry floor. To end the battle, I emptied a tankard of cold water on the opponents, who then hastily retreated. While mopping up the mess, I slipped and fell on my butt. When I regained my dignity, I found both cats purring softly and harmoniously—one at each end of my couch.

5   Sometimes when the Colonel is on the lam, he will silently run into the laundry room where he'll bivouac in a basket of warm, freshly dried laundry. That action is cause for a summary court martial punishable by tossing the offender outside. All too soon he's granted clemency by another family member who was not privy to the Colonel's recent conviction.

6   This same family member was also responsible for the third member of our troika. He came into our lives last July while I was re-building fence on our property in Idaho. During this work, my wife Diana drove up in her Toyota Corolla with a scrawny, orange kitten sitting on her lap. Through the car window, she handed me the little beast. Purring louder than the car's engine, the kitten vibrated like a wind-up toy in the palm of my hand. Later, while Diana and I sat swatting mosquitoes and enjoying an evening campfire, we took turns petting the little kitty as it leapt from my lap to Diana's and back. His hyperactivity soon earned him his name, Sergeant Murphy. He was constantly hungry and ate more frequently than my horses. We brought him home and he quickly

gained weight during the next few weeks. Because he was young, small, and intelligent, Sergeant Murphy soon made his presence known to the General and Colonel.

7   Now that they are inseparable comrades, my troika often tests their tactical talents. Such war games take place in the barn where General Schwartskoff takes command from atop a haystack. Last week, for example, I witnessed one of these maneuvers when I was feeding my horses their evening meal. Sergeant Murphy had concealed himself near the haystack while Colonel North reconnoitered the barn listening for indications of mouse movement. Then with a flick of his orange tail, the Colonel revealed his position. He had spotted his prey and leapt on it. The hapless mouse was doomed. Snarls exploded into deep guttural growls and screeching cat sirens as Sergeant Murphy and Colonel North simultaneously landed atop the mouse. As both trained killers attached each other, their small enemy escaped. Meanwhile, General Schwartskoff deposited his own small victory on our doorstep and then rubbed against the door to be let in. When Diana admitted the troika, I completed my chores and returned to the living room with relaxation on my mind. As expected, I found all members of the Interior Guard fast asleep on my couch. Taking command, I tossed the troika outside for their midnight watch and then returned to my nicely warmed, comfortable couch.

Thesis and Organization

1. What does Sammons' introduction lead you to expect about his system of division and classification?
2. Paragraphs 2–6 combine division and classification by discussing the cats according to rank and characteristics. What cat goes where and why?
3. Paragraph 7 concludes the essay by bringing all the cats together. How does their interaction reinforce their classification?
4. Think about Sammons' system of division and classification and the personalities of his cats. What is his thesis?

Technique and Style

1. What connection(s) can you find between Sammons' first and last paragraphs? What name would you give this strategy?
2. How would you describe Sammons' tone? What examples can you cite to support your opinion?

3. *Coherence* is what gives an essay the impression of unity, and it is brought about by the writer carefully linking ideas to each other. What examples can you find that give Sammons' essay coherence?
4. Paragraph 6 introduces another person into the essay, Sammons' wife Diana. In what ways does that addition add or detract from the overall effect of the essay?
5. Reread the essay, marking any word that has a military association. What reasons can you think of for this metaphoric use of language?

Suggestions for Writing

Think of the kinds of friends you have and see if you can work out a system of division and classification you can fit them into. Perhaps you have some who are generals whereas others are sergeants and privates. Or perhaps you can divide them up into good, better, and best friends or another more individualized classification. If the subject of friends doesn't appeal, think of pets you have had or places that you enjoy. Once you have your subject and categories picked out, then brainstorm for examples that you can use, placing them in their appropriate categories. When you draft your paper, use what you learned from writing description and narration to bring your examples to life.

The New York Walk: Survival of the Fiercest

Caryn James

Division and classification may seem to play a small part in Caryn James's essay, but it's a crucial one, for misreading the kind of man who hassles women on a city street can have serious consequences. Central to James's essay is the initial division between "a harmless gesture and a threat" (13). Faced with either, most women adopt the " 'don't mess with me' glare" that James finds natural. But most also wonder about the long-term effects of that glare on the glarer. As the essay explains, James lives in New York City. Her essay was, appropriately, published in the New York Times *on October 17, 1993.*

WHAT TO LOOK FOR   *As you write, you'll probably discover that you use a number of rhetorical modes. James, for example, begins and ends with narration and description, and the body of her essay incorporates division and classification, example, process, cause and effect, and comparison and contrast. The mixture of modes may make the essay hard to classify, but it also gives it variety.*

KEY WORDS AND PHRASES

gridlock (1)	moot (12)
Times Square (1)	tinged (12)
maneuver (5)	Holly Golightly (12)
sidling (6)	Tiffany's (12)
naïf (8)	'burbs (12)
Darwinian (9)	savor (13)
cobblestoned (10)	fluke (13)
psychic (11)	Broadway (13)
residue (12)	

1   I know better than to talk back to guys who hassle women on the street. But on one weird August afternoon, I was caught in pedestrian gridlock in Times Square and the humidity turned my common sense to mush. A young man so average-looking he belonged in a Nike commercial planted himself on the sidewalk in

front of me, purposely blocking my path, and offered some not-poetic variation on "Hey, baby."

2   What I did next was something no short, slight, sane person should ever do: I stamped my little foot and snapped at him in unprintable terms to get out of my way, right now! And while I was wondering why I had chosen a response that was both ineffectual *and* ridiculous, the street hassler smiled, stepped aside and said in a good-natured, singsong voice, "You're gonna learn to love me."

3   Humor is a desirable quality in a man, but this remark did not make him a person to take home. He was visibly affected by some chemical or other, so I made sure to stay behind him as he woozed his way toward traffic. A basic rule of navigating the New York sidewalks, like driving anyplace, is that it's safer to be behind the drunk driver or drug-addled walker than in front of him.

4   And I didn't want him to see that my deliberately off-putting scowl was turning into a laugh.

5   For an instant I had almost lost the protective covering, the "don't mess with me" glare, that so many of us wear on crowded urban streets. Then I remembered that danger is real—the humor made him seem harmless, but his swaying toward an intersection suggested someone seriously out of control—and that walking in the city is a precise defensive maneuver.

6   This is especially, though not exclusively, true for women. Men are hassled, too, but physical size and social conditioning have made women more likely to be picked on. Walking can become an exhausting series of paralyzing questions. Should you slow down for the guy who seems, quite obviously, about to ask for directions? (I tried it once and was asked to join a theater group.) When is someone being innocently friendly, and when is he sidling up to get a better grip on your wallet or purse? When is a comment an invisible weapon, and when is it just a remark?

7   What's more, 30 years of raised feminist consciousness has taught us all that when men yell out to women on the street, whether to comment on a smile or issue a crude invitation, no compliment is involved. The average street hassler is not a fussy type, and while he may keep an eye out for a 17-year-old with no thighs, he will happily go after whoever crosses his line of vision: your mother, your granny, your self.

8   So most women have mastered the New York Walk for avoiding unpleasant encounters: eyes ahead but with good peripheral

vision, bag clutched to your side, a purposeful stride and an un-
friendly look. If someone talks to you, think of him as an obscene
phone caller. Hang up. Do not acknowledge that he exists. In a
big city, this is as necessary as locking your doors, and only a naïf
would think otherwise.

9   Most of the time, this survival strategy doesn't bother me. I've
always thought that my chilly, don't-talk-to-strangers New England
upbringing has given me a Darwinian advantage; I've been naturally selected for this urban life. Ignoring strangers who talk to me
in Times Square—people to whom I have not, after all, been properly introduced—makes me feel right at home.

10   I could have evolved differently. My sister transplanted herself
to Virginia, and while walking with her there on a civilized cob-
blestoned street once, I was shocked to hear her say: "You know,
you don't have to grab your bag like that. You're not in New York
anymore."

11   At moments like that, it's easy to wonder about the psychic cost
of living in a city where such guardedness becomes second nature.
Is it even possible, when you step into your house or office, to
drop the hostile mask quite so easily or thoroughly as you imagine
you can?

12   What residue of snarling distrust must build up over the years,
so slowly you'd never notice it accumulating? Those are finally
moot questions for someone like me, for whom New York will always be tinged with Holly Golightly glamour. Assuming a defensive posture while walking down the street seems a reasonable
trade-off for the advantages of living here. Just as a matter of personal preference, I'd rather be hassled outside the Metropolitan
Museum or Tiffany's than on a farm or in the 'burbs. (Don't say it
doesn't happen.)

13   Maybe the best one can do is to savor those rare episodes during which it is easy to tell the difference between a harmless gesture and a threat. On another summer day, by a fluke in the law of
averages, I happened to be the only person walking by a real-life
cliché: a scaffold full of construction workers having lunch at a site
on Broadway. As I passed, glare in place and prepared for anything, they started to sing a cheerful version of an oldies song:
"There she goes, a-walkin' down the street/Singin' doo-wah-diddy-
diddy-dum-diddy-do."

14   Hours later as I left my office, several blocks away, I passed a
man who gave a big surprised wave. "Hey, I know you!" he said

with a friendly smile of recognition as he passed by. "We sang to you!" I almost said hello.

Thesis and Organization

1. What is the point of James's opening narrative?
2. Paragraph 6 briefly describes various categories of men who approach women on the street. What are they?
3. Paragraph 7 tells the reader that "no compliment is involved." What is?
4. The essay ends with an example of "a harmless gesture" (13). What is James's reaction?
5. Think about the division that James makes, her glare and its "psychic cost" (11), and in your own words, state the thesis.

Technique and Style

1. Though the essay is certainly a literate one, James includes a number of words that best fit the category of slang. What, if anything, do they add to the essay?
2. What evidence can you find to disprove the idea that the essay deals only with the hassling of women?
3. How would you describe James's tone?
4. Where in the essay does James use process? Cause and effect?
5. Explain whether you find James's mixing of modes adds or detracts from the essay.

Suggestions for Writing

We interact with strangers in many different ways according to many different circumstances. The next time you find yourself in one of those situations, note how people act. Likely spots to observe them are traffic jams, elevators, lines (at a bank, supermarket, movie, cafeteria), train stations, and airports. Think about how various people act and what categories they fall into. When you draft your paper, make your categories come alive through description, narration, and example.

Gads! It's Garlic

Laurel Dewey

Laurel Dewey, writing as the Humorous Herbalist, is a regular columnist for the Carbondale, Colorado, Valley Journal, *a weekly newspaper with a readership as varied as the characters on* Northern Exposure. *As someone who believes in herbal therapy, she first makes a distinction between herbs that are good for you and those that are not. Having made that division, she usually continues by discussing the various categories of use to which the herb can be put, in this case garlic. She is careful to place a disclaimer at the end of each piece, warning readers that "this column is not meant to take the place of your physician, nor is it intended to treat, diagnose or prescribe." She is careful to warn even those who share her belief in herbal therapy, telling those who are pregnant or nursing to consult their physician before trying out what she discusses. The essay was published in October, 1993.*

WHAT TO LOOK FOR   *Sometimes a writer will choose a topic that has an obvious negative association. Often the best way to deal with the negative is head on, which is what Dewey does with her subject of garlic.*

KEY WORDS AND PHRASES

antibiotic (3)	*gangrene (5)*
nutrients (3)	*penicillin (5)*
pharmaceutical (3)	*enzyme (7)*
Marseilles (4)	

1   I told a friend recently about the flu-fighting qualities of garlic. I mentioned that by taking a clove or two a day, she could build an invisible shield against those galloping germs. She thought about it for a second, then said, "Sure, that makes sense. Because everybody—sick or not sick—won't want to get near you!"

2   Good point.

3   But seriously, garlic truly *is* one of the best herbs around for fighting the flu as well as being an honest-to-goodness *natural* antibiotic. However, this antibiotic doesn't rob your system of vital

nutrients and vitamins. I'm not saying pharmaceutical antibiotics don't have a place in the healing world—there are times when you need a strong drug to knock an infection out of your body. But relying on them continually for the slightest cold or flu symptoms eventually strips the body of its ability to fight the next invading germ until your system is left raw and unprotected.

4   Garlic, on the other hand, works as both a preventative and a healing helper when the flu bug bites. But don't take my word for it—take a look at history. During the plague of 1772 which ravaged the population in Marseilles, four common thieves roamed the streets, plundering the infected, dead bodies for riches. Never once did they contract the deadly virus. When they were arrested, the officials wanted to know what "magic" potion they used to fight the plague. They confessed the magic was a simple combo of fresh garlic cloves marinated in wine vinegar.

5   Garlic made many heroic appearances throughout both World Wars when the availability of antibiotics was scarce. Fresh garlic was cut and pressed onto wounds to disinfect them and prevent gangrene. The Soviet army thought so highly of garlic they nicknamed it "Russian penicillin."

6   Clearly, this is one herb that has proven itself to be both valuable and effective. Its ability to be absorbed into the blood system and begin its powerful job is nothing short of amazing. In fact, if you mash up half a bulb of fresh garlic and spread it across the soles of your feet, within an hour you'll start to taste the garlic on your tongue. In the interest of science, I tried this experiment. (Okay, I'll admit, it was a slow Sunday, but I wanted to see if all the hoopla was worth whooping about.) So, there I was with the mashed garlic taped to the bottom of my bare foot and within an hour, that distinct garlic flavor did indeed do a dance across my taste buds.

7   What's the magic stuff that adds the zip to this beloved bulb? Primarily the active ingredients are alliin, allicin and sulphur compounds. Allicin is the strong antibiotic member, alliin turns into an antibiotic agent when it meets the digestive enzyme allinase, and the sulphur compounds work to strengthen the immune system, lower high blood pressure and aid in the fight of internal and external infection.

8   But you're saying "Hey, garlic stinks . . . literally." And I say, okay, eat a clove or two, then chew on parsley, or an orange peel,

or swish lemon and water in your mouth. Or you can always try the odorless, garlic oil supplements. These are okay, but the fresh clove—eaten whole or sliced through a garlic press—retains a higher level of the infection-fighting properties. Cooking with fresh garlic is a good way to thread it into your diet. However, over-cooking it or boiling it almost reduces the allicin content entirely. With prevention of illness being a top priority these days, garlic seems a natural booster when it comes to bolstering the immune system. Just two fresh cloves of garlic taken each day can help cleanse your blood and regulate your system so that germs have a harder time planting their seed.

9   Garlic oil is an excellent remedy for earache or irritations brought on by infection, coldness, water or fungus. This can be used on young children as well as adults. Simply prick a capsule of garlic oil and gently drip two to three drops into each ear. (Even if the problem is only in one ear, it's always best to treat both ears so that the infection doesn't transfer to the good ear.) After adding the garlic oil, loosely plug the ear with a cotton ball and avoid drafts or cold temperatures. You can leave the cotton plug in for up to eight hours while the garlic works on the infection. As al-ways, if the ear continues to ache, throb or affect your balance, see a doctor immediately.

10   While garlic works wonders on your body, it's also a bang-up supplement for your pooch or pussycat. Adding one to two fresh cloves of garlic to your pet's food each day is a great way to keep them healthy. It also helps to keep fleas, ticks, flies and bugs away from their fur. Once again, the garlic will work it's way through their system, penetrating their skin and fur. The odor, nearly unde-tectable to humans, is downright disagreeable to bugs and the like. Ear mites can also be run out of town by using one to two drops of garlic oil in each of your pet's ears.

11   Garlic water—made by combining two bulbs of fresh garlic to a gallon of water and letting it sit in the sun for several days—acts as a natural pesticide for trees, flowers and vegetable gardens. It doesn't take much of this mixture to do the trick. A light spray of the combo laced across the plants is enough to combat the flying intruders. Too much of the strong scent and your garden will start to smell like the 7th Street Bus Terminal. Trust me, that's not a good smell.

12   The way I see it, an apple a day may keep the doctor away, but a daily clove of garlic or two will make you feel like new!

Thesis and Organization

1. What paragraph or paragraphs introduce the essay?
2. What are the ways that garlic can be used?
3. Categorize those uses according to the problems they can solve. What are they?
4. Dewey's thesis isn't stated in one sentence but instead is made up of bits and pieces of a number of sentences. What is her thesis?
5. The essay ends with a call to action that plays on a familiar saying. How effectively does it conclude the essay?

Technique and Style

1. In paragraphs 4 and 5, Dewey includes some examples drawn from history. What do they add to the essay?
2. Dewey relies upon process to explain what makes garlic work (7). How necessary is the process to the rest of the essay?
3. What reasons can you think of for Dewey using quotation marks around the word *magic* (4).
4. Dewey uses her personal experience to begin the essay and again in paragraph 6. What does it contribute to the essay?
5. In paragraph 8, Dewey addresses the reader directly. What effect does that achieve?

Suggestions for Writing

Most people would associate garlic with one thing: food. So too we're apt to think of an object as serving only one purpose, yet we know that any item can have a number of uses, some of which are not so obvious. Safety pins, paper clips, staples, coins, even kitty litter can be used in a number of inventive ways. Think of an underrated object and then jot down its uses. Each use is apt to fit a separate category, probably according to the problem it solves. When you draft your paper, you may find that you want to devote a separate paragraph to each use, but if you're going to write about a large number of uses, then try to combine some into a larger category.

I ntense!

Richard Brookhiser

An editor for the National Review, *author of numerous articles and a book,* The Way of the WASP: How It Made America and How It Can Save It *(1990), Richard Brookhiser is an astute observer of people and society and their quirks. The subtitle of Brookhiser's essay— "Reflections on a Paradoxical Personality Type"—points out a particular quirk, so be on the lookout for what's paradoxical about the truly intense. You'll also find that the essay weaves definition into its division. The essay was first published in* The Atlantic *in May 1993, then reprinted in* The Utne Reader *in the November/December issue of that same year.*

WHAT TO LOOK FOR   *If you are writing a reflective kind of essay, a collection of thoughts on a particular subject, you may find it difficult to find a way to bring those thoughts together. Brookhiser does it by weaving his ideas around a conversation with his wife, who provides a kind of audience for his thoughts. You can use a similar device if you set up an opening dialogue.*

KEY WORDS AND PHRASES
pothead *(4)*	Marilyn *(6)*
capacity *(4)*	psychic *(8)*
resilient *(5)*	Francis of Assisi *(11)*
Goebbels *(6)*	grievance *(11)*
Lenin *(6)*	exfoliation *(11)*
Trotsky *(6)*	home stretch *(12)*

1   My wife and I were having lunch. She was talking. "What do my friends mean," she asked, "when they call me intense?"

2   I didn't know what to answer at first, not because I didn't know what she was talking about but because I knew so perfectly that it was hard to put into words.

3   My wife is five feet tall. Of the pocket dictionary of pet names I have bestowed on her over the years, most of which have had a half-life of about a month, one was "bundle," short for "bundle of energy." When I think of her as a car, I think of a sports car, usu-

ally a Miata, red—or the cars in the cartoons I watched on TV as a kid, which walked down highways on tire feet and had eyelashes over their headlights and grins for grillwork. If a pet squirrel accomplished anything by running around in a wheel—if the shaft of the wheel turned on a gas jet, which heated a tea kettle, whose steam floated a small parachute that brushed a light switch as it rose—and if the squirrel understood the process and desired the result, then my wife could be that squirrel.

4   *Intense,* I told my wife, was the word my pothead friends used in college, in the '70s, when they were at that stage of being stoned in which they were fully conscious of the activities of the unstoned but lacked the desire or the capacity to participate in any way. What normal activity is to the stoned, the activity of those who are intense is to those who are normal.

5   I was not making any headway, so I decided to list intense people. "Hillary is intense," I said. "Bill is not." Our forty-second president: hand pumper, hugger, hugger of the tree hugger, smiler, glows with the flow, interested in a hundred policies, committed to about three. Resilient, intelligent, eager to please and be pleased—he is all these things. But he is not intense. The first lady: author of articles in law journals, this year earning less money than her husband probably for the first time in her life, lived in Arkansas not because she was born there but because she chose to. She is intense. My wife began to see.

6   I went through other presidents. Bush: not intense. Reagan: not intense. Carter: intense. Ford: come on. Nixon: so intense that he will probably live, on pure intensity, to give a sound bite at Clinton's funeral. Johnson: not intense (paradoxical—I'll get back to it). Kennedy: not intense. Eisenhower: very intense, though he pretended not to be. George Washington: the most intense president we have ever had. Goebbels, I added, was also intense, though Hitler was not. Lenin was intense. Trotsky was not. Madonna is intense, Marilyn was not.

7   "Give me explanations!" my wife howled. How intense of her, I thought. Here goes.

8   The defining quality of intense is that the motor never stops. The engine always runs, the battery always hums. Within the psychic boiler room of the intense person there is always at least a skeleton crew, and that crew never takes a break.

9   Intense cuts across such categories as good and evil, great and mediocre, success and failure, happiness and the lack of it. Jimmy

Carter in office was decent, piddling, unsuccessful, and troubled, whereas Lenin was wicked, grand, triumphant, and possibly happy (he was known to laugh at the murder of his enemies). But from each man came the whir of wheels endlessly turning.

10   Activity, to be intense, must also be deliberate, directed, self-propelled. Intense requires an exercise of will. This is what distinguishes the achievements of the intense from those of the non-intense.

11   You can be busy without being intense. This thoughtless quality characterizes busy but not intense types—Lyndon Johnson, William F. Buckley Jr., and Francis of Assisi. Even when they seem to be consciously choosing, their choices are driven by uncontrollable personal forces (in Johnson's case, ambition and grievance). Their activity is an exfoliation of their natures. They do not do, they are.

12   Are the intense ever happy? As often as anyone else in this world. The intense are happy when they're coming down the home stretch. Do the intense ever rest? Never.

13   Are you intense? This is the sort of question no one can ever answer for himself. Each of us thinks he is more complicated than anyone else does, possibly more complicated than anyone actually is. If you want to know which you are, ask a friend. If you do, you are probably intense.

Thesis and Organization

1. Paragraphs 1–3 serve as an introduction. What do they lead you to expect about the author's tone?
2. Brookhiser sets out one definition in paragraph 4. What other paragraphs help define the central term?
3. Division enters paragraphs 5 and 6, then is followed by definition. Where does Brookhiser return to his division?
4. Multiple examples make up paragraphs 5, 6, 9, and 11. What are the advantages of using so many examples?
5. Like many reflective essays, this one contains no one sentence that can work as the thesis. Instead, the reader must deduce the thesis from bits and pieces of Brookhiser's ideas about intense people. What is the thesis?

Technique and Style

1. Brookhiser uses analogy in paragraph 3. How effective do you find his comparisons?

2. What does Brookhiser achieve by the comparison in paragraph 11?

3. What does the dialogue add to the essay?

4. Brookhiser brings in the topic of happiness in paragraph 12. What reasons can you think of for introducing that idea?

5. Who is the "you" in paragraphs 11 and 13?

Suggestions for Writing

You can write your own "Intense!" essay by drawing up your own list of friends or public figures, using Brookhiser's definition or your own. Or, if you prefer, pick another category and figure out who belongs where. Think of who (or what) is "with it" or "not with it"; funny, not funny; in or out; lazy or not lazy. For examples, draw upon the world of public figures or well-known characters from mythology, books, television, or film. If your examples are not that well known, make sure you provide enough information about them so that your reader can see how they fit your categories. You may want to have a working thesis to keep you on track, and then in your final draft, switch from an explicit to an implied thesis.

*T*he Plot Against People

Russell Baker

Russell Baker has discovered the principles behind the continuing battle between humans and inanimate objects. He discusses these principles as he neatly divides things into three categories and then places objects into his classifications. The author of several collections of essays and an autobiography, Russell Baker has a syndicated column that also appears as a regular feature in the New York Times, *where this essay was published in 1968.*

WHAT TO LOOK FOR   *Transitions between paragraphs can be wooden, so obvious that they leap off the page to say "Look at me! I'm a transition." The more effective variety is subtle, and one way to bring that about is to pick up a key word from the previous sentence and repeat it in the first sentence of the paragraph that follows. After you've read Baker's essay, go back over it searching for his transitions between paragraphs.*

KEY WORDS AND PHRASES
inanimate (1)	*conciliatory (12)*
inherent (10)	*barometers (13)*
negotiated (11)	*aspire (15)*

1   Inanimate objects are classified into three major categories—those that don't work, those that break down and those that get lost.

2   The goal of all inanimate objects is to resist man and ultimately to defeat him, and the three major classifications are based on the method each object uses to achieve its purpose. As a general rule, any object capable of breaking down at the moment when it is most needed will do so. The automobile is typical of the category.

3   With the cunning typical of its breed, the automobile never breaks down while entering a filling station with a large staff of idle mechanics. It waits until it reaches a downtown intersection in the middle of the rush hour, or until it is fully loaded with family and luggage on the Ohio Turnpike.

4   Thus it creates maximum misery, inconvenience, frustration and irritability among its human cargo, thereby reducing its owner's life span.

5   Washing machines, garbage disposals, lawn mowers, light bulbs, automatic laundry dryers, water pipes, furnaces, electrical fuses, television tubes, hose nozzles, tape recorders, slide projectors—all are in league with the automobile to take their turn at breaking down whenever life threatens to flow smoothly for their human enemies.

6   Many inanimate objects, of course, find it extremely difficult to break down. Pliers, for example, and gloves and keys are almost totally incapable of breaking down. Therefore, they have had to evolve a different technique for resisting man.

7   They get lost. Science has still not solved the mystery of how they do it, and no man has ever caught one of them in the act of getting lost. The most plausible theory is that they have developed a secret method of locomotion which they are able to conceal the instant a human eye falls upon them.

8   It is not uncommon for a pair of pliers to climb all the way from the cellar to the attic in its single-minded determination to raise its owner's blood pressure. Keys have been known to burrow three feet under mattresses. Women's purses, despite their great weight, frequently travel through six or seven rooms to find a hiding space under a couch.

9   Scientists have been struck by the fact that things that break down virtually never get lost, while things that get lost hardly ever break down.

10   A furnace, for example, will invariably break down at the depth of the first winter cold wave, but it will never get lost. A woman's purse, which after all does have some inherent capacity for breaking down, hardly ever does; it almost invariably chooses to get lost.

11   Some persons believe this constitutes evidence that inanimate objects are not entirely hostile to man, and that a negotiated peace is possible. After all, they point out, a furnace could infuriate a man even more thoroughly by getting lost than by breaking down, just as a glove could upset him far more by breaking down than by getting lost.

12   Not everyone agrees, however, that this indicates a conciliatory attitude among inanimate objects. Many say it merely proves that furnaces, gloves and pliers are incredibly stupid.

13   The third class of objects—those that don't work—is the most curious of all. These include such objects as barometers, car clocks, cigarette lighters, flashlights, and toy train locomotives. It is inaccurate, of course, to say that they never work. They work once, usually for the first few hours after being brought home, and then quit. Thereafter, they never work again.

14   In fact, it is widely assumed that they are built for the purpose of not working. Some people have reached advanced ages without ever seeing some of these objects—barometers, for example—in working order.

15   Science is utterly baffled by the entire category. There are many theories about it. The most interesting holds that the things that don't work have attained the highest state possible for an inanimate object, the state to which things that break down and things that get lost can still only aspire.

16   They have truly defeated man by conditioning him never to expect anything of them, and in return they have given man the only peace he receives from inanimate society. He does not expect his barometer to work, his electric locomotive to run, his cigarette lighter to light or his flashlight to illuminate, and when they don't, it does not raise his blood pressure.

17   He cannot attain that peace with furnaces and keys and cars and women's purses as long as he demands that they work for their keep.

Thesis and Organization

1. In what ways does the introduction, paragraphs 1–2, set up both the system of classification and the major principle at work among inanimate objects?

2. Paragraphs 3–6 explain the first category. What effects does the automobile achieve by breaking down? How do those effects support Baker's contention about "the goal of all inanimate objects"? What other examples does Baker put into his first category? What example does not fit?

3. Paragraphs 7–12 present the second classification. What causes, reasons, or motives are attributed to the examples in this group?

4. Paragraphs 13–16 describe the third group. What are its qualities? Why might Baker have chosen to list it last? What principle of organization can you discern beneath Baker's ordering of the three groups?

5. Consider how each group frustrates and defeats people together with the first sentence of paragraph 2. Combine this information into a sentence that states the author's thesis.

Technique and Style

1. In part, the essay's humor arises from Baker's use of anthropomorphism, his technique of attributing human qualities to inanimate objects. How effectively does he use the technique?
2. Baker has a keen eye for the absurd, as illustrated by paragraph 10. What other examples can you find? What does this technique contribute to the essay?
3. Baker's stance, tone, and line of reasoning, while patently tongue-in-cheek, are also mock-scientific. Where can you find examples of Baker's explicit or implied "scientific" trappings?
4. The essay's transitions are carefully wrought. What links paragraph 3 to paragraph 2? Paragraph 7 to paragraph 6? Paragraph 10 to paragraph 9? Paragraph 12 to paragraph 11?
5. How an essay achieves unity is a more subtle thing. What links paragraph 8 to paragraph 6? Paragraph 9 to paragraphs 3–6? Paragraph 16 to paragraph 2? Paragraph 17 to paragraphs 10–12 and paragraphs 3–5?

Suggestions for Writing

Write your own "plot" essay, imagining something else plotting against people. Suggestions: clothes, food, pets, the weather, plants, traffic. Take a "scientific" stance.

Comparison and Contrast

"What's the difference?" gets at the heart of **comparison and contrast,** and it is a question that can fit into any context. In college, it often turns up in the form of essay questions; in day-to-day life, it implies the process behind most decisions: "What shall I wear?" "Which movie will I see?" "Should I change jobs?" All these questions involve choices that draw upon comparison and contrast. Like description, narration, example, and classification, comparison and contrast forces you to observe, but here you are looking for similarities and differences. In a way, comparison and contrast is the simplest form of division and classification in that you are examining only two categories, or perhaps only one example from the two categories. "Which sounds better, tapes or records?" compares two categories; "Which sounds better, compact discs or records?" compares two items in the same category.

No matter what you select, however, you need to be sure that the comparison is fair. Deciding where to go out to dinner often depends on how much you are willing to spend, so comparing a fast-food place to an elegant French restaurant doesn't appear to have much of a point. If neither is worth the money, however, you have an assertion to work from, but you have to work carefully.

Sometimes the similarities will not be readily apparent. Huey Newton and Martin Luther King, Jr., were both African-Americans, and for most of us the similarity ends there. In "Of Prophets and Protesters," however, Robert C. Maynard shows us that many more similarities tie the two together. Both cared deeply about their people and the poor, both were passionate speakers, both affected their generations, both led movements that affected American history, both died violently, both left legacies. There the similarity ends. One was admired, the other despised; one advocated nonviolence, the other violence; one believed in democracy, the other in socialism; one was in the mainstream of the civil rights movement, the other on the radical fringe.

Essays that depend primarily on other modes, such as description, narration, and definition, often use comparison and contrast to heighten a difference or clarify a point, but the pieces in this section rely on comparison and contrast as their main principle of organization, even though their purposes differ.

AUDIENCE AND PURPOSE   If you intend to inform your audience, you'll find the essay that follows by Robert C. Maynard useful. Maynard cannot assume that his audience is as familiar with Huey Newton as they are with Martin Luther King, Jr., so he must spell out some details. In doing so and in pondering the similarities and differences of the two figures, Maynard assumes a thoughtful, meditative tone. He distances himself from the two figures so that he sees them for what they stand for instead of the flesh-and-blood people they were.

Shana Alexander also leaves the reader with much to think about, though her satirical tone tips the essay toward persuasion. Along the way to her final point she needs to fill in a lot of gaps, for the reader is apt to know as little about "new-style" funerals in Nashville as old-style justice in New Guinea. The essays by James Gorman and Suzanne Britt, however, are written primarily to entertain, and both have a satirical edge as well. Gorman compares a Cairn Terrier to a Macintosh computer and in doing so makes the reader take another look at how the computer industry markets its products. So, too, Suzanne Britt's humorous defense of the fat forces us to think again about the values of our culture, even though her essay is fundamentally humorous.

ANALOGY   One useful form of comparison is **analogy**, for it can emphasize a point or illuminate an idea. If you are writing about an abstraction, for example, you can make it more familiar by using an analogy to make it concrete and therefore more understandable. An intangible word such as *rumor* becomes more distinct, more memorable, if you write of it as cancer. Or if you are explaining a process, analogy can often make the unfamiliar familiar; many a tennis instructor has said, "Hold your racquet as though you are shaking hands with a person."

An analogy is an extended **metaphor**, in which a primary term is equated with another quite dissimilar term. The process of writing, for example, is a far cry from making music, but that's the metaphor at the heart of Lara Tucker's description of how she writes. She extends the metaphor into an analogy, describing how the performers and instruments combine to create music so that the reader can understand how, too, the different parts of the writing process work together.

So in exposition, analogy clarifies—because by making x analogous to y, you bring all the associations of y to bear on x. You'll find that Nancy Sakamoto's essay draws upon sports analogies to explain "The Conversational Ballgame," the differences in conversational styles between Americans and Japanese. Americans converse, she says, as though they are playing tennis or volleyball, tossing conversation back and forth. The Japanese, however, converse as though they are bowling—they stand in line to talk, "wait their turn," and each bowls a different ball, "with a suitable pause between turns."

But to use analogy well, you have to use it cautiously. Often writers use it quite sparingly, working one into a sentence or paragraph instead of using it as the basic structure for an entire essay. Sakamoto uses analogy to clarify her comparison, not as a basis for argument.

METHOD OF COMPARISON   Comparison-and-contrast essays group information so that the comparison is made by **blocks** or **point by point** or by a combination of the two. If you were to write an essay explaining the differences between an American feast, such as Thanksgiving, and a Chinese one, here is what the two major types of organization would look like in outline form:

Type	Structure	Content
Block	Paragraph 1	Introduction
	Block A, paragraphs 2–4	American culture
	Point 1	Preparation
	Point 2	Courses & types of food
	Point 3	Manners
	Block B, paragraphs 5–7	Chinese culture
	Point 1	Preparation
	Point 2	Courses & types of food
	Point 3	Manners
	Paragraph 8	Conclusion

Type	Structure	Content
Point by Point	Paragraph 1	Introduction
	Point 1, paragraph 1	Preparation
		Chinese
		American
	Point 2, paragraph 3	Courses & types of food
		Chinese
		American

And so on. As you can see, sticking rigorously to one type of organization can get boring, predictable, so writers often mix the two.

In "Fashions in Funerals," for example, Shana Alexander first discusses a funeral (of sorts) in New Guinea, then the "new-style" funeral that has come to pass in Nashville. Her concluding paragraph brings together the two blocks of information. Robert C. Maynard, however, relies on point-by-point comparison, grouping King and Newton together in paragraphs that make particular points. Outlining an essay readily reveals which type of organization the writer depends on.

OTHER MODES   A close look at any of the essays that follow will show how you can use other modes, such as description, narration, and cause and effect, to help flesh out the comparison and contrast. In "That Lean and Hungry Look," for example, Suzanne Britt relies heavily on description and example to clarify her comparisons, and she adds narration to give credibility to her assertions. On the other hand, Robert C. Maynard's analysis of Huey Newton and Martin Luther King, Jr., employs cause and effect. What was it about these men, Maynard wonders, that so influenced the course of American history? What do their very different lives have in common?

THESIS AND ORGANIZATION   The one-sentence thesis placed at the end of an introductory paragraph certainly informs the reader of your subject and stance, but you might find your paper more effective if you treat your thesis more subtly, trying it out in different forms and positions. While some of the essays in this chapter save their major assertion until last, others combine ideas from various points in the essay to form a thesis. In "Fashions in Funerals" and "Of Prophets and Protesters," each author builds to a final point that is the essay's explicit or implied thesis. Suzanne Britt, however, weaves bits and pieces of thesis throughout her whole essay, although her thesis is implied. As for

James Gorman, the reader will have to decide. His essay's organization, however, is clear-cut.

USEFUL TERMS

Analogy   *Analogy* examines a subject by comparing it point by point to something seemingly unlike but more commonplace and less complex. An analogy is also an extended *metaphor*.

Block comparison   A comparison of x to y by grouping all that is to be compared under x and then following with the same information under y.

Comparison and contrast   If you examine two or more subjects by exploring their similarities and differences, you would be using comparison and contrast. Similarities and differences are usually developed through literal and logical comparisons within like categories.

Metaphor   An implied but direct comparison in which the primary term is made more vivid by associating it with a quite dissimilar term. "Life is a bed of roses" is a familiar metaphor.

Point by point   A comparison that examines one or more points by stating the point, then comparing x to y, and then continuing to the next point.

IDEAS FOR WRITING   Think back to a decision you made recently. It may be an important one as in "Where should I go to college?" or an unimportant one as in, "What shall I have for lunch?" Then in your journal or as a draft for an essay, jot down what your choices were and narrow the list to the two most important ones. You then have a working paper for a comparison and contrast.

▋ POINTERS FOR USING COMPARISON AND CONTRAST

Exploring the Topic

1. **What are the similarities?** What characteristics do your two subjects share? Are the two so similar that you have little to distinguish them? If so, try another subject; if not, pare down your list of similarities to the most important ones.

2. **What are the differences?** In what ways are your two subjects different? Are they so different that they have little in common? If so, make sure you can handle a humorous tone or try another subject; if not, pare down your list of differences to the most important ones.

3. **Should you emphasize similarities or differences?** Which pattern of organization best fits your material? Block? Point by point? A combination of the two?
4. **What examples will work best?** If your reader isn't familiar with your topic, what examples might be familiar? What examples will make clear what may be unfamiliar?
5. **What metaphor does your subject suggest?** Given the metaphor and your subject, what characteristics match? How can the metaphor be extended into an analogy? How can you outline the analogy as an equation? What equals what?
6. **What other modes are appropriate?** What modes can you draw upon to help support your comparison and the organization of the essay? Do you need to define? Where can you use description? Narration? Example? Do any of your comparisons involve cause and effect?
7. **What is your point? Your purpose?** Do you want to entertain, inform, persuade? Given your point as a tentative thesis, should you spell it out in the essay or imply it? If you are writing to inform, what information do you want to present? If you are writing to persuade, what do you want your reader to do?
8. **What persona do you want to create?** Is it best for you to be a part of the comparison and contrast or to be an observer? Do you have a strongly held conviction about your subject? Do you want it to show? Does your persona fit your audience, purpose, and material?

Drafting the Paper

1. **Know your reader.** Use your first paragraph to set out your major terms and your general focus, and to prepare the reader for the pattern of organization and tone that will follow. Reexamine your list of similarities and differences to see which ones may well be unfamiliar to your reader. Jot down an illustration or brief description by each characteristic that the reader may not be familiar with. If your reader is part of the group you are examining, tread carefully, and if your teacher may have a bias about your topic, try to figure out what the bias is so you can counter it. Reread your paper from the perspective of the reader who is biased so that you can check your diction as well as your choice of examples and assertions.
2. **Know your purpose.** If you are writing to persuade, keep in mind the reader's possible bias or neutral view and see how you can use your persona as well as logical and emotional appeals to get the reader on your side. Informative papers run the risk of telling the reader something that person already knows, so use description, detail, example, and diction to present your information in a new light. If your paper's main purpose is

to entertain, these techniques become all the more crucial. Try adding alliteration, allusions, paradox, and puns to the other techniques you draw upon.

3. **If you use an analogy, double-check it.** Make sure your analogy is an extended metaphor, not a statement of fact. See what you want to emphasize. Also make sure that placement is effective by trying out the analogy in different positions. Perhaps it works best as a framing device or standing alone in a sentence or paragraph.

4. **Use other modes to support your comparison.** Description and example are probably the most obvious modes to use, but also consider narration, cause and effect, definition, and analogy. Perhaps a short narrative would add interest to your paper, or perhaps cause and effect enters into your comparisons. Definition may be vital to your thesis, and analogy may help clarify or expand a point.

5. **Check your pattern of organization.** If you are using block comparison, make sure you have introduced your two subjects and that your conclusion brings them back together. In the body of the paper, make sure that what you cover for one, you also cover for the other. In point-by-point comparison, check to see that your points are clearly set out. You may want to use both types of organization, though one will probably predominate.

6. **Make a point.** Perhaps you want to use your comparison to make a comment on the way we live, perhaps to clarify two items that people easily confuse, perhaps to argue that one thing is better than the other. Whatever your point, check it to make sure it is an assertion, not a mere fact. Whether your purpose is to inform or to persuade, take a stand and make sure that your thesis clearly implies or states it.

What's a Metaphor for the Way I Write?

Lara Tucker

Lara Tucker, who wrote the piece that follows in 1992, has since earned a Master's in Fine Arts from the Writer's Workshop at the University of New Orleans and is a substitute teacher in the public school system in North Carolina. She wrote the analogy as part of a take-home final examination, responding to the instruction "Write a brief essay that develops a metaphor for your writing process." She's still making music.

WHAT TO LOOK FOR *Tucker uses the question-and-answer format to strike a conversational tone, one that starts with a quick response followed by a sentence fragment. As you read her essay, try to hear it as well, or read it aloud and the tone will come through loud and clear. Try to spot the techniques she uses to create it.*

KEY WORDS AND PHRASES
hep-cat

It's music. The composition of different sounds that come together to create a whole piece. First I hear one note from one instrument, then another begins, then another, and another. It's a big gathering of musicians who have played often enough with one another, just not all the time. After all, they have their day jobs. They are fairly good, not amazing, musicians, but they know their craft with an inner ear. Together they can make the music something special, if they practice enough before they go on. The sax player has been playing a lot longer than the piano-man, but they know each other's strengths and try to smooth over each other's weaknesses. Besides, there's the guitar guy, the bass player, the hep-cat drummer, and the tambourine shaker to take into account. They work together, albeit with some fighting, to deepen the harmonies, reflect the differences, and do their solos. Whether it's rock and roll, rhythm and blues, ballads, pop, sophisticated jazz—they like it all. And they are willing to find the notes inside their instruments that will put a piece together to get a rhythm going.

The idea is to get the audience to say "I like that groove—I like what that music is doing!"

Thesis and Organization

1. State the analogy in your own words.
2. What principle lies behind the sequencing of the sentences in the paragraph?
3. Spell out the various stages of the analogy and what stands for what.
4. What effect does Tucker want to have on the listener/reader?
5. What is the essay's thesis?

Technique and Style

1. In your own words, describe the kind of person Tucker reveals herself to be in her writing.
2. How would you characterize Tucker's diction? Is it formal? Informal? What? What effect does she achieve with her choice of diction level?
3. What does Tucker imply about writing by pointing out that the musicians have "day jobs"?
4. How would you describe what Tucker values about writing?
5. When Tucker writes "there's the guitar guy" she is using the passive voice. Rewrite the sentence substituting an active verb for "there's." What is gained? Lost?

Suggestions for Writing

Think about how you write, defining the process as beginning with your first thought on a subject and ending with your final revision. Are there stages you can identify? Emotions? Generalize upon your experience to write a short essay describing what you find as an appropriate analogy for the way you write.

$\mathcal{C}$onversational Ballgames

Nancy Sakamoto

As you will discover from reading the following essay, Nancy Sakamoto is an American married to a Japanese. Living in two cultures and teaching English to Japanese students, she naturally analyzes how people use language differently. This essay is the result of that analysis and first appeared in Polite Fictions *(1982).*

WHAT TO LOOK FOR *An analogy is an extended metaphor or simile, a comparison of two seemingly dissimilar things. A good analogy does double duty. It clarifies what is being explained by comparing the unfamiliar to the familiar while at the same time it intensifies the explanation, making it more vivid and therefore more memorable. Think about how Sakamoto's analogies affect the reader as you read the essay.*

KEY WORDS AND PHRASES
bounded (5)   *belatedly (16)*

1   After I was married and had lived in Japan for a while, my Japanese gradually improved to the point where I could take part in simple conversations with my husband and his friends and family. And I began to notice that often, when I joined in, the others would look startled, and the conversational topic would come to a halt. After this happened several times, it became clear to me that I was doing something wrong. But for a long time, I didn't know what it was.

2   Finally, after listening carefully to many Japanese conversations, I discovered what my problem was. Even though I was speaking Japanese, I was handling the conversation in a western way.

3   Japanese-style conversations develop quite differently from western-style conversations. And the difference isn't only in the languages. I realized that just as I kept trying to hold western-style conversations even when I was speaking Japanese, so my English students kept trying to hold Japanese-style conversations even when they were speaking English. We were unconsciously playing entirely different conversational ballgames.

4   A western-style conversation between two people is like a game of tennis. If I introduce a topic, a conversational ball, I expect you to hit it back. If you agree with me, I don't expect you simply to agree and do nothing more. I expect you to add something—a reason for agreeing, another example, or an elaboration to carry the idea further. But I don't expect you always to agree. I am just as happy if you question me, or challenge me, or completely disagree with me. Whether you agree or disagree, your response will return the ball to me.

5   And then it is my turn again. I don't serve a new ball from my original starting line. I hit your ball back again from where it has bounded. I carry your idea further, or answer your questions or objections, or challenge or question you. And so the ball goes back and forth, with each of us doing our best to give it a new twist, an original spin, or a powerful smash.

6   And the more vigorous the action, the more interesting and exciting the game. Of course, if one of us gets angry, it spoils the conversation, just as it spoils a tennis game. But getting excited is not at all the same as getting angry. After all, we are not trying to hit each other. We are trying to hit the ball. So long as we attack only each other's opinions and do not attack each other personally, we don't expect anyone to get hurt. A good conversation is supposed to be interesting and exciting.

7   If there are more than two people in the conversation, then it is like doubles in tennis, or like volleyball. There's no waiting in line. Whoever is nearest and quickest hits the ball, and if you step back, someone else will hit it. No one stops the game to give you a turn. You're responsible for taking your own turn. But whether it's two players or a group, everyone does his best to keep the ball going, and no one person has the ball for very long.

8   A Japanese-style conversation, however, is not at all like tennis or volleyball. It's like bowling. You wait for your turn. And you always know your place in line. It depends on such things as whether you are older or younger, a close friends or a relative stranger to the previous speaker, in a senior or junior position, and so on.

9   When your turn comes, you step up to the starting line with your bowling ball, and carefully bowl it. Everyone else stands back and watches politely, murmuring encouragement. Everyone waits until the ball has reached the end of the alley and watches to see if

it knocks down all the pins, or only some of them, or none of them. There is a pause, while everyone registers your score.

10   Then, after everyone is sure that you have completely finished your turn, the next person in line steps up to the same starting line, with a different ball. He doesn't return your ball, and he does not begin from where your ball stopped. There is no back and forth at all. All the balls run parallel. And there is always a suitable pause between turns. There is no rush, no excitement, no scramble for the ball.

11   No wonder everyone looked startled when I took part in Japanese conversations. I paid no attention to whose turn it was and kept snatching the ball halfway down the alley and throwing it back at the bowler. Of course the conversation died. I was playing the wrong game.

12   This explains why it is almost impossible to get a western-style conversation or discussion going with English students in Japan. I used to think that the problem was their lack of English language ability. But I finally came to realize that the biggest problem is that they, too, are playing the wrong game.

13   Whenever I serve a volleyball, everyone just stands back and watches it fall, with occasional murmurs of encouragement. No one hits it back. Everyone waits until I call on someone to take a turn. And when that person speaks, he doesn't hit my ball back. He serves a new ball. Again, everyone just watches it fall.

14   So I call on someone else. This person does not refer to what the previous speaker has said. He also serves a new ball. Nobody seems to have paid any attention to what anyone else has said. Everyone begins again from the same starting line, and all the balls run parallel. There is never any back and forth. Everyone is trying to bowl with a volleyball.

15   Now that you know about the difference in the conversational ballgames, you may think that all your troubles are over. But if you have been trained all your life to play one game, it is no simple matter to switch to another, even if you know the rules. Knowing the rules is not at all the same thing as playing the game.

16   Even now, during a conversation in Japanese I will notice a startled reaction and belatedly realize that once again I have rudely interrupted by instinctively trying to hit back the other person's bowling ball. It is no easier for me to "just listen" during a conversation, than it is for my Japanese students to "just relax" when speaking

with foreigners. Now I can truly sympathize with how hard they must find it to try to carry on a western-style conversation.

Thesis and Organization

1. The introduction (1–3) sets out the problem and then narrows it down. What is the problem?
2. Sakamoto's analysis of the problem begins in paragraph 4. In what ways is western-style conversation similar to tennis?
3. How is Japanese-style conversation similar to bowling?
4. The essay moves from block-by-block comparison to a different kind of organization in paragraphs 12–14. Explain how paragraphs 12–14 are organized.
5. Paragraphs 15 and 16 conclude the essay. Given what Sakamoto says in her introduction and her conclusion, what is her thesis?

Technique and Style

1. Where in the essay does Sakamoto bring in her personal experience? What does it add?
2. Sakamoto's analogies are drawn from sports, but what other areas would provide a good pair of analogies?
3. The organization mixes two types of comparison. Explain whether or not you think the combination is successful.
4. Sakamoto switches pronouns in the essay, moving between the first person *I* and the second person *you*. What reasons can you think of for the shift?
5. How would you describe the audience for whom the essay is written?

Suggestions for Writing

Think of two people who are alike in an important way, yet very different in other respects. Perhaps you have two friends who lead quite different lives but at the same time share some similar habits or tastes. The similarity can provide your paper with the overriding connection between the two people, leaving you free to develop how the two people contrast. Or think about the way two people approach the same problem from different directions. One, for example, may need to have complete silence to study, whereas the other cannot study unless the television set is blasting. Or consider writing a paper comparing how you go about writing a paper and how someone else does it differently. Maybe you have to stew about ideas, jot down notes, start and stop. If that's the case, talk to someone in your class whose habits are very different, someone who may seem to dash off a draft almost without effort. The results may be the same, papers on similar subjects for the same class and perhaps earning the same grade, but the processes involved in creating the papers are quite dissimilar.

F ashions in Funerals

Shana Alexander

The jungles of new Guinea are a long way from Nashville, Tennessee, but Shana Alexander compares the funeral customs of the two places to show that two different cultures are perhaps not so far apart after all. The piece was included in Alexander's collection of essays, Talking Woman *(1976).*

WHAT TO LOOK FOR *Getting started, writing that opening paragraph, can often be difficult. One way to search for ideas is to flip through your local newspaper or a magazine with an eye out for an unusual story. That may be just what got Shana Alexander thinking. Whatever brought the story of the New Guinea "funeral" to mind, she uses a narrative to begin her essay, and that's a technique you can adopt for your own writing.*

KEY WORDS AND PHRASES
ensued (1) entrepreneur (3)
mausoleum (3) crypt (4)

1   A man in the remote jungles of New Guinea not long ago murdered another man with an ax. Tribal justice ensued. First the murderer was shot and killed with an arrow, and then seven other members of the tribe cut him up and ate him.

2   When word of the feast reached civilization, the authorities concluded that on this occasion justice had literally been served, and perhaps a bit too swiftly, so they hauled the seven cannibals into court, where a wise Australian judge dismissed all the charges, and acquitted the seven men. "The funerary customs of the people of Papua and New Guinea," he explained, "have been, and in many cases remain, bizarre in the extreme."

3   What, I wonder, would the judge have to say about the new, high-rise mausoleum now under construction in Nashville, Tennessee? When completed, this model of modern funerary design will be twenty stories high, fully air-conditioned, and capable of holding 65,000 bodies. A second slightly less deluxe tower on an adjoining site will have facilities to entomb 63,500 more.

Nashville's enterprising mortician entrepreneur points out that his high-rise mortuary will be self-contained on only 14 acres, whereas it would require 129 acres to contain all these caskets in the, uh, conventional manner.

4   Well, not exactly caskets. In the new-style funeral, you will be laid out—after embalming, of course—on something called a "repose," described as a "bedlike structure," complete with white sheets, pillow, and blanket. When the ceremonies are ended, bed, pillow, sheet, and blanket are all whisked away; a fiberglass lid snaps down over what remains; and—zap—it's into the wall, stacked seven-high, with a neat bronze marker attached to the face of the crypt.

5   The forward-looking undertaker who thought all this up is already respected, in the trade, for bringing to Nashville the one-stop funeral.

6   But the most important advantage of the high-rise mausoleum is that by putting everything-but-everything under one roof you cut down on the high cost of dying. Maybe so, maybe so. But I can't help thinking it would be even cheaper to die in New Guinea, where the funerary customs are certainly no less bizarre, and a lot more practical.

Thesis and Organization

1. Which paragraphs emphasize New Guinea? Which emphasize Nashville? What sentence summarizes the point the author wishes to make about New Guinea?

2. What sentence serves as a transition between New Guinea and Nashville? What sentence summarizes the point the author wishes to make about Nashville?

3. What paragraph covers both New Guinea and Nashville? What sentence presents that paragraph's major assertion? Explain how that sentence is or is not the thesis of the essay.

4. What is Alexander's attitude toward "the new-style funeral"? Is she attempting to persuade the reader to adopt that attitude or is she simply informing the reader about the latest fashion in funerals and making a comment about it? What evidence can you find in the essay to support your view? Has she convinced you of anything? Why or why not?

Technique and Style

1. How would you characterize the author's tone? Is it earnest, light-hearted, sarcastic, ironic, tongue-in-cheek, what? What examples can you find to support your answer? Is the tone effective? Why or why not?

2. Where in the essay does the author use narration? Description? How do those modes support the author's use of comparison and contrast?
3. Why might Alexander have chosen to begin the essay in the third person with an objective point of view? Where and why does she introduce first person? Second person? How does her choice of point of view relate to her thesis?
4. How would you characterize the author's level of diction? Is it colloquial? Conversational? Formal? Fancy? What examples support your view? What relationship do you find between Alexander's tone and her level of diction?
5. Where in the essay does Alexander use fragments? What important parts of speech do those sentences lack? Rewrite the sentences as complete sentences. What is lost? Gained?

Suggestions for Writing

Compare and contrast two fads or fancies from different times or cultures: gold-fish swallowing or flagpole sitting in the 20s versus one of the odder pursuits of today; the Icarus myth versus hang-gliding; tattooing in primitive cultures versus nail polish and lipstick in sophisticated societies; killing enemies with primitive weapons versus killing people you don't even know with cars; polygamous marriage versus serial marriage.

*T*hat Lean and Hungry Look

Suzanne Britt

Our culture may worship the "lean and hungry look," but the more fools they, Suzanne Britt implies in her point-by-point comparison of thin people and fat ones. The essay appeared in Newsweek's *"My Turn" column in 1976.*

WHAT TO LOOK FOR   *Allusions are a form of comparison that make a connection between what the writer is focusing on and the reader's knowledge of cultural or historical events or quotations. Britt uses allusions ironically, but they can take on any spin the writer gives them. Allusions can also help you come up with ideas for what you are writing about. If, for example, you had to write a paper on trees, you could get some help from a dictionary of quotations. You'll find an index in the back of such a dictionary that will list all the quotations that mention trees.*

KEY WORDS AND PHRASES

metabolisms (3)	*rutabagas (10)*
inert (3)	*prognose (11)*
wizened (4)	*convivial (12)*
nebulous (5)	*gyrate (12)*
mulched (9)	*gluttonous (12)*
machinations (10)	

1   Caesar was right. Thin people need watching. I've been watching them for most of my adult life, and I don't like what I see. When these narrow fellows spring at me, I quiver to my toes. Thin people come in all personalities, most of them menacing. You've got your "together" thin person, your mechanical thin person, your condescending thin person, your tsk-tsk thin person, your efficiency-expert thin person. All of them are dangerous.

2   In the first place, thin people aren't fun. They don't know how to goof off, at least in the best, fat sense of the word. They've always got to be a-doing. Give them a coffee break, and they'll jog around the block. Supply them with a quiet evening at home, and they'll fix the screen door and lick S&H green stamps. They say

137

things like "there aren't enough hours in the day." Fat people never say that. Fat people think the day is too damn long already.

3   Thin people make me tired. They've got speedy little metabolisms that cause them to bustle briskly. They're forever rubbing their bony hands together and eyeing new problems to "tackle." I like to surround myself with sluggish, inert, easygoing fat people, the kind who believe that if you clean it up today, it'll just get dirty again tomorrow.

4   Some people say the business about the jolly fat person is a myth, that all of us chubbies are neurotic, sick, sad people. I disagree. Fat people may not be chortling all day long, but they're a hell of a lot *nicer* than the wizened and shriveled. Thin people turn surly, mean and hard at a young age because they never learn the value of a hot-fudge sundae for easing tension. Thin people don't like gooey soft things because they themselves are neither gooey nor soft. They are crunchy and dull, like carrots. They go straight to the heart of the matter while fat people let things stay all blurry and hazy and vague, the way things actually are. Thin people want to face the truth. Fat people know there is no truth. One of my thin friends is always staring at complex, unsolvable problems and saying, "The key thing is . . . ." Fat people never say that. They know there isn't any such thing as the key thing about anything.

5   Thin people believe in logic. Fat people see all sides. The sides fat people see are rounded blobs, usually gray, always nebulous and truly not worth worrying about. But the thin person persists. "If you consume more calories than you burn," says one of my thin friends, you will gain weight. It's that simple." Fat people always grin when they hear statements like that. They know better.

6   Fat people realize that life is illogical and unfair. They know very well that God is not in his heaven and all is not right with the world. If God was up there, fat people could have two doughnuts and a big orange drink anytime they wanted it.

7   Thin people have a long list of logical things they are always spouting off to me. They hold up one finger at a time as they reel off these things, so I won't lose track. They speak slowly as if to a young child. The list is long and full of holes. It contains tidbits like "get a grip on yourself," "cigarettes kill," "cholesterol clogs," "fit as a fiddle," "ducks in a row," "organize," and "sound fiscal management." Phrases like that.

8   They think these 2000-point plans lead to happiness. Fat people know happiness is elusive at best and even if they could get the kind thin people talk about, they wouldn't want it. Wisely, fat people see that such programs are too dull, too hard, too off the mark. They are never better than a whole cheesecake.

9   Fat people know all about the mystery of life. They are the ones acquainted with the night, with luck, with fate, with playing it by ear. One thin person I know once suggested that we arrange all the parts of a jigsaw puzzle into groups according to the size, shape and color. He figured this would cut the time needed to complete the puzzle by at least 50 percent. I said I wouldn't do it. One, I like to muddle through. Two, what good would it do to finish early? Three, the jigsaw puzzle isn't the important thing. The important thing is the fun of four people (one thin person included) sitting around a card table, working a jigsaw puzzle. My thin friend had no use for my list. Instead of joining us, he went outside and mulched the boxwoods. The three remaining fat people finished the puzzle and made chocolate, double-fudged brownies to celebrate.

10   The main problem with thin people is they oppress. Their good intentions, bony torsos, tight ships, neat corners, cerebral machinations and pat solutions loom like dark clouds over the loose, comfortable, spread-out, soft world of the fat. Long after fat people have removed their coats and shoes and put their feet up on the coffee table, thin people are still sitting on the edge of the sofa, looking neat as a pin, discussing rutabagas. Fat people are heavily into fits of laughter, slapping their thighs and whooping it up, while thin people are still politely waiting for the punch line.

11   Thin people are downers. They like math and morality and reasoned evaluation of the limitations of human beings. They have their skinny little acts together. They expound, prognose, probe and prick.

12   Fat people are convivial. They will like you even if you're irregular and have acne. They will come up with a good reason why you never wrote the great American novel. They will cry in your beer with you. They will put your name in the pot. They will let you off the hook. Fat people will grab, giggle, guffaw, gallumph, gyrate and gossip. They are generous, giving and gallant. They are gluttonous and goodly and great. What you want when you're down is soft and jiggly, not muscled and stable. Fat people know this. Fat people have plenty of room. Fat people will take you in.

Thesis and Organization

1. How does the introduction prepare the reader for the essay's pattern of organization? Its tone? Its thesis?
2. Paragraphs 2–5 and 8–10 use point-by-point comparison to support the essay's thesis. What point or points are raised in each of those paragraphs?
3. Why might the author change her paragraph structure in paragraphs 6 and 7 and paragraphs 11 and 12? In each pair of paragraphs, which paragraph deals with what type of person? Why might the author have chosen to present them in that order? How does the order of paragraphs 11 and 12 affect Britt's thesis?
4. The thesis of essay is obvious, but its purpose is somewhat complex. The humorous tone of the essay and the author's wordplay suggest that the essay's purpose is to entertain, but the author's unusual perspective provides the reader with a fresh way of looking at a familiar topic; at the same time the reader suspects that underneath the humor there may lurk a serious point and a persuasive one. Citing evidence from the essay, make a case for what you think is the author's main purpose.

Technique and Style

1. The title of the essay is an allusion that is picked up in the first sentence. What is being alluded to? What other allusion can you spot in paragraph 1? In paragraph 9? What do the allusions add to the essay's persona?
2. Britt relies heavily on details to make her points vivid. How many specific details can you find in paragraph 10? What assertion about thin people is supported by details? What assertion about fat people is implied by details?
3. Frequently, the author relies on a short declarative sentence to open a paragraph. What effect does this technique have on the paragraph? On the essay as a whole?
4. Britt achieves her comic effect by taking words at their face value, by putting clichés to use as clichés, and by employing alliteration. Where in the essay do you find examples of these techniques? Choose a sentence that uses one of the techniques and analyze its specific effect. What does it contribute to the thesis and purpose of the essay and to its tone and persona?

Suggestions for Writing

Make a humorous or sarcastic case for the villain instead of the hero; the ordinary instead of the beautiful; the poor instead of the rich; the hungry instead of the fed; the loser instead of the winner.

$\boxed{M}$an, Bytes, Dog

James Gorman

Few people would think of evaluating a dog in terms of the character-istics of a computer, but that's what James Gorman does to discover which is man's best friend. This unlikely comparison appeared in the New Yorker *in 1984.*

WHAT TO LOOK FOR   *Comparing two very dissimilar things can often get a writer into trouble if the major point is a serious one. Gorman, however, uses the dissimilarity to construct a satire that has an underlying serious statement about dogs and computers.*

KEY WORDS AND PHRASES
microcanine (8)   BASIC (17)
peripheral (9)   criterion (18)
eponymously (11)

1   Many people have asked me about the Cairn Terrier. How about memory, they want to know. Is it IBM compatible? Why didn't I get the IBM itself, or a Kaypro, Compaq, or Macintosh? I think the best way to answer these questions is to look at the Macintosh and the Cairn head on. I almost did buy the Macintosh. It has terrific graph-ics, good word-processing capabilities, and the mouse. But in the end I decided on the Cairn, and I think I made the right decision.

2   Let's start out with the basics:

Macintosh
Weight (without printer): 20 lbs.
Memory (RAM): 128 K
Price (with printer) $3,090

Cairn Terrier
Weight (without printer): 14 lbs.
Memory (RAM): Some
Price (with printer) $250

3   Just on the basis of price and weight, the choice is obvious. An-other plus is that the Cairn Terrier comes in one unit. No printer is

141

necessary, or useful. And—this was a big attraction to me—there is no user's manual.

4   Here are some of the other qualities I found put the Cairn out ahead of the Macintosh.

5   **Portability:** To give you a better idea of size, Toto in *The Wizard of Oz* was a Cairn Terrier. So you can see that if the young Judy Garland was able to carry Toto around in that little picnic basket, you will have no trouble at all moving your Cairn from place to place. For short trips it will move under its own power. The Macintosh will not.

6   **Reliability:** In five to ten years, I am sure, the Macintosh will be superseded by a new model, like the Delicious or the Granny Smith. The Cairn Terrier on the other hand, has held its share of the market with only minor modifications for hundreds of years. In the short term, Cairns seldom need servicing, apart from shots and the odd worming, and most function without interruption during electrical storms.

7   **Compatibility:** Cairn Terriers get along with everyone. And for communications with any other dog, of any breed, within a radius of three miles, no additional hardware is necessary. All dogs share a common operating system.

8   **Software:** The Cairn will run three standard programs, SIT, COME, and NO, and whatever else you create. It is true that, being microcanine, the Cairn is limited here, but it does load the programs instantaneously. No disk drives. No tapes.

9   Admittedly, these are peripheral advantages. The real comparison has to be on the basis of capabilities. What can the Macintosh and the Cairn do? Let's start on the Macintosh's turf—income-tax preparation, recipe storage, graphics, and astrophysics problems:

	Taxes	Recipes	Graphics	Astrophysics
Macintosh	yes	yes	yes	yes
Cairn	no	no	no	no

10   At first glance it looks bad for the Cairn. But it's important to look beneath the surface with this kind of chart. If you yourself are leaning toward the Macintosh, ask yourself these questions: Do you want to do your own income taxes? Do you want to type all your recipes into a computer? In your graph, what would you put on the x axis? The y axis? Do you have any astrophysics problems you want solved?

11   Then consider the Cairn's specialties: playing fetch and tug-of-

war, licking your face, and chasing foxes out of rock cairns (eponymously). Note that no software is necessary. All these functions are
part of the operating system:

	Fetch	Tug-of-war	Face	Foxes
Cairn	yes	yes	yes	yes
Macintosh	no	no	no	no

12   Another point to keep in mind is that computers, even the Macintosh, only do what you tell them to do. Cairns perform their functions all on their own. Here are some of the additional capabilities
that I discovered once I got the Cairn home and housebroken:

13   **Word Processing:** Remarkably, the Cairn seems to understand
every word I say. He has a nice way of pricking up his ears at
words like "out" or "ball." He also has highly tuned voice recognition.

14   **Education:** The Cairn provides children with hands-on experience at an early age, contributing to social interaction, crawling ability, and language skills. At age one, my daughter could say "Sit,"
"Come," and "No."

15   **Cleaning:** This function was a pleasant surprise. But of course
cleaning up around the cave is one of the reasons dogs were developed in the first place. Users with young (below age two) children
will still find this function useful. The Cairn Terrier cleans the floor,
spoons, bib, and baby, and has an unerring ability to distinguish
strained peas from ears, nose, and fingers.

16   **Psychotherapy:** Here the Cairn really shines. And remember,
therapy is something that computers have tried. There is a program
that makes the computer ask you questions when you tell it your
problems. You say, "I'm afraid of foxes." The computer says,
"You're afraid of foxes?"

17   The Cairn won't give you that kind of echo. Like Freudian ana-
lysts, Cairns are mercifully silent; unlike Freudians, they are infinitely
sympathetic. I've found that the Cairn will share, in a nonjudgmental
fashion, disappointments, joys, and frustrations. And you don't have
to know BASIC.

18   The last capability is related to the Cairn's strongest point, which
was the final deciding factor in my decision against the Macintosh—
user-friendliness. On this criterion, there is simply no comparison.
The Cairn Terrier is the essence of user friendliness. It has fur, it
doesn't flicker when you look at it, and it wags its tail.

Thesis and Organization

1. Paragraph 1 begins by setting out the answers to some of the standard journalistic points: *who, what, where, when, why,* and *how.* What answers does paragraph 1 provide?
2. Paragraph 2 summarizes the "basics," and paragraph 3 draws a conclusion from them. What is the thesis suggested by paragraphs 1–3?
3. Paragraphs 5–12 compare the Cairn to the Macintosh. What is the basis of comparison in each paragraph? Which paragraphs focus on the Cairn, the Macintosh, both? Which pattern of comparison dominates, the point-by-point or block?
4. What sentence introduces paragraphs 13–18? Which paragraphs focus on the Cairn, the Macintosh, both? Which pattern of comparison dominates, the point-by-point or block?
5. Reconsider the thesis of the essay from a broader perspective by summarizing what the dog can do that the computer cannot. What comment might the author be making about dogs? Pets? Computers? Machines? About their relative worth? Consider the essay as a satire, and state its thesis.

Technique and Style

1. Explain how the author's use of punctuation and spelling in the title establishes the tone of the essay.
2. Humor often stems from improbably juxtapositions. Given that the fundamental comparison fits that idea, what other examples can you find of Gorman's using this technique?
3. What effect does the author achieve by including the two charts? What do the charts contribute to the satire?
4. The tone of the essay is at times informal, almost as though the author were talking to the reader. How is that tone reinforced by point of view? By diction? By the examples Gorman includes? Why did he choose his tone?
5. In paragraphs 5, 8, and 16, Gorman relies on the short sentence. Choose an example from one of those paragraphs and rewrite it, combining the sentence with another. What is gained? Lost?

Suggestions for Writing

Compare two quite dissimilar subjects in order to make a satiric point about one of them. Suggestions: going to a party versus studying, raising a garden versus children, owning a bicycle versus a car, eating junk food versus cooking, playing poker versus football. Or if you prefer, write a serious paper evaluating two products to determine which is better.

Of Prophets and Protesters

Robert C. Maynard

At first thought, the lives of Huey Newton and Martin Luther King, Jr., would seem to have more differences than similarities. After all, Newton epitomized a radical approach to asserting one's civil rights while King espoused nonviolence. Robert Maynard, however, finds some significant commonalities: concern, passion, charisma, and— unhappily—violent death. Maynard's essay was published in 1989, appearing in his syndicated column carried by the Times-Picayune *of New Orleans.*

Until his death in 1993, Maynard, one of the most prominent African Americans in American journalism, was the editor and publisher of The Oakland Tribune *and well known for his efforts to encourage minority journalists. As for Martin Luther King, Jr., biographies abound, and information on Huey Newton is readily available. The most recent account of Newton's life is Hugh Pearson's* The Shadow of the Panther: Huey Newton and the Price of Black Power in America *(Addison-Wesley, 1994).*

WHAT TO LOOK FOR *When you write about a controversial subject, you have to be careful not to arouse the reader's negative associations. As you read Maynard's essay, notice how he deals with readers who may think of Huey Newton as a racist and radical.*

KEY WORDS AND PHRASES
charismatic (2)   articulating (7)
instigation (3)   advocated (8)
chic (5)   tangible (10)

1   If Huey Newton and Martin Luther King, Jr., ever met, they certainly formed no bond. They are bound nonetheless today by the common threads of how they lived and how each died. In one of history's curious accidents, their deaths help tell the tale of their times.

2   Dr. King and Huey Newton shared a deep concern for their people and for the plight of the poor. They aroused the passions of their generations. They were charismatic figures whose words

were remembered and repeated. In different ways, the movements they led helped change America.

3   Dr. King was gunned down in Memphis, probably at the instigation of a hate group. Newton was gunned down in West Oakland, probably the victim of criminal street activity. The full extent of his own criminal involvement is not altogether clear.

4   What is clear is the first half-light of history is how the two men differed. The work of one is revered in much of the nation, yet the activity of the other was reviled.

5   Newton was representative in the sixties and seventies of sharp and chic radical diversion from the mainstream of the civil rights movement. There were others, such as Stokely Carmichael and H. Rap Brown. Their criticism of Dr. King and the nonviolent movement was that it was too passive, even "Uncle Tom."

6   I covered many of those leaders before and after the split in the movement. I found the differences fascinating. So were some of the similarities. All agreed on one basic tenet: Racism was destroying black lives by the millions.

7   Newton, Carmichael, and Brown, though all critics of Dr. King, differed in their styles and approaches. They shared with each other and with Dr. King a great talent at articulating the nature of the inequities in our society.

8   The radicals differed among themselves and with Dr. King in the solutions they advocated. Newton and the Panthers were socialists and allied themselves with other fringe groups in the white community. Carmichael and Brown preached black nationalism and racial separation.

9   Dr. King preached democracy. He resisted those who would change ours to a socialist system. He also had no patience for those who advanced the idea that black people should have a state of their own. Dr. King believed black Americans contributed mightily to the shaping of America and were entitled to their fair share of the American dream.

10   The struggle of differing views did not die with Dr. King in 1968. Some of those arguments went full force into the decade of the seventies. By then, the Voting Rights Act and other reforms of the nonviolent movement began showing tangible results.

11   The fringe movements died. Their leaders had their 15 minutes of fame. H. Rap Brown took a Muslim life-style and name, and

leads a very low-profile life. Stokely Carmichael pops up now and again, but he has a small following.

12   Dr. King, even in death, continues to command the con-science of the nation. This is so because his choice of a remedy was to resort to basic American principles of justice, fairness and equality.

13   To see the urban underclass is to recognize how much remains to be done. It is also worth noting that the violent streets that spawned the radical movements remain violent streets. It was on those streets that Huey Newton's life ended.

14   His death is a reminder that the civil rights movement spawned prophets and protesters. Dr. King pronounced a prophecy that remains a challenge to the conscience of our soci-ety. And, although Huey Newton and Dr. King differed on solu-tions, their deaths are joined as reminders of the nation's unfin-ished business.

Thesis and Organization

1. What tentative thesis does paragraph 1 suggest?
2. Which paragraphs focus on similarities?
3. Which paragraphs focus on differences? On both similarities and differ-ences?
4. Paragraphs 10–14 deal with the time since Martin Luther King, Jr.'s, death. What has changed? What has not changed?
5. Consider your answer to question 1 and the last sentence in paragraph 14. What is the essay's thesis?

Technique and Style

1. In what ways does the title fit the essay?
2. Huey Newton was a controversial figure who many readers may think of negatively. What is Maynard's view of Newton? How does he take negative opinions of Newton into account?
3. Maynard frequently uses parallelism to emphasize his points. Choose one example and rewrite the sentence so that the parallelism disap-pears or is strengthened. What is gained? Lost?
4. To what extent does Maynard rely on first person? What reasons can you find for his use of it?

5. Alliteration, the use of similar initial sounds, is a technique usually associated with poetry, not prose. What examples can you find in Maynard's essay? What do they add?

Suggestions for Writing

Think about two people who were different yet shared an impact on those about them. You can probably come up with two who influenced you significantly—relatives, teachers, religious people. If you want to write on a less personal subject, think of figures who influenced their fields, those in sports, music, film, medical research, history, politics.

Process

*I*f you have ever been frustrated in your attempts to put together a barbecue grill or hook up a stereo system, you know the value of clear and complete directions. And if you have tried to explain how to get to a particular house or store, you also know that being able to give clear directions is not as easy as it first seems. This practical how-to kind of **process analysis** is one we deal with every day in recipes, in user's manuals, and in instruction booklets. Basic to this process is dividing the topic into the necessary steps, describing each in sufficient detail, and then sequencing the steps so they are easy to follow. You can also help by anticipating trouble spots. If you are writing a set of directions, for example, you might start by describing the parts that must be put together so that you familiarize the reader with them and also force a quick inventory. And if the plans call for 12 screws but include 15, telling the reader that the package includes 3 extra will stave off the inevitable "I must have done it wrong" that leftover parts usually elicit.

But writing directions is only one kind of process analysis. "How did it happen?" and "How does it work?" are questions that get at other sorts of processes, the scientific and the historical. Lab reports exemplify scientific process analysis, as do the kinds of papers you find published in *Scientific American* or the *New England Journal of Medicine*. Like the practical how-to process paper, the report of an experiment or explanation of a physical process clearly marks the steps in a sequence. The same is true of essays that rely on historical process, though sometimes it's harder to discern the steps. A paper that analyzes how the United States became involved in the Vietnam War, for instance, identifies the major stages of involvement and their chronology, the steps that led up to open warfare. Essays that focus on a historical process often condense time in a way that practical or scientific process analysis does not, but the chronology itself is still important.

Although process analysis is a kind of writing usually associated with specialized subjects—how to do *x*, how *y* works, or how *z* came about—it also finds its way into less formal prose. If you were to write about how you got interested in a hobby, for instance, you would be using process analysis, as you would if you were writing an explanatory research paper on the history of Coca-Cola. Process analysis is also useful as a means of discovery. If you were to analyze the process you go through to revise a draft of one of your papers, you might find out that you overemphasize a particular stage or leave out a step. As a way of thinking and expressing ideas, process analysis tends to be underrated because it is equated with the simpler forms of how-to writing.

AUDIENCE AND PURPOSE   The concept of audience is crucial to process essays, for you must know just how familiar the reader is with the topic in order to know what needs to be explained and how to explain it. Christina Erwin's "A Room Without a View," for instance, assumes the audience is a general one that shares her dislike of cleaning up but does not know just what her particular task entails. What the reader doesn't know then guides Erwin's selection of detail and example. Maneka Gandhi writes about lipstick, however, and has a different problem, for she is aware that her readers already know what lipstick looks like. How it got that way and what goes into it are not so readily apparent, so what the readers don't know gives Gandhi a good deal to say. Anyone who has ever been a student is familiar with cramming, but how to do it well is not so widely known, and that is the focus of Jill Young Miller's essay.

What you have to say may be surprising, in which case you need to present the information in a believable way. At the same time, you have to be careful to adjust the information to the level of the audience. The process involved in friends' growing apart can be explained in terms so personal that only the writer could appreciate it, but Michael T. Kaufman is careful to gear his description to the general reader who may have experienced something similar. And he places his personal narrative into a larger, more general context.

On the other hand, if you know not only more but also more specialized information than the reader, you must be careful to adjust the information to the level of the audience. Sometimes a writer explores a process to inform the reader, sometimes to persuade, but always the writer has an assertion in mind and is trying to affect the reader. In her essay "Death by Fasting," for example, Joan Graf depicts the physiology of starvation, outlining the stages the body goes through. In doing so, she must explain scientific terms so that she doesn't baffle her reader. Michael T. Kaufman's essay on friendship, Naomi Wolf's advice to women graduates, and Jill Young Miller's essay on cramming may be intended to inform, but all have an assertive edge. That edge becomes more distinct in the essays by Maneka Gandhi and Joan Graf as an informative purpose combines with a persuasive one.

SEQUENCE   Chronology is as crucial to process as it is to narration. In fact, it is inflexible. What provides the stick in lipstick has to precede what makes it look and smell good. Kaufman's friendship with Hector had to be close before he could feel the loss of distance. The writer must account for all the important steps. If time is crucial to the process, the writer must account for it also, although in a historical process essay, time is apt to be compressed or de-emphasized to underscore a turning point, such as Kaufman's reading of an announcement in the drama section of the newspaper. And undergirding the concept of sequence, of course, is the pattern of cause and effect; crucial to Kaufman's essay is the source of his stereotyping.

DETAIL AND EXAMPLE   In writing a process analysis, you will draw upon the same skills you use for description, narration, and example papers, for without supporting details and examples to further and describe the process, a process essay can be tedious indeed. Wolf's "A Woman's Place" employs examples from different times and sources, drawing upon statistics, allusion, and quotation. Graf intertwines her account of the physiology of fasting with the facts of a particular example, an IRA prisoner's starvation and death. Incorporating references to current events or adding a narrative example or even an amusing aside can make what otherwise might be a list into an interesting paper.

TRANSITIONS   To make the stages of the process clear, you will need to rely on logically placed **transitions** that lead the reader from one stage to the next. Most writers try to avoid depending only on obvious links, such as *first, next, next,* and instead use chronology, shifts in tense, and other indicators of time to indicate sequence. Graf indicates chronology at first with "early in a fast" and "by the third day," and then shifts to "other adjustments," "side effects," and "last stages."

THESIS AND ORGANIZATION The body of a process essay almost organizes itself because it is made up of the steps you have identified, and they must occur in a given sequence. Introductions and conclusions are trickier, as is the thesis, for you must not only set out a process but also make an assertion about it. The author of "Of My Friend Hector and My Achilles Heel," for instance, concludes the essay with a look at why the friendship drifted apart, what stereotyping contributed, and how the two could become friends again. Maneka Gandhi begins her essay by implying her thesis in her first two paragraphs. Christina Erwin, on the other hand, opts for an implied thesis that evolves out of the process she describes. Jill Young Miller and Joan Graf, however, set their process analysis within frameworks. Miller uses a narrative about a particular student to open and close her explanation of the process of cramming for tests. So, too, Graf frames the process of fasting within a particular setting, but she uses the contemporary political situation to add a persuasive edge to her description of a scientific process. In all of these essays, the thesis confronts the reader with a point, implicit or explicit, about the process involved, and in so doing heads off the lethal response, "So what?"

USEFUL TERMS
Chronology The time sequence involved in events; what occurred when.
Process analysis Process analysis examines a topic to discover the series of steps or acts that brought or will bring about a particular result. Whereas cause and effect emphasizes *why*, process emphasizes *how*.
Transition A word, phrase, sentence, or paragraph that carries the reader smoothly from point A to point B. Some transitions, such as time markers (*first, next,* and the like) are obvious; others are more subtle, such as a repeated word or phrase or a synonym for a key term. Transitions provide coherence by linking ideas together and thus improve readability.

IDEAS FOR WRITING Thinking through a process can be helpful if the process involved is one you use often and have developed almost unconscious practices for. Breaking out the process into definite steps can sometimes reveal a gap or show where time is wasted. Try out this idea in your journal or a draft for an essay by analyzing a process you're quite familiar with—studying, taking tests, writing a paper, reading a textbook.

▩ POINTERS FOR USING PROCESS

Exploring the Topic

1. **What kind of process are you presenting?** Is it a practical, "how-to" one? A historical one? A scientific one? Some mixture of types?
2. **What steps are involved?** Which are crucial? Can some be grouped together? Under what headings can they be grouped?
3. **What is the sequence of the steps?** Are you sure that each step logically follows the one before it?
4. **How familiar is your reader with your subject?** Within each step (or group of steps), what information does the reader need to know? What details can you use to make that information come alive? What examples? What connections can you make to what the reader *does* know?
5. **Is setting or context important?** If so, what details of the setting or context do you want to emphasize?
6. **What is the point you want to make about the process?** Is your point an assertion? Will it interest the reader?

Drafting the Paper

1. **Know your reader.** Using two columns, list what your reader may know about your topic in one column and what your reader may not know in the other. If you are writing about a practical process, figure out what pitfalls your reader may fall into. If you are writing about a historical or scientific process, make sure your diction suits your audience. Be on the lookout for events or actions that need further explanation to be understood by a general audience. If your reader is apt to have a bias against your topic, know what the bias is. If your topic is familiar, shape your first paragraph to enlist the reader's interest; if the topic is unfamiliar, use familiar images to explain it.
2. **Know your purpose.** If you are writing to inform, make sure you are presenting new information and that you are making an assertion about your topic. Don't dwell on information that the reader already knows if you can possibly avoid it. If you are writing to persuade, remember that

you do not know whether your audience agrees with you. Use your persona to lend credibility to what you say, and use detail to arouse your reader's sympathies.

3. **Present the steps in their correct sequence.** Make sure that you have accounted for all the important steps or stages in the process and that they are set out in order. If two or more steps occur at the same time, make sure you have made that clear. If time is crucial to your process, see that you have emphasized that point. If, on the other hand, the exact time at which an event occurred is less important than the event, make sure you have stressed the event and have subordinated the idea of time.

4. **Use details and examples.** Whether you are writing an informative or a persuasive essay, use details and examples that support your purpose. If you are explaining how to make your own ice cream, for example, draw upon what the reader knows about various commercial brands and flavors to bolster your case for making your own. After all, your reader may not want to take the time and trouble for that process and therefore may have to be enticed into trying it. Choose details and examples that combat your reader's attitude if that attitude is apt to be a negative one.

5. **Double-check your transitions.** First mark your stages with obvious transitions or with numbers. After you have turned your notes into a working draft, review the transitions you have used, checking to see that they exist, that they are clear, and that they are not overly repetitious or obvious. Make sure each important stage (or group of stages) is set off by a transition. See if you can indicate shifts by using tense or words and phrases that don't call attention to themselves as transitions.

6. **Make a point.** What you say about a subject is far more interesting than the subject itself, so even if you are writing a practical process essay, make sure you have a point. A paper on topic such as "how to change a tire" becomes unbearable without a thesis. Given an assertion about changing a tire—"Changing my first flat was as horrible as I had expected it to be"—the paper at least has a chance.

*H*ow to Cram

Jill Young Miller

Cramming, deeply embedded as a way of student life, often turns up in nightmares as panic over having to take an exam for a course you never signed up for. Real or imagined, the situations that drive us to cram are known too well to us all. Appropriately enough, the essay was published in Campus Voice *(1987), a magazine distributed free on many college campuses.*

WHAT TO LOOK FOR   *Often when you write a process analysis you may find you use the imperative form of verbs, as in "Next, take . . . ." But the imperative need not sound rude or bossy. As you read Miller's essay, keep your ear tuned to how her imperatives sound.*

KEY WORDS AND PHRASES
chronic (1)   *acronyms (24)*
Chaucer (2)   *salvaged (30)*
elaborate (2)

1   Frances Avila learned the hard way not to expect miracles overnight. A chronic crammer, the New York University senior did the usual for her midterm in "Major British Writers" last fall: she pulled an all-nighter. Fighting off fatigue and anxiety, Avila forced herself to concentrate on the novels and her notes through dawn, breaking only to splash cold water on her face. Near noon, she closed her books to head for the test.

2   The first question—"Expand on the gap between her front teeth"—was a lulu. Avila didn't recognize the allusion to Chaucer's Wife of Bath, even though she'd read the section only hours before. "Not only did I blank out, but I was also frightened," she recalls. "I didn't expect the test to be that elaborate." The bad situation only got worse. She fumbled through 14 more stray lines before plunging into part two, which wasn't any easier. Avila had studied innumerable facts for hours, but she knew only one thing for sure: she was in trouble.

3   "I failed the exam," she explains, "because I had to compare and contrast two poets from different time periods. In order to do

155

that, I had to elaborate on all the details within the poetry. But I'd absorbed just enough information the night before to understand what I was reading and not enough to catch all the details."

4   Sound familiar? Almost all of us had stood (and sleepwalked) in Avila's shoes at one time or another. Sometimes push comes to shove, crunch comes to cram, and before you know it, you have to read 450 pages in six hours. Pour on the caffeine, you mumble.

5   About 90 percent of all students cram, estimates Don Dansereau, a psychology professor at Texas Christian University, who defines cramming as "intense studying the night before or the day of a test." Quips Ric Schank, a University of Florida senior, "Down here, it's the rule rather than the exception."

6   Despite its popularity, cramming gets low marks from educators and memory experts, who claim that the last-minute nature of the act kills your chances for payoff at test time.

7   A quick stroll down memory lane explains why. Most experts identify three types of memory: immediate, short-term, and long-term. You use your immediate memory as you read this, remembering each word just long enough to make the transition to the next.

8   Short-term memory is limited, too. For example, you use it when you look up a phone number, close the book, and dial. Short-term memory can supposedly hold a maximum of seven items for only a few seconds.

9   Long-term memory is the big daddy, the one that holds everything you know about the world. It's the memory that last-minute learners need to respect.

10   How well you organize information on its way into your long-term memory determines how quickly you can retrieve it later, or whether you retrieve it at all. Think of a backpack you'd take on a hike, says Laird Cermak, a research psychologist at the Boston Veterans Administration Hospital and the author of *Improving Your Memory* (McGraw-Hill, 1975). "If your backpack is organized and you get bit by a snake, you can go right for the snakebite kit," he explains.

11   The magic lies in spacing your study over days, weeks, or even months. That gives you time to mull over the new stuff, relate it to what you already know, and organize it for exam-time recall. "The reason you forget the information is not because it was learned the night before," Cermak explains. "It's because when you crammed

you didn't give yourself good ways to remember it in the future."
In other words, last-minute studying limits the number of mental
retrieval routes you can create.

12　　But it doesn't take a psychologist to explain why cramming often fails. "You throw things into your mind, knowing that you're
going to spit them out in a couple of hours and forget them. It's not
a good way to learn at all," says NYU journalism senior David
Reilly.

13　　No quick-and-dirty detours to long-term retention and instant
recall exist. But if you're forced into a late-night, last-minute study
session, the results don't have to be disastrous. Here's some advice
to help make the morning after less anxious than the night before:

14　　**Find out what kind of test you're in for.** If you cram, you're
likely to fare better on multiple-choice and fill-in-the-blank tests
because they jog your memory with cues, Cermak says.

15　　**Find a quiet place to study.** When Avila crams, she seeks out
a small room at the library that's devoid of distractions. "I'm cornered," she says. "I have no choice but to look at the print."

16　　If you like to study with music in the background, go for something without lyrics and keep the volume down low. Classical music such as Bach can have a soothing effect if your nerves are im-
peding your studies, says Danielle Lapp, a memory researcher at
Stanford University and the author of *Don't Forget! Easy Exercises
for a Better Memory at Any Age* (McGraw-Hill, 1987).

17　　**Compose a scene that you can re-create during the exam.**
If you can, study at the desk or in the room where you'll take the
test, or do something while you study that you can do again when
you take the test. For example, Dansereau suggests that you chew
grape gum. "The flavor acts a cuing device," he explains.

18　　**Build your concentration.** Spend ten minutes warming up
with a novel or magazine before you tackle a tough chapter. Says
Cermak, "It helps you block out whatever else is going on."

19　　**Watch what you eat and drink.** Avoid heavy meals and alcohol. Both could make you drowsy, cautions Lapp. If you need a
cup of coffee to perk up, fine. But putting too much caffeine in
your system can make you jittery and break your concentration.

20　　**Mark your book.** Even if you only have time to read the chapter once, it helps to highlight important terms and sections. Identifying the key words and passages requires you to be mentally alert
and forces you to be an active rather than a passive reader.

21   **Spend time repeating or discussing facts out loud.** Recitation promotes faster learning because it's more active than reading or listening. (Try it out when you study for your next foreign language vocabulary quiz.) Discussion groups are helpful for this reason.

22   **Take short breaks at least every few hours.** They'll help you beat fatigue, which takes a heavy toll on learning. Two hour-long sittings separated by a 15-minute break are more productive than one two-hour session in which your mind wanders throughout the second half. It doesn't matter what you do during those breaks; just take them.

23   **Experiment with memory techniques.** They impose structure on new information, making it easier to remember at test time. The "house" method is one of the oldest. Let's say you want to remember a list of sequential events for a history exam. Try to imagine the events taking place in separate but connected rooms of your house. When the test asks you to recall the events, take a mental amble through the rooms.

24   Another simple technique involves acronyms. You may have learned the names of the Great Lakes (Huron, Ontario, Michigan, Erie, and Superior) with this one: HOMES.

25   **Try some proven learning strategies.** Richard Yates, a counselor and time management expert at Cleveland State University, recommends the SQ3R method: survey, question, read, recite, review. Survey the material to formulate a general impression; rephrase titles and headings into questions; read through the material quickly to find the main points and the answers to your questions; recite those main ideas, taking brief notes; and review. Even when you're pressed for time, the strategy can help. "It may take a little longer," says Yates, "but it's worth the effort."

26   **Get some sleep.** UF's Schank quit all-nighters after his freshman year. "I'd go into a final and be so wired from staying up all night that I'd lose my concentration," he says. "I'd miss questions that I knew I wouldn't miss if I were in a good frame of mind." Now he crams until about 3 A.M., sleeps for about four hours, and hits the books again at 8 A.M.

27   Psychologists and memory researchers can't specify how much sleep you need—everyone has his or her own threshold—but they do stress its importance. Says Lapp, "You're better off getting some

sleep so that your mind is rested for the exam than you are cramming the whole night." Just don't forget to set that alarm clock before you go to bed.

28   For an early-morning exam, it's best to do heavy-duty studying right before you go to sleep. In other words, unless you've got back-to-back exams, don't cram and then do something else for a few hours before a test. Freshly learned material is remembered much better after a period of sleep than after an equal period of daytime activity.

29   **Relax.** It may sound simplistic, but it's key to good test performance. "Anxiety is enemy number one of memory," Lapp explains. She compares a student taking a test to a singer performing on-stage. "There's no way a completely anxious singer can utter a sound," she says.

30   Cramming is like going to the dentist; if you have to do it, you want it to be as painless and as productive as it can be. After all, no one goes to college to take a semester-long class and promptly forget all the new information that's been taught. At least Frances Avila didn't. After her disastrous midterm, she didn't dare risk cramming for her "Major British Writers" final exam. This time, she spaced her studying over a period of weeks, earned an A, and salvaged her grade for the semester.

31   That doesn't mean she's quit cramming for good—in fact, she hasn't even tried to. Instead she's perfected her technique. Ditto for Reilly, who's tried unsuccessfully to break the habit. "Every semester I kick myself a million times and scream that I'm not going to cram next semester," he laments. "But it never seems to work."

Thesis and Organization

1. The steps to follow are given in paragraphs 14–29, which leaves almost half the essay taken up by introduction and conclusion. Examine paragraphs 1–13 and identify the use of narration, example, and definition.
2. Analyze the role of narrative in the introduction and conclusion. What effect does Miller achieve with the story of Avila?
3. How necessary is Miller's definition of cramming? Of types of memory? Explain the relation between the two.
4. What principle do you find behind the sequencing of paragraphs 14–29? How does that principle relate to Miller's informative purpose?

5. Consider what Miller tells you about studying, memory, cramming, and Avila. In your own words, state her thesis.

Technique and Style

1. Miller's paragraphs are shorter than you would usually find in an essay of this length. How can you justify the relative shortness of her paragraphs?
2. What point of view does Miller use in the essay? What reasons can you find for that choice?
3. The imperative can be rude and bossy, as in the command "Shut the door." How would you characterize Miller's use of the imperative? How does she avoid using it rudely?
4. What sources does Miller use in her essay? What purpose do they serve in relation to Miller's information? Her credibility? Why provide full citations in paragraphs 10 and 16?
5. What kind of person does Miller seem to be? If you were taking a study skills course, would you want her as a teacher? Why or why not?

Suggestions for Writing

Think about the steps in a process you know well and write your own "how-to" essay. Suggestions: worrying creatively, handling stress, coping with obnoxious people, throwing a curve ball, returning a serve, spiking a volleyball; making the perfect burger, frying the perfect egg, baking the perfect brownie.

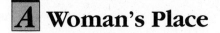

A Woman's Place

Naomi Wolf

Naomi Wolf was working on her doctorate at Princeton University when she adapted her dissertation into The Beauty Myth, *a best-selling book published in 1991. As the title of that book implies, Wolf concerns herself with issues that affect women. Her most recent work is* Power Feminine: How to Love the Feminist Movement Again, *which appeared in 1993. The essay that follows is adapted from a commencement address she gave at Scripps College, a women's college in California.*

WHAT TO LOOK FOR   *Many writers steer away from beginning a sentence with* and *because they are afraid of creating a sentence fragment. But as long as the sentence has a subject and main verb, it can begin with* and *(or, like this one, with* but *or any other conjunction) and still be an independent clause, a complete sentence, with the conjunction serving as an informal transition. To see how effective this kind of sentence can be, notice Wolf's last paragraph.*

KEY WORDS AND PHRASES

Dick Cavett (2)	*equity (14)*
Elis (4)	*Virginia Woolf (16)*
chrysalis (9)	*Antigone (16)*
Djuna Barnes (9)	*Joan of Arc (16)*
precipitously (11)	*Audre Lorde (18)*
tithe (13)	*Emma Goldman (12)*

1   Even the best of revolutions can go awry when we internalize the attitudes we are fighting. The class of 1992 is graduating into a violent backlash against the advances women have made over the last 20 years. This backlash ranges from a Senator using "The Exorcist" against Anita Hill, to beer commercials with the "Swedish bikini team." Today I want to give you a backlash survival kit, a four-step manual to keep the dragons from taking up residence inside your own heads.

2   My own commencement, at Yale eight years ago, was the Graduation from Hell. The speaker was Dick Cavett, rumored to have been our president's "brother" in an all-male secret society.

3   Mr. Cavett took the microphone and paled at the sight of hundreds of female about-to-be Yale graduates. "When I was an undergraduate," I recall he said, "there were no women. The women went to Vassar. At Vassar, they had nude photographs taken of the women in gym class to check their posture. One year the photos were stolen, and turned up for sale in New Haven's red-light district." His punchline? "The photos found no buyers."

4   I'll never forget that moment. There we were, silent in our black gowns, our tassels, our brand new shoes. We dared not break the silence with hisses or boos, out of respect for our families, who'd come so far; and they kept still out of concern for us. Consciously or not, Mr. Cavett was using the beauty myth aspect of the backlash: when women come too close to masculine power, someone will draw critical attention to their bodies. We might be Elis, but we still wouldn't make pornograpy worth buying.

5   That afternoon, several hundred men were confirmed in the power of a powerful institution. But many of the women felt the shame of the powerless: the choking on silence, the complicity, the helplessness. We were orphaned from our institution.

6   I want to give you the commencement talk that was denied to me.

7   Message No. 1 in your survival kit: redefine "becoming a woman." Today you have "become women." But that sounds odd in ordinary usage. What is usually meant by "You're a real woman now"? You "become a woman" when you menstruate for the first time, or when you lose your virginity, or when you have a child.

8   These biological definitions are very different from how we say boys become men. One "becomes a man" when he undertakes responsibility, or completes a quest. But you, too, in some ways more than your male friends graduating today, have moved into maturity through a solitary quest for the adult self.

9   We lack archetypes for the questing young woman, her trials by fire; for how one "become a woman" through the chrysalis of education, the difficult passage from one book, one idea to the next. Let's refuse to have our scholarship and our gender pitted against each other. In our definition, the scholar learns womanhood and the woman learns scholarship; Plato and Djuna Barnes, mediated

to their own enrichment through the eyes of the female body with its wisdoms and its gifts.

10   I say that you have already shown courage: Many of you graduate today in spite of the post-traumatic stress syndrome of acquaintance rape, which one-fourth of female students undergo. Many of you were so weakened by anorexia and bulimia that it took every ounce of your will to get your work in. You negotiated private lives through a mine field of new strains of VD and the ascending shadow of AIDS. Triumphant survivors, you have already "become women."

11   Message No. 2 breaks the ultimate taboo for women: *Ask for money in your lives*. Expect it. Own it. Learn to use it. Little girls learn a debilitating fear of money—that it's not feminine to insure we are fairly paid for honest work. Meanwhile, women make 68 cents for every male dollar and half of marriages end in divorce, after which women's income drops precipitously.

12   Never choose a profession for material reasons. But whatever field your heart decides on, for god's sake get the most specialized training in it you can and hold out hard for just compensation, parental leave and child care. Resist your assignment to the class of highly competent, grossly underpaid women who run the show while others get the cash—and the credit.

13   Claim money not out of greed, but so you can tithe to women's political organizations, shelters and educational institutions. Sexist institutions won't yield power if we are just patient long enough. The only language the status quo understands is money, votes and public embarrassment.

14   When you have equity, you have influence—as sponsors, shareholders and alumnae. Use it to open opportunities to women who deserve the chances you've had. Your B.A. does not belong to you alone, just as the earth does not belong to its present tenants alone. Your education was lent to you by women of the past, and you will give some back to living women, and to your daughters seven generations from now.

15   Message No. 3: Never cook for or sleep with anyone who routinely puts you down.

16   Message No. 4: Become goddesses of disobedience. Virginia Woolf wrote that we must slay the Angel in the House, the censor within. Young women tell me of injustices, from campus rape coverups to classroom sexism. But at the thought of confrontation,

they freeze into niceness. We are told that the worst thing we can do is cause conflict, even in the service of doing right. Antigone is imprisoned. Joan of Arc burns at the stake. And someone might call us unfeminine!

17   When I wrote a book that caused controversy, I saw how big a dragon was this paralysis by niceness. "The Beauty Myth" argues that newly rigid ideals of beauty are instruments of a backlash against feminism, designed to lower women's self-esteem for a political purpose. Many positive changes followed the debate. But all that would dwindle away when someone yelled at me—as, for instance, cosmetic surgeons did on TV, when I raised questions about silicone implants. Oh, no, I'd quail, people are mad at me!

18   Then I read something by the poet Audre Lorde. She'd been diagnosed with breast cancer. "I was going to die," she wrote, "sooner or later, whether or not I had ever spoken myself. My silences had not protected me. Your silences will not protect you. . . . What are the words you do not yet have? What are the tyrannies you swallow day by day and attempt to make your own, until you will sicken and die of them, still in silence? We have been socialized to respect fear more than our own need for language."

19   I began to ask each time: "What's the worst that could happen to me if I tell this truth?" Unlike women in other countries, our breaking silence is unlikely to have us jailed, "disappeared" or run off the road at night. Our speaking out will irritate some people, get us called bitchy or hypersensitive and disrupt some dinner parties. And then our speaking out will permit other women to speak, until laws are changed and lives are saved and the world is altered forever.

20   Next time, ask: What's the worst that will happen? Then push yourself a little further than you dare. Once you start to speak, people *will* yell at you. They *will* interrupt, put you down and suggest it's personal. And the world won't end.

21   And the speaking will get easier and easier. And you will find you have fallen in love with your own vision, which you may never have realized you had. And you will lose some friends and lovers, and realize you don't miss them. And new ones will find you and cherish you. And you will still flirt and paint your nails, dress up and party, because as I think Emma Goldman said, "If I can't dance, I don't want to be part of your revolution." And at last you'll know with surpassing certainty that only one thing is more frightening than speaking your truth. And that is not speaking.

Thesis and Organization

1. Wolf's essay could easily be retitled "How to Survive the Backlash." What is the backlash?
2. Why does Wolf include the anecdote about Dick Cavett? How is it related to the backlash?
3. What are the four steps for survival?
4. What gender-based stereotypes does Wolf attack?
5. Wolf's essay gives advice and explains how to survive, but it also comments on women's place in society today. Combine those comments with her advice and the result will be the thesis.

Technique and Style

1. What saying does Wolf's title refer to? How does her title set up her essay?
2. Throughout the essay, Wolf uses allusion—Anita Hill (1), Plato and Djuna Barnes (9), Virginia Woolf (16), Audre Lorde (18), and Emma Goldman (21). Use an encyclopedia to look up one of these allusions so that you can explain to the class how it is (or is not) appropriate.
3. To explore the effect of Wolf's repeated use of *and* in her last paragraph, try rewriting it. What is gained? Lost?
4. The original audience for the essay was women, but it was republished for an audience that also includes men. Explain whether or not men would find the essay offensive. Is it anti-male?
5. Wolf is obviously a feminist, but think of feminism as a continuum ranging from conservative to radical. Based on this essay, what kind of feminist is Wolf? What evidence can you find for your opinion?

Suggestions for Writing

All of us at one time or another have played a role we didn't believe in or didn't like. These roles can vary greatly: Dutiful Daughter, Responsible Sibling, Perfect Husband (or Wife), Brave Man, Happy Homemaker—the list can go on and on. Think about the roles you have had to play and how you broke out of them. Choose one and draft a paper explaining "How to Survive" or "How to Break Out."

A Room Without a View

Christina Erwin

The title of the essay plays on A Room With A View, *the title of a novel by E. M. Forster, an English novelist (1879–1970). The novel was made into a film in 1986 and had therefore become generally familiar to many readers. Christina Erwin graduated from the University of New Orleans in the spring of 1994. Among writers, she particularly admires Erma Bombeck, and as you read the essay, you'll find echoes of Bombeck's good-natured but wry humor.*

WHAT TO LOOK FOR   *Many a how-to essay plunges into a predictable string of* first, next, next, next, *followed by* finally. *You can avoid that trap by following Erwin's technique, using spatial relationships to establish sequence.*

KEY WORDS AND PHRASES
lava flow (4)	*hieroglyphics (8)*
Freud (5)	*sedimentary bed (11)*
hawk (7)	*fossilized (11)*
salves (8)	

1   It's the most often used room in my house, yet no one ever admits to have been in there. It's the place we visit each evening when we retire and every morning when we awaken. It's the bathroom. And the two-foot deep cabinet housed within is a room in itself but without a view. It is a volcano on the verge of eruption.

2   Under the pressure of a six P.M. deadline, I knew I'd have to work quickly for my house to pass my mother-in-law's white-glove inspection. I had completed the major events of my cleaning the day before, bulldozing through the laundry, sandblasting the dirty dishes. All that remained was the detail work.

3   After dusting the tops of the canned peas in my pantry, removing the corn chips from beneath the sofa cushion, and fluffing the pillow in my dog's bed, I knew I had to face it: the dreaded bathroom cabinet. Donning rubber gloves, a gas mask, and hip boots, I prepared for combat.

4   Opening the door to the cabinet, I was buried in a lava flow of once-tried shampoos, half-used deodorants, powders, lotions, and hairsprays that failed to make good on their promises. There is no such thing as "all-day hold."

5   If Freud were alive today, he wouldn't have to psychoanalyze his patients to learn how they tick. He could simply peek in their bathroom cabinets (a skill he could learn from my mother-in-law). His diagnosis of my cabinet—repulsion with body odor, obsession with body hair—incurable! simply having hair on our heads (which I am still blessed with, although my husband is not so lucky) is not enough for us; we also insist that it be a certain color, thickness, softness, length, and height.

6   If ever a hair product was advertised, I've probably tried it at least once, be it gel, mousse, spray or color—and it was probably still in that cabinet, waiting to be sprung from hair-care penitentiary. I threw out as many bottles as I could bear to part with, creating a toxic mixture in the bottom of the garbage can that I feared would eat its way through to the floor.

7   Beyond the hair-goo, I found medicines that no one in my family would admit to ever having needed. Hemorrhoid ointments, diarrhea tablets, antacids, even petroleum jelly lay hidden in shame behind the classier drugstore items, the ones over-packaged in plastic, endorsed by fashion models. Has someone like Cindy Crawford ever done an ad for wart remover? Would Paul Newman ever hawk athlete's foot powder? I doubt it.

8   I sorted the pills, balms, and salves into three piles—still usable; past the expiration date; and past recognition, those tubes and plastic bottles with labels resembling hieroglyphics. The last two piles I pitched into the trash can, which was beginning to glow.

9   Buried at the back of the cabinet, I found a twelve-roll bargain pack of toilet paper. My husband hides it there, sure that people will think we're weird if there are more than four rolls visible at one time, a fear that his mother instilled in him. What would Dr. Freud have said about that skeleton in our cabinet?

10   Behind the T.P. I found the plunger (that would have saved me a bill from the plumber last week when the kitchen sink backed up), the bonnet-style hairdryer my mother gave me when I moved out, and the hammer we lost while hanging the new shower curtain rod. I also came across a broken steam iron and an overdue book for which I'd received threats of torture from the librarian.

11   I had worked my way down to the sedimentary bed of solo earrings, razor blades, and toenail clippers. While examining a fossilized aspirin, I heard the doorbell ring. I knew it was her. Quickly, I shoved my latest discoveries back into the cabinet and then covered the whole mess with a large beach towel. The battle was over. I waved a white toilet brush in surrender and answered the door.

Thesis and Organization

1. What paragraph or paragraphs provide the introduction?
2. What are the steps in the process Erwin describes?
3. What does the essay imply (good-naturedly) about our culture?
4. How would you describe the attitude of the writer toward cleaning?
5. Given your answer to 4 and the subject of the essay, what is the thesis?

Technique and Style

1. The essay uses two analogies, one from geology (1, 4, 11) and one from war (3, 11). Choose one and explain what it adds to the essay.
2. Exaggeration or hyperbole is a standard comic technique. Select one example from the essay and explain how it achieves its effect.
3. Erwin places the clean-up within the broader context of her mother-in-law's visit. What does that context add to the essay?
4. What effect is achieved by delaying the subject of the first paragraph until the third sentence?
5. Coherence, literally the quality of sticking together, is a characteristic of good prose, prose in which each paragraph flows naturally into the next so that the essay appears a seamless whole. What techniques can you spot in Erwin's essay that contribute to its coherence.

Suggestions for Writing

Sooner or later, all of us have had to take on an unpleasant job, usually one that we have put off as long as possible. Think of all the unpleasant or difficult things you have had to do. Choose one as a basis for a "how-to" paper. The fact that the job is unpleasant or difficult is apt to make examples and steps come readily to mind. If that idea doesn't appeal, write a paper that takes a positive approach to a usually negative action, such as "How to Procrastinate" or "How to Tell a White Lie."

Of My Friend Hector And My Achilles Heel

Michael T. Kaufman

The title plays on the names of major figures in Greek mythology. During the Trojan War, Hector, a Trojan, was killed in battle by Achilles, a Greek, who in turn was killed when an arrow struck his heel, his only vulnerable spot. According to myth, Achilles's mother tried to make him immortal by dipping him into the river Styx, but she had to hold him by his heel, which, therefore, remained unprotected. From this tale, we get both "Achilles heel" as a synonym for a weak spot and the "Achilles tendon."

Kaufman may have an Achilles heel, but as he explains in his essay, Hector was his childhood friend. In adulthood, however, Kaufman may well have murdered Hector symbolically. Author of the "About New York" column in the New York Times, *Kaufman's essay was published in the supplement* Education Life *in 1992.*

WHAT TO LOOK FOR   *Process essays frequently depend on time markers that are often so obvious that they leap off the page. As you read Kaufman's essay, look for how he indicates time so that if you write an essay that depends on chronology, you too can indicate time subtly.*

KEY WORDS AND PHRASES

tenement (2)	versatile (13)
walkup (2)	assumptions (13)
linoleum (3)	retrospect (14)
avocado (4)	reinforced (14)
presumably (8)	concocted (14)
perfunctory (9)	decades (16)
longshoreman (11)	conveyed (16)
Peter Falk (12)	consigned (16)
"The Prisoner of Second Avenue" (12)	

1   This story is about prejudice and stupidity. My own.

2   It begins in 1945 when I was a 7-year-old living on the fifth floor of a tenement walkup on 107th Street between Columbus

and Manhattan Avenues in New York City. The block was almost entirely Irish and Italian, and I believe my family was the only Jewish one around.

3   One day a Spanish-speaking family moved into one of the four apartments on our landing. They were the first Puerto Ricans I had met. They had a son who was about my age named Hector, and the two of us became friends. We played with toy soldiers and I particularly remember how, using rubber bands and wood from orange crates, we made toy pistols that shot off little squares we cut from old linoleum.

4   We visited each other's home and I know that at the time I liked Hector and I think he liked me. I may even have eaten my first avocado at his house.

5   About a year after we met, my family moved to another part of Manhattan's West Side and I did not see Hector again until I entered Booker T. Washington Junior High School as an 11-year-old.

6   The class I was in was called 7SP–1; the SP was for special. Earlier, I recall, I had been in the IGC class, for "intellectually gifted children." The SP class was to complete the seventh, eighth and ninth grades in two years and almost all of us would then go to schools like Bronx Science, Stuyvesant or Music and Art, where admission was based on competitive exams. I knew I was in the SP class and the IGC class. I guess I also knew that other people were not.

7   Hector was not. He was in some other class, maybe even 7–2, the class that was held to be the next-brightest, or maybe 7–8. I remember I was happy to see him whenever we would meet, and sometimes we played punchball during lunch period. Mostly, of course, I stayed with my own classmates, with other Intellectually Gifted Children.

8   Sometimes children from other classes, those presumably not so intellectually gifted, would tease and taunt us. At such time I was particularly proud to have Hector as a friend. I assumed that he was tougher than I and my classmates and I guess I thought that if necessary he would come to my defense.

9   For high school, I went uptown to Bronx Science. Hector, I think, went downtown to Commerce. Sometimes I would see him in Riverside Park, where I played basketball and he worked out on the parallel bars. We would acknowledge each other, but by this

time the conversations we held were perfunctory—sports, families, weather.

10   After I finished college, I would see him around the neighborhood pushing a baby carriage. He was the first of my contemporaries to marry and to have a child.

11   A few years later, in the 60's, married and with children of my own, I was once more living on the West Side, working until late at night as a reporter. Some nights as I took the train home I would see Hector in the car. A few times we exchanged nods, but more often I would pretend that I didn't see him, and maybe he also pretended he didn't see me. Usually he would be wearing a knitted watch cap, and from that I deduced that he was probably working on the docks as a longshoreman.

12   I remember quite distinctly how I would sit on the train and think about how strange and unfair fate had been with regard to the two of us who had once been playmates. Just because I had become an intellectually gifted adult or whatever and he had become a longshoreman or whatever, was that any reason for us to have been left with nothing to say to each other? I thought it was wrong and unfair, but I also thought that conversation would be a chore or a burden. That is pretty much what I thought about Hector, if I thought about him at all, until one Sunday in the mid–70's, when I read in the drama section of this newspaper that my childhood friend, Hector Elizondo, was replacing Peter Falk in the leading role in "The Prisoner of Second Avenue."

13   Since then, every time I have seen this versatile and acclaimed actor in movies or on television I have blushed for my assumptions. I have replayed the subway rides in my head and tried to fathom why my thoughts had led me where they did.

14   In retrospect it seems far more logical that the man I saw on the train, the man who had been my friend as a boy, was coming home from an Off Broadway theater or perhaps from a job as a waiter while taking acting classes. So why did I think he was a longshoreman? Was it just the cap? Could it be that his being Puerto Rican had something to do with it? Maybe that reinforced the stereotype I concocted, but it wasn't the root of it.

15   No, the foundation was laid when I was 11, when I was in 7SP–1 and he was not, when I was in the IGC class and he was not.

16   I have not seen him since I recognized how I had idiotically kept tracking him for years and decades after the school system had tracked both of us. I wonder now if my experience was that unusual, whether social categories conveyed and absorbed before puberty do not generally tend to linger beyond middle age. And I wonder, too, that if they affected the behavior of someone like myself who had been placed on the upper track, how much more damaging it must have been for someone consigned to the lower.

17   I have at times thought of calling him, but kept from doing it because how exactly does one apologize for thoughts that were never expressed? And there was still the problem of what to say. "What have you been up to for the last 40 years?" Or "Wow, was I wrong about you!" Or maybe just, "Want to come over and help me make a linoleum gun?"

Thesis and Organization

1. Kaufman describes the process of his relationship with Hector, how it came to be. What are the stages he notes?
2. What time periods correspond to those stages?
3. At what point in the essay does Kaufman clarify what he means by his "prejudice and stupidity" (1)?
4. What are the causes behind Kaufman's assumptions?
5. In paragraph 16, Kaufman generalizes upon his experience. What thesis for the essay does that paragraph suggest?

Technique and Style

1. Kaufman's first paragraph is made up of one short sentence and a fragment. Look up *sentence fragment* in a handbook of grammar. To what extent does Kaufman's use agree with the handbook?
2. Paragraphs 6–8 describe the years when Kaufman's prejudices were formed. How did he see himself then? How does he see himself now?
3. The length of Kaufman's paragraphs is determined by the column width of the page on which the essay was printed. If that constraint did not exist, which paragraphs could be combined? What would be gained? Lost?
4. Given the essay's point and content, how effective is the title?
5. Kaufman ends his essay by referring to an incident in his introduction. Explain whether or not the reference is effective.

Suggestions for Writing

Human nature often leads us to stereotype people or to jump to conclusions that later turn out to be wrong. Think of a time when you labeled someone wrongly or assumed something that proved untrue. Jot down what you assumed and list those things that led to that conclusion. Then write out what you found to be true. You can use your first list as the basis of your introduction. The body of your paper can explain how you made those assumptions and how they changed.

ou Sure You Want to Do This?

Maneka Gandhi

Ever wonder what goes into a single tube of lipstick? Maneka Gandhi tells us, though she also warns us that we may find out more than we wanted to know. Gandhi writes a regular column in the Illustrated Weekly *of India, although this essay was published in the* Baltimore Sun *(1989). A strong voice on the current political scene in India, Maneka Gandhi speaks out in favor of vegetarianism as well as protecting the environment and animal rights.*

WHAT TO LOOK FOR *Process analysis essays that are built around chronology sometimes fall into predictable transitions such as* first, second, next, then. *Gandhi avoids the obvious even though chronology is important to her discussion. Be on the lookout for how she gets from one stage to the other.*

KEY WORDS AND PHRASES
metamorphoses (2) *molten (6)*
hydrogenated (3) *iridescent (8)*

1   Are you one of those women who feel that lipstick is one of the essentials of life? That to be seen without it is the equivalent of facial nudity? Then you might like to know what goes into that attractive color tube that you smear on your lips.

2   At the center of the modern lipstick is acid. Nothing else will burn a coloring sufficiently deeply into the lips. The acid starts out orange, then sizzles into the living skin cells and metamorphoses into a deep red. Everything else in the lipstick is there just to get this acid into place.

3   First lipstick has to spread. Softened food shortening, such as hydrogenated vegetable oil, spreads very well, and accordingly is one of the substances found in almost all lipsticks. Soap smears well, too, and so some of that is added as well. Unfortunately, neither soap nor shortening is good at actually taking up the acid that's needed to do the dyeing. Only one smearable substance will do this to any extent: castor oil.

4   Good cheap castor oil, used in varnishes and laxatives, is one of the largest ingredients by bulk in every lipstick. The acid soaks into the castor oil, the castor oil spreads on the lips with the soap and shortening till the acid is carried where it needs to go.

5   If lipstick could be sold in castor oil bottles there would be no need for the next major ingredient. But the mix has to be transformed into a rigid, streamlined stick, and for that nothing is better than heavy petroleum-based wax. It's what provides the "stick" in lipstick.

6   Of course, certain precautions have to be taken in combining all these substances. If the user ever got a sniff of what was in there, there might be problems of consumer acceptance. So a perfume is poured in at the manufacturing stage before all the oils have cooled—when it is still a molten lipstick mass.

7   At the same time, food preservatives are poured into the mass, because apart from smelling rather strongly the oil in there would go rancid without some protection. (Have you smelled an old lipstick? That dreadful smell is castor oil gone bad.)

8   All that's lacking now is shine. When the preservatives and the perfume are being poured in, something shiny, colorful, almost iridescent—and, happily enough, not even too expensive—is added. That something is fish scales. It's easily available from the leftovers of commercial fish-packing stations. The scales are soaked in ammonia, then bunged in with everything else.

9   Fish scales, by the way, mean that lipstick is not a vegetarian product. Every time you paint your lips you eat fish scales. So lipsticks without them actually are marked "vegetarian lipstick."

10   Is that it then? Shortening, soap, castor oil, petroleum wax, perfume, food preservatives and fish scales? Not entirely. There is still one thing missing: color.

11   The orange acid that burns into the lips turns red only on contact. So that what you see in the tube looks like lip color and not congealed orange juice, another dye has to be added to the lipstick. This masterpiece of chemistry and art will be a soothing and suggestive and kissable red.

12   But it has very little to do with what actually goes on your face. That, as we said, is—but by now you already know more than you wanted to.

Thesis and Organization

1. What does paragraph 1 make clear about the essay's audience and subject? What expectations does it set up for the reader?
2. Which paragraphs focus on the ingredients that make lipstick work?
3. Which paragraphs focus on making lipstick attractive?
4. Consider the title of the essay and what Gandhi has to say about what goes into a tube of lipstick. What is her thesis?
5. Given the thesis of the essay, do you find Gandhi's purpose more informative than argumentative or the reverse? Explain.

Technique and Style

1. Considering what you have learned about Gandhi's thesis and purpose, how would you characterize the tone of the essay?
2. What provides the transitions between paragraphs 3 and 4? Between paragraphs 10 and 11? How effective do you find this device?
3. Examine the verbs Gandhi uses in paragraphs 2 and 3. What do they contribute to the essay's tone?
4. Paragraph 9 is more of an aside, a "by the way" comment, than a furthering of the essay's forward motion. What reasons can you think of that make the paragraph appropriate?
5. The last paragraph contains two references that at first may seem vague. What does "it" refer to in paragraph 12's first sentence. What does "That" refer to in the second sentence? Would a summary add to or detract from the conclusion? Explain.

Suggestions for Writing

Think about other items we take for granted and then find out if their ingredients contain a few surprises. You might start with a product (hot dogs, marshmallows, frozen pies, shampoo) first noting the ingredients listed on the package and then consulting an unabridged dictionary.

Death by Fasting

Joan Stephenson Graf

"Death by Fasting" sets a scientific process, how the body reacts to prolonged starvation, within a political context, the hunger strike. Here, the hunger strikers are members of the Irish Republican Army held prisoner by the British. Bobby Sands was the first prisoner to die. Graf's essay appeared more than ten years ago in Science 81, *a publication of the American Association of the Advancement of Science, but the troubles in Ireland live on.*

WHAT TO LOOK FOR   *Much of what is published in the social and physical sciences uses process analysis, and now and then that information needs to be written for a nonscientific audience. You may run into the same problem if you are writing a paper on a subject you are very familiar with that is nonetheless aimed at a general audience. When and if that time comes, you'll find Graf's essay a good model. Pay particular attention to how she adjusts technical terms and information.*

KEY WORDS AND PHRASES

overlord (2)	*anemia (7)*
partitioning (2)	*emaciated (7)*
profligate (4)	*anorexia nervosa (9)*

1   Bad news travels fast in Northern Ireland. Women and children blow whistles and bang dustbin lids on the pavement to telegraph a grim message: Every 11 days, on the average, a convicted member of the Irish Republican Army dies of starvation in the Maze prison near Belfast.

2   The hunger strike, a strategy IRA inmates are using to pressure their British overlords to reclassify them as political prisoners rather than common criminals, has caught the attention of the entire world. IRA leaders advise prisoners when to begin their fasts so that they will have the most political impact. Last winter, for example, the IRA planned 27-year-old Bobby Sands's fast so that he would die on the anniversary of the bloody Easter Rising of 1916 that led to the original partitioning of Ireland.

3   But Sands did not die on Easter. The human body does not conform precisely to timetables calculated for an "average" person,
one who can survive fasting for 50 to 70 days, assuming he has
water. Sands lasted 66 days.

4   Early in a fast, the body is comparatively profligate in burning
its fuels. A normal, nonfasting person's principal source of energy
is sugar, or glucose. The brain in particular needs glucose to function, but the body's reserve of it, stored in the liver in the form of a
starchy carbohydrate glycogen, is exhausted in less than a day.
When that supply runs out, the body makes its own glucose from
the next most available source, protein in the muscles. If protein
were the only energy supply, however, vital muscles in the heart,
kidneys, spleen, and intestines would quickly be destroyed, and
death would follow soon thereafter.

5   So as early as the first day of the fast, certain tissues begin sup-
plementing their glucose supply with energy derived from fat,
which comprises 15 to 20 percent of an average person's body
weight. By the third day, when most people lose their hunger
pangs, the brain is getting most of its energy from ketone bodies,
which are formed in the liver from fatty acids.

6   To protect its vital organs and to conserve energy, the body
makes a lot of other adjustments as well. The metabolic rate drops,
pulse slows, blood pressure lowers. A starving person feels chilly.
The body's thermostat cranks down a notch, an energy-saving
strategy akin to maintaining a house at 65 degrees during the winter. According to reports from Belfast, the hunger strikers spend a
lot of time in a bed under sheepskin rugs.

7   Fasting produces a lot of side effects: anemia, dry skin, ulcer-
ated mouth, abnormal heart rhythm, erosion of bone mineral, difficulty in walking, blindness, loss of hearing, speech impairment,
decrease in sexual drive. Those who visited Bobby Sands in his final days were shocked at his sunken cheeks, emaciated frame, and
rapidly thinning brown hair.

8   In the last stages of starvation, when fat is depleted, the body
draws exclusively from its protein reserves. At the end of his fast,
when his insulating muscle was consumed, Sands was gently laid
on a waterbed to cushion his frail skeleton.

9   "The body essentially digests itself," says Arnold E. Andersen, a
psychiatrist at Johns Hopkins Medical Institution who treats
women suffering from anorexia nervosa, an affliction of young

women who exist on a semistarvation diet. "There is a point at which the organs simply stop functioning." Autopsies of the Irish prisoners turn up no single cause of death.

10   As hunters and gatherers, our ancestors adapted to survive when harvests were poor. But the body's heroic efforts to save itself while awaiting better nutritional times simply cannot outlast the determined resolve of the Irish hunger strikers.

Thesis and Organization

1. Process essays emphasize *how* something happens, but other concerns such as *who, what, when, where,* and *why* are also apt to be important. Where in this essay does the author first bring out *where? Who? What? Why?* What device does she use to indicate *when?*
2. At what point does the essay begin to focus on *how?* When does the focus shift again?
3. The mode of cause and effect, like the modes of process and narration, involves sequence. Cause must precede effect. Paragraphs 4, 5, 6, and 7 use cause and effect. Select one of these paragraphs and analyze the cause-and-effect relationship involved.
4. Consider only the scientific process that the author presents. If that alone were the subject of the essay, what would be the author's primary assertion about the subject? Now consider also the political context that the author provides. Given both the process and its context, what is the author's major assertion?
5. What emotions does the author want to elicit from the reader? Is she informing the reader about what some members of the IRA are experiencing or is she persuading the reader to share a particular conviction or take a particular action? What evidence can you cite?

Technique and Style

1. Paragraphs 1–3 set out the overall political context for the essay, but paragraphs 4 and 5 make no mention of it. Where in paragraphs 6–10 is the political context brought back in? How does the author's reintroduction of the context relate to her thesis? Purpose? Why might she have chosen to omit it from paragraphs 4 and 5?
2. The essay deals with two levels of conflict: the IRA versus the British and the body versus itself. How does paragraph 10 bring the two conflicts together? What does the paragraph imply about the nature of the Irish hunger striker's "determined resolve"? How does the implication relate to the essay's thesis?

3. The essay first appeared in *Science 81,* a magazine published by the American Association for the Advancement of Science "to bridge the gap between science and citizen." How does the essay serve the magazine's general purpose?
4. Graf chooses her details with care: "sheepskin rugs" (6); "sunken cheeks, emaciated frame, and rapidly thinning brown hair" (7); "a waterbed to cushion his frail skeleton" (8). What purpose do these details reveal? How is their purpose related to that of the essay?
5. Paragraphs 4–9 contain a great deal of technical information. What examples can you cite to show that the author is *not* writing to a technically sophisticated audience?

Suggestions for Writing

Make your own "death by" arguments, researching the physiological process involved and placing it within a politically sensitive context. Use the *Readers' Guide to Periodical Literature* and *The New York Times Index* to find newspaper material to refer to in your argument. Suggestions: death by radiation (the danger of nuclear waste disposal); death by industrial poisoning (hazardous waste); death by diet (the liquid protein fad); death by digging (black lung disease); death by accident (the lawsuits filed over blood transfusions).

Cause and Effect

ause-and-effect essays investigate why X happens and what results from X. Though writers examine both **cause and effect**, most will stress one or the other. Process analysis focuses on *how;* causal analysis emphasizes *why.* Causal analysis looks below the surface of the steps in a process and examines why they occurred; it analyzes their causes and effects. All of the examples mentioned in the introduction to process analysis (page 149) can be turned into illustrations of causal analysis.

Let's say you've followed the directions that came with your new stereo system and have finally reached the moment of truth when you are ready to push the switch marked "Power." You push, it clicks, but then nothing happens. The receiver is on, as are the turntable and tape deck, but no sound comes out of the speakers. Probably you first check for the most immediate possible cause of the problem, the hookups. Are all the jacks plugged into the correct sources? Are they secure? Are the speaker wires attached correctly? If everything checks out, you start to search for less immediate causes only to discover that the wrong switch was depressed on the receiver, and it is tuned to a nonexistent compact disc player. You push "Tape," and music fills the room. The problem is solved.

Essays that analyze cause and effect usually focus on one or the other. If you are writing about your hobby, which, let's say, happens to be tropical fish, you could emphasize the causes. You might have wanted a pet but were allergic to fur; you might have been fascinated with the aquarium in your doctor's office, and your aunt gave you two goldfish and a bowl. Reasons such as these are causes that you would then have to sort out in terms of their importance. But if you wished to focus on effect, you might be writing on how your interest in tropical fish led to your majoring in marine biology.

You can quickly see how causal analysis can get confusing in that a cause leads to an effect which can then become another cause. This kind of causal chain undergirds Benjamin Franklin's point that "a little neglect may breed great mischief . . . for want of a nail the shoe was lost; for want of a shoe the horse was lost; and for want of a horse the rider was lost."

You can avoid the traps set by causal analysis if you apply some of the skills you use in division and classification and in process analysis:

1. Divide your subject into two categories, causes and effects.
2. Use process analysis to identify the steps or stages that are involved and list them under the appropriate heading, causes or effects.
3. Sort out each list by dividing the items into primary or secondary causes and effects, that is, those that are relatively important and those that are relatively unimportant.

When you reach this final point, you may discover that an item you have listed is only related to your subject by time, in which case you should cross it out.

If you were writing a paper on cheating in college, for instance, your notes might resemble these:

	Possibilities	**Examples**	**Importance**
Causes	Academic pressure	Student who needs an A	Primary
	Peer pressure	Everybody does it	Primary
	System	Teachers tolerate it	Secondary
		No real penalty	
	Moral climate	Cheating on income taxes	Secondary
		False insurance claims	
		Infidelity	
		Break up of family unit	
Effects	Academic	Grades meaningless	Primary
	Peers	Degree meaningless	Primary
	System	Erodes system	Secondary
	Moral climate	Weakens moral climate	Secondary

The train of thought behind these notes chugs along nicely. Looking at them, you can see how thinking about the moral climate might lead to speculation about the cheating that goes uncaught on tax and insurance forms, and for that matter the cheating that occurs in a different context, that of marriage. The idea of infidelity then sets off a causal chain: infidelity causes divorce, which causes the breakup of families. Pause there. If recent statistics show that a majority of students have cheated and if recent statistics also reveal a large number of single-parent households, it isn't safe to conclude that one caused the other. The relationship is one of time, not cause. Mistaking a **temporal relationship** for a causal one is a **logical fallacy** called *post hoc* reasoning.

It is also easy to mistake a **primary cause** or effect for a **secondary cause**. If the notes above are for an essay that uses a narrative framework, and if the essay begins by relating an example of a student who was worried about having high enough grades to get into law school, the principle behind how the items are listed according to importance makes sense. To bring up his average, the student cheats on a math exam, justifying the action by thinking, "Everybody does it." The essay might then go on to speculate about the less apparent reasons behind the action, the system and the moral climate. For the student who cheated, the grade and peer pressure are the more immediate or primary causes; the system and climate are the more remote or secondary causes.

AUDIENCE AND PURPOSE   What you know or can fairly safely assume about the intended audience determines both what to say and how to say it. Writing about the beginnings of the magazine *Sassy,* Elizabeth Larsen, for instance, assumes her readers will be unaware of the causes behind the major shift in the magazine's editorial philosophy. But when George Felton writes about the cause-and-effect relationships involved in the current trend in advertising, he knows he is writing to readers bombarded by advertisements and commercials. He can drop brand names and know they will be recognized.

Most readers are equally aware of Joseph Perkins' topic of teenage pregnancy, but the scope of the problem and the efforts being made on behalf of the fathers involved are news. Also new to many readers is what a person feels like when taken for a criminal. In "Black Men and Public Space," Brent Staples details those emotions in such a way that his audience feels the full irony of the situations he describes. And while his readers may take up whistling Vivaldi or look twice before scuttling to the other side of the street, they will not be offended by Staples's essay.

An awareness of the reader and that person's possible preconceptions also guide Deborah Black's "The Single Parent Family," for the topic she addresses is one that raises strong emotions, particularly when the word *welfare* is introduced. Some of her readers may be single parents, some may be on welfare, and some may react negatively to the idea of government-sponsored financial support. Black as well as all of the writers must be careful not to step on their readers' toes.

FALSE CAUSAL RELATIONSHIPS   As the introduction to this chapter points out, it is easy to mistake a temporal relationship for a causal relationship and to assign significance to something relatively unimportant. But if you carefully analyze the essays included in this chapter, you will see how their writers solved these problems. Elizabeth Larsen, writing in "Censoring Sex Information: The Story of *Sassy*," is careful to point out that the advertisers' objections to the magazine's content were based not on morals but on money, thus identifying the true cause for the loss of advertising accounts.

Multiple examples form the base of Brent Staples's "Black Men and Public Space," but Staple's essay is more expressive than argumentative. He explores not only the effect he—a black man—has on others as he walks the darkened city streets but also the feelings those effects elicit in him. He mentions, for instance, that "women are particularly vulnerable to street violence, and young black males are drastically overrepresented among the perpetrators of that violence." The next sentence shows how that fact is irrelevant to him: "Yet these truths are no solace against the kind of alienation that comes of being ever the suspect, a fearsome entity with whom pedestrians avoid making eye contact."

VALID CAUSAL RELATIONSHIPS   Evidence and logical reasoning are essential to cause-and-effect essays, although Joe Klein beings "The Education of Berenice Belizaire" with a narrative example. Had he rested his whole point on that one example, he could be accused of hasty generalization, a logical fallacy. He is careful, therefore, to broaden out his one example by placing it in a context, quoting a teacher who comments on how eager immigrants are to learn and then citing the overall contribution immigrants have made to the city of New York, both in the past and present. Joseph Perkins's sequence of causal relationships is much more complex, so Perkins relies heavily on statistics and interviews to explain the nature of the problem—young un-married fathers, single-mother households, and the welfare system—and its solution. All of the writers included in this chapter draw upon many sources for their evidence. Whether statistics, interviews, popular culture, folklore, scientific studies, quotations, or personal experience, varied sources can provide you with a wide variety of examples to use as supporting evidence.

THESIS AND ORGANIZATION   Although a cause can lead to an effect that then becomes a cause leading to another effect and so on, most essays are organized around either cause or effect: why some immigrants succeed, why poverty plagues the black community, what happens if a magazine's editorial staff decides to provide information about sex, what "Healthism" really means, what effects being a black male and walking the streets at night have not only on city dwellers but on the walker.

USEFUL TERMS

Cause and effect   You would use cause and effect to examine a topic to discover, explain, or argue why a particular action, event, situation, or condition occurred.

Logical fallacy   An error in reasoning. Assigning a causal relationship to a temporal one and reaching a conclusion based on one example are both logical fallacies.

Primary cause   The most important cause or causes.

Secondary cause   The less important cause or causes.

Temporal relationship   Two or more events related by time rather than anything else.

IDEAS FOR WRITING   In your journal or as notes for a paper, write down a decision you reached recently. Perhaps you decided on a major or bought an expensive piece of equipment or changed jobs or volunteered to do something. Once you have a list, you can decide whether you want to focus on cause—those reasons that led you to that decision—or effect, the results of the decision. When you have made that choice, you may find it helpful to work up an outline similar to the one

on p. 182. Also, think about what point you want to make so as you organize your thoughts you have a working thesis in mind.

■ POINTERS FOR USING CAUSE AND EFFECT

Exploring the Topic

1. **Have you stated the topic as a question that asks why X happened?**
   What are the possible causes? The probable causes? Rank the causes in
   order of their priority.
2. **Have you stated the topic as a question that asks what results from
   X?** What are the possible effects? The probable effects? Rank the effects
   in order of their priority.
3. **Is a temporal relationship involved?** Review your lists of causes and
   effects and rule out any that have only a temporal relationship to your
   subject.
4. **Which do you want to emphasize, cause or effect?** Check to make
   sure your focus is clear.
5. **What is your point?** Are you trying to show that something is so or to
   explore your topic?
6. **What evidence can you use to support your point?** Do you need to
   cite authorities or quote statistics? If you depend on personal experience,
   are you sure your experience is valid, that is, representative of general
   experience?
7. **What does your reader think?** Does your audience have any preconceived ideas about your topic for which you need to account? What are
   they? How can you deal with them?
8. **What role do you want to play in the essay?** Are you an observer or a
   participant? Is your major intention to inform, to persuade, or to entertain? What point of view best serves your purpose?

Drafting the Paper

1. **Know your reader.** Figure out what attitudes your reader may have
   about your topic. If the cause-and-effect relationship you are discussing
   is unusual, you might want to shape your initial attitude so that it is
   as skeptical as your reader's. On the other hand, you may want to start with
   a short narrative that immediately puts the reader on your side. Consider
   how much your reader is apt to know about your topic. If you are the
   expert, make sure you explain everything that needs to be explained but
   without doing so condescendingly.
2. **Know your purpose.** Adjust your tone and persona to suit your purpose. If you are writing a persuasive paper, make sure your persona is

credible and that you focus your ideas so that they may change the mind of a reader who initially does not agree with you—or short of that, that your ideas make the reader rethink his or her position. If you are writing an informative paper, choose a persona and tone that will interest the reader. Tone and persona are even more crucial to essays written to entertain, where the tone can range from the ironic to the lighthearted.

3. **Emphasize a cause or effect.** Essays that focus on cause more than likely will cover a variety of probable reasons that explain the result. Though there may be only one effect or result, you may want to predict other possible effects in your last paragraph. For instance, an essay that explores the causes of violence examines a number of reasons or causes for the result or effect—violence—but may conclude by speculating on the possible effects of the rising crime rate. On the other hand, essays that focus on effect more than likely will cover a number of possible effects that are produced by a single cause, though again you may want to speculate on other causes. If you are writing about the effects of smoking, at some point in the essay you may want to include other harmful substances in the air such as coal dust, hydrocarbons, and carbon monoxide.

4. **Check for validity.** Don't hesitate to include quotations, allusions, statistics, and studies that will support your point. Choose your examples carefully to buttress the relationship you are trying to establish, and be sure you don't mistake a temporal relationship for a causal one.

5. **Make a point.** The cause-and-effect relationship you examine should lead to or stem from an assertion: video games not only entertain, they also stimulate the mind and improve coordination; video games are not only habit-forming, they are also addictive.

*T*he Single-Parent Family

Deborah Black

One of many older students returning to school, Deborah Black is now a senior, concentrating on a pre-law major. Her three children—Delores, Meredith, and Deborah Jean—continue to cheer her on toward graduation, and she expects to receive her degree in may of 1995. She then plans to go on to law school. She wrote "The Single-Parent Family" when she was enrolled in a freshman composition class in 1992.

WHAT TO LOOK FOR   *While writing that takes a conversational tone comes relatively easy for many students, those same writers often have difficulty when they have to write more formal essays. As you read Black's essay, be thinking about the strategies she uses to achieve her academic tone—her diction, syntax, paragraphing, and sense of authority.*

KEY WORDS AND PHRASES

parity (1)   intact (4)
median (3)

1   As a result of their parents' inability to preserve their marriages or to marry at all, almost a quarter of U.S. kids live in single-parent households, the majority headed by females. David Blankenhorn, president of the Institute for American Values, a New York family-issues research group, says that as an expectation of childhood the experience of fatherlessness is approaching a rough parity with the experience of having a father.

2   Generally, children from single-parent families have more trouble while growing up and bear more scars than children from two-parent families. This is contrary to the longstanding opinion that children recover quickly from divorce and flourish in families of almost any shape. Sara McLanahan, a Princeton University sociologist who studies children of divorce as they enter adulthood, says, "Almost anything you can imagine not wanting to happen to your children is a consequence of divorce" (Magnet 44).

3   Children in single-parent families have less than one third of the median per capita income of kids from two-parent families. Seventy-five percent of single-parent children will sink into poverty before they reach eighteen years of age, versus 20% of the kids from two-parent families. Had family breakdown not deprived many families of a male breadwinner, the child poverty rate would have declined in the 80's.

4   Growing up in a single-parent family marks not only the child's external economic circumstances, but also his or her psyche. A study from the National Center of Health Statistics has found that children from single-parent homes were 100 to 200% more likely than those from intact families to have emotional and behavioral problems and 50% more likely to have learning disabilities.

5   Judith Wallerstein, co-author of *Second Chances: Men, Women & Children a Decade after Divorce,* made some startling discoveries in her 15-year study of children of divorce. She was alarmed by the magnitude of pain and fear expressed by the children when their parents divorced. She believed these wounds would not heal and could be harmful years later.

6   Males in the study, even those who were bright, had difficulty learning and behaving well after divorce. Female children did much better, even better than girls from intact families. But Wallerstein found the girls' success tended to be "fragile." Says she: "These girls were on super behavior, consciously trying to be good little girls at a high inner cost" (Magnet 44). By young adulthood males and females were having equal difficulty forming loving, intimate relationships.

7   Can the single parent provide a positive role model for male and female children? Joseph White in his book *The Psychology of Blacks: An Afro-American Perspective* tells us that the single parent can provide a positive role model for his or her children. He cites examples of black single-parent families who have used the extended family to help rear children who are fatherless or motherless. This extended family provides a safety net for these children of divorce and poverty. White feels that going to workshops, discussion groups, and community forums can help the single parent cope with his or her dual roles and responsibilities.

8   The welfare system has a new program that is a valuable resource in providing troubled families with a chance for a better future. Project Independence is a program that gives a single parent

an opportunity to further his or her education, thus enabling the parent to get not just a job but a career that will allow him or her to adequately provide for the family. This program provides child care, transportation, remediation, and financial aid. Additionally, single parents in this program receive food stamps, Medicaid, and a welfare check. The people who run this program are caring, dedicated individuals who encourage participants to set realistic goals and then help them to achieve these goals.

9   Being in this program has brought many changes in my life. After my divorce, I was alone, confused, and scared. I was undereducated and had no job skills that would make me marketable for employment. Like many people I thought that going on welfare was like admitting defeat. This program eliminated this viewpoint and gave me the opportunity to start a new life.

10   Can I be both mother and father to my three girls? The answer is yes. Though I never would have chosen this path, it is the one I have to travel. Much of the time I feel like I am experiencing multiple personalities: mother, father, and college student. One of the most important things to me is to be a good role model for my children. Every day they see me studying, working, and trying to get ahead. I also try to teach them how to be self-sufficient, how to cope with life's difficulties, and how to keep the lines of communication open between us.

11   The support systems that a parent enlists can help him or her to be a successful parent. Project Independence, Success at 6, Head Start, and Families First are important programs that can help struggling families in America. The success of future generations depends on our collective willingness to recognize the problems and support the solutions to them.

WORKS CITED

Magnet, M. (1992, August). The American Family, 1992. *Fortune,* pp. 42–47.

White, J. L. (1984). *The Psychology of Blacks: An Afro-American Perspective.* Englewood Cliffs, NJ: Prentice-Hall.

Thesis and Organization

1. The essay opens with a statistic and a statement about what it means. What does the number of children living in single-parent households imply about the future?

2. Paragraphs 2–6 explain how living in a single-parent household affects children. What are those effects?
3. The essay's focus changes in paragraph 7, shifting to the idea of single parents as role models. What can "cause" the single parent to become a good role model?
4. How does being a good role model affect children?
5. Consider the problem Black poses and the solution she provides. What is her thesis?

Technique and Style

1. How many sources does Black use in her essay? What effect do they have on her authority to write knowledgeably about her subject?
2. Paragraph 9 brings in Black's personal experience. Is the essay stronger or weaker because of it?
3. Some people have negative views about welfare programs and the people on them. How does Black counter those opinions?
4. How would you describe the Deborah Black that you find in this essay? How does the impression she creates support her thesis?
5. Explain whether or not the essay leans more toward argument than explanation. What support can you find for your interpretation?

Suggestions for Writing

Being a parent is one of the most difficult jobs there is, one full of unexpected traps, dangers, and successes. Choose one of your parents and think about the effect that person has had on you. You will probably find yourself thinking of particular times and events, each one of which can serve as an example. Jot down those examples so you can choose among them, selecting the ones that best serve your purpose. Your thesis will be a general statement about the overall effect the person had on you, and the examples will explain how that effect came about. If you don't want to write on that subject, consider the kind of parent you would like to be and the effect you would like to have on your children. How to bring about those effects would then be the body of your paper.

Censoring Sex Information: The Story of *Sassy*

Elizabeth Larsen

As much as American teenagers need information about sex, the editors of Sassy *discovered it's sex, not sex education, that sells. Elizabeth Larsen was on* Sassy's *editorial staff when that lesson became clear. She now works for the* Utne Reader, *where this essay was published in 1990.*

WHAT TO LOOK FOR   *When dealing with causal relationships it's easy to fall into the habit of overusing transitions that set out a causal relationship such as* therefore, so, because, consequently, thus, *and the like. You'll find that Larsen, in paragraphs 5–8, avoids these obvious transitions, so see if you can spot how she gets from one paragraph to another.*

KEY WORDS AND PHRASES

unanimous (1)	*celluloid (4)*
couched (1)	*scenarios (4)*
abstinence (2)	*phenomenal (5)*
prototype (3)	*vocal (8)*
per capita (3)	*Jerry Falwell (8)*

1   At the first editorial meeting of *Sassy* magazine, in 1987, the staff sat around the editor in chief's office discussing how to make our new magazine different from other teenage publications. The unanimous first priority was to provide sex education: since we had read the competition during our own adolescence, we knew the sex information published by teen magazines was scarce and usually couched in judgmental terms.

2   We had a good reason to put this issue high on our agenda. The United States has the highest teen pregnancy rate of any similarly industrialized Western nation, and we felt this was not an issue that would go away by just telling teens to say no. The rock stars and athletes speaking out against drugs and drunk driving on TV weren't making any pitches for virginity. The situation had be-

come even more confusing for teenagers because of the attention that abstinence was getting as the only sure way to prevent AIDS. Our readers were left with a lot of unanswered questions that we felt were important to address.

3   *Sassy*'s initial advertisers did not feel as strongly as its editors about leading the sex education of America's youth. Many were concerned about an article in the prototype issue entitled "Sex for Absolute Beginners," which had previously run in *Dolly, Sassy*'s Australian counterpart. The article answered questions ranging from "Can I get pregnant?" and "What is an orgasm?" to "Am I homosexual?" and "Is masturbation wrong?" A few advertisers were offended by the thought of their own teenage daughters reading the information and decided not to advertise, while others reluctantly signed contracts, fearing that if the magazine were a huge success, they couldn't afford to be left out. It became clear to me later that their concerns were business rather than moral ones when I realized that many of the same companies who objected to "Sex for Absolute Beginners" in *Sassy* nevertheless advertised without complaint in *Dolly*—the most widely read teenage magazine in the world in terms of circulation per capita. For what the advertisers understood long before the editors did is that sex may sell billions of dollars of U.S. products every year, but responsible, direct information about sex directed toward U.S. teenagers would not.

4   In the first issue, *Sassy* printed an article entitled "Losing Your Virginity." We ran this because we felt that at least one reason so many teens were having sex was that the media had successfully convinced them that losing their virginity was going to be the biggest moment of their lives. Our strategy was to provide our readers with more realistic accounts to debunk the celluloid stereotype. After setting up some alternative scenarios, we left the moral decisions to the reader while providing detailed information about birth control and sexually transmitted diseases and answers to frequently asked questions such as, "Will it hurt?" "Can he tell I'm a virgin?" "What if I change my mind?" and "How long will it take?"

5   The reader response to this article was phenomenal. *Sassy* and the article's author received hundreds of letters saying that finally someone had spoken to them in a way with which they felt comfortable. Mail started pouring in to the "Help" column, which I wrote, making apparent that we had only scratched the surface of

a teenager's reality. What was most disconcerting to us was the tone of fear and shame these letters portrayed. Many young women were desperate for answers—we even received phone calls requesting advice. The next few articles we ran on sex were all in response to these frantic letters asking about pregnancy, abortion, incest, suicide, and homosexuality.

6   "The Truth About Boys' Bodies," "Getting Turned On," "And They're Gay," "My Girlfriend Got Pregnant," and "Real Stories About Incest" were articles written to let girls know that whatever choices they made about their sexuality weren't shameful as long as they were responsible about safe sex, birth control, and emotional self-care.

7   Much of our reader response was positive. Mothers and even grandmothers called to say that they had read our articles with their daughters and granddaughters and as a result felt closer to each other. There was also relief among some parents that we had explained something important they were uncomfortable communicating. On the other hand, there was also a fair share of irate screaming directed our way. Most of these callers felt the information we printed was "pornographic" and reeled off the old saw that information just encourages young women to have sex. Perhaps the most alarming phone call came from a father who screamed, "Anything my daughter learns about sex, she'll learn from me!" before he slammed down the receiver. These people canceled their subscriptions—a routine response to a publication one disagrees with and something we had counted on.

8   What we hadn't counted on was the mass reader/advertiser boycott led by a woman whose kids didn't even read *Sassy*. As a member of a group called Women Aglow was to show us, it is possible in this country for a vocal minority to bring about what amounts to censorship. Through the Jerry Falwell-supported publication *Focus on the Family*, Women Aglow organized a letter-writing campaign aimed at our major advertisers in which they threatened to boycott their products if those companies continued to advertise in *Sassy*. Within a matter of months *Sassy* had lost nearly every ad account, and we were publishing what we jokingly called *The Sassy Pamphlet*. We were told that to stay in business we must remove the "controversial" content from the magazine. That was reluctantly done, and today *Sassy* has regained its advertisers but not its detailed information on sex education.

9   Sadly, what was to a few young editors just a sobering lesson about the power of advertising was a great loss to young women, who need the information *Sassy* once provided.

Thesis and Organization

1. How does paragraph 1 answer the questions *who, where, when, why, how?*
2. What reasons does paragraph 2 state as what caused the editorial staff to focus on sex information?
3. How did that focus affect the advertisers? What primary cause lay behind that response?
4. Paragraphs 5–8 detail the readers' and advertisers' responses. What were they?
5. Reread paragraphs 3, 8, and 9. What do you conclude is the essay's thesis?

Technique and Style

1. How would you characterize the author's tone? Angry? Disappointed? Demoralized? What? On the whole, is it objective or subjective?
2. Given that tone, how would you describe the author's persona? Do you find it credible? Why or why not?
3. How would you define the author's purpose? Expressive, argumentative, informative, or some mixture? Explain.
4. What does the author gain by her use of the first-person plural, *we?*
5. What does the use of quotations add to the essay? What might be lost without them?

Suggestions for Writing

Think about times when you have met censorship head-on. Perhaps there were films you weren't allowed to see, books you couldn't read, topics you couldn't discuss, or places you couldn't go. Or perhaps censorship has been an issue in your family, church, or community. No matter what subject you choose, you might start by looking up *censorship* in an unabridged dictionary.

B lack Men and Public Space

Brent Staples

Any woman who walks along city streets at night knows the fear Brent Staples speaks of, but in this essay we learn how that fear can affect the innocent. We see and feel what it is like to be a tall, strong, young black man who enjoys walking at night but innocently terrifies any lone woman. His solution to his night walking problems gives a delightful twist to nonviolent resistance.

The irony of Staples's situation was not lost on Jesse Jackson. Speaking in Chicago in 1993, he pointed out an equally distressing irony: "There is nothing more painful to me at this stage in my life than to walk down the street and hear footsteps and start thinking about robbery. Then [I] look around and see someone white and feel relieved."

Brent Staples holds a PhD in psychology from the University of Chicago and writes on politics and culture for the New York Times *editorial board. His memoir,* Parallel Time: Growing Up in Black and White, *is published by Pantheon Books. The essay reprinted here was first published in* Harpers *in 1986. He's still whistling.*

WHAT TO LOOK FOR   *Before you read the essay, look up the dash in a handbook of usage so you'll be on the lookout for Staples's use of it. He uses it in two different ways, but always appropriately.*

KEY WORDS AND PHRASES

impoverished (1)	*retrospect (6)*
uninflammatory (1)	*intimidation (7)*
tyranny (2)	*perilous (8)*
foyer (2)	*ad hoc (8)*
warrenlike (5)	*labyrinthine (8)*
bandolier (5)	*affluent (9)*
lethality (6)	*constitutionals (12)*

1   My first victim was a woman—white, well-dressed, probably in her early twenties. I came upon her late one evening on a deserted street in Hyde Park, a relatively affluent neighborhood in an otherwise mean, impoverished section of Chicago. As I swung onto the avenue behind her, there seemed to be a discreet, uninflammatory

distance between us. Not so. She cast back a worried glance. To her, the youngish black man—a broad 6 feet 2 inches with a beard and billowing hair, both hands shoved into the pockets of a bulky military jacket—seemed menacingly close. After a few more quick glimpses, she picked up her pace and was soon running in earnest. Within seconds she disappeared into a cross street.

2   That was more than a decade ago. I was 22 years old, a graduate student newly arrived at the University of Chicago. It was in the echo of that terrified woman's footfalls that I first began to know the unwieldy inheritance I'd come into—the ability to alter public space in ugly ways. It was clear that she thought herself the quarry of a mugger, a rapist, or worse. Suffering a bout of insomnia, however, I was stalking sleep, not defenseless wayfarers. As a softy who is scarcely able to take a knife to a raw chicken—let alone hold one to a person's throat—I was surprised, embarrassed, and dismayed all at once. Her flight made me feel like an accomplice in tyranny. It also made it clear that I was indistinguishable from the muggers who occasionally seeped into the area from the surrounding ghetto. That first encounter, and those that followed, signified that a vast, unnerving gulf lay between nighttime pedestrians—particularly women—and me. And I soon gathered that being perceived as dangerous is a hazard in itself. I only needed to turn a corner into a dicey situation, or crowd some frightened, armed person in a foyer somewhere, or make an errant move after being pulled over by a policeman. Where fear and weapons meet—and they often do in urban America—there is always the possibility of death.

3   In that first year, my first away from my hometown, I was to become thoroughly familiar with the language of fear. At dark, shadowy intersections, I could cross in front of a car stopped at a traffic light and elicit the *thunk, thunk, thunk, thunk* of the driver—black, white, male, or female—hammering down the door locks. On less traveled streets after dark, I grew accustomed to but never comfortable with people crossing to the other side of the street rather than pass me. Then there were the standard unpleasantries with policemen, doormen, bouncers, cabdrivers, and others whose business it is to screen out troublesome individuals *before* there is any nastiness.

4   I moved to New York nearly two years ago and I have remained an avid night walker. In central Manhattan, the near-constant crowd cover minimizes tense one-on-one street encounters. Elsewhere—in SoHo, for example, where sidewalks are narrow

and tightly spaced buildings shut out the sky—things can get very taut indeed.

5   After dark, on the warrenlike streets of Brooklyn where I live, I often see women who fear the worst from me. They seem to have set their faces on neutral, and with their purse straps strung across their chests bandolier-style, they forge ahead as thought bracing themselves against being tackled. I understand, of course, that the danger they perceive is not a hallucination. Women are particularly vulnerable to street violence, and young black males are drastically overrepresented among the perpetrators of that violence. Yet these truths are no solace against the kind of alienation that comes of being ever the suspect, a fearsome entity with whom pedestrians avoid making eye contact.

6   It is not altogether clear to me how I reached the ripe old age of 22 without being conscious of the lethality nighttime pedestrians attributed to me. Perhaps it was because in Chester, Pennsylvania, the small, angry industrial town where I came of age in the 1960s, I was scarcely noticeable against a backdrop of gang warfare, street knifings, and murders. I grew up one of the good boys, had perhaps a half-dozen fistfights. In retrospect, my shyness of combat has clear sources.

7   As a boy, I saw countless tough guys locked away; I have since buried several, too. They were babies, really—a teenage cousin, a brother of 22, a childhood friend in his mid-twenties—all gone down in episodes of bravado played out in the streets. I came to doubt the virtues of intimidation early on. I chose, perhaps unconsciously, to remain a shadow—timid, but a survivor.

8   The fearsomeness mistakenly attributed to me in public places often has a perilous flavor. The most frightening of these confusions occurred in the late 1970s and early 1980s, when I worked as a journalist in Chicago. One day, rushing into the office of a magazine I was writing for with a deadline story in hand, I was mistaken for a burglar. The office manager called security and, with an ad hoc posse, pursued me through the labyrinthine halls, nearly to my editor's door. I had no way of proving who I was. I could only move briskly toward the company of someone who knew me.

9   Another time I was on assignment for a local paper and killing time before an interview. I entered a jewelry store on the city's affluent Near North Side. The proprietor excused herself and re-

turned with an enormous red Doberman pinscher straining at the end of a leash. She stood, the dog extended toward me, silent to my questions, her eyes bulging nearly out of her head. I took a cursory look around, nodded, and bade her good night.

10 Relatively speaking, however, I never fared as badly as another black male journalist. He went to nearby Waukegan, Illinois, a couple of summers ago to work on a story about a murderer who was born there. Mistaking the reporter for the killer, police officers hauled him from his car at gunpoint and but for his press credentials would probably have tried to book him. Such episodes are not uncommon. Black men trade tales like this all the time.

11 Over the years, I learned to smother the rage I felt at so often being taken for a criminal. Not to do so would surely have led to madness. I now take precautions to make myself less threatening. I move about with care, particularly late in the evening. I give a wide berth to nervous people on subway platforms during the wee hours, particularly when I have exchanged business clothes for jeans. If I happen to be entering a building behind some people who appear skittish, I may walk by, letting them clear the lobby before I return, so as not to seem to be following them. I have been calm and extremely congenial on those rare occasions when I've been pulled over by the police.

12 And on late-evening constitutionals I employ what has proved to be an excellent tension-reducing measure: I whistle melodies from Beethoven and Vivaldi and the more popular classical composers. Even steely New Yorkers hunching toward nighttime destinations seem to relax, and occasionally they even join in the tune. Virtually everybody seems to sense that a mugger wouldn't be warbling bright, sunny selections from Vivaldi's *Four Seasons*. It is my equivalent of the cowbell that hikers wear when they know they are in bear country.

Thesis and Organizations

1. Reread paragraph 1. What expectations does it evoke in the reader? For paragraph 2, state in your own words what Staples means by "unwieldy inheritance." What effects does that inheritance have?
2. The body of the essay breaks into three paragraph blocks. In paragraphs 3–5, what effects does the author's walking at night have on others? On himself?

3. In paragraphs 6 and 7, Staples refers to his childhood. Why had he been unaware of his effect on others? What effect did the streets he grew up on have on him?
4. Staples uses examples in paragraphs 8–10. What do all three have in common? What generalization does Staples draw from them?
5. Summarize the causes and effects Staples brings out in paragraphs 11 and 12, and in one sentence, make a general statement about them. What does that statement imply about being a black male? About urban life? About American culture? Consider your answers to those questions and in one sentence state the thesis of the essay.

Technique and Style

1. A large part of the essay's impact lies in the ironic contrast between appearance and reality. What details does Staples bring out about himself that contrast with the stereotype of the mugger?
2. In paragraph 1, Staples illustrates the two uses of the dash. What function do they perform? Rewrite either of the two sentences so that you avoid the dash. Which sentence is better and why?
3. Trace Staples's use of time. Why does he start where he does? Try placing the time period mentioned in paragraphs 6 and 7 elsewhere in the essay. What advantages does their present placement have? What is the effect of ending the essay in the present?
4. Examine Staples's choice of verbs in the second sentence of paragraph 5. Rewrite the sentence using as many forms of the verb *to be* as possible. What differences do you note?
5. Staples concludes the essay with an analogy. In what ways is it ironic? How does the irony tie into the essay's thesis?

Suggestions for Writing

Think about a situation you have been in where a stereotype determined your effect on others. Age, race, gender, physique, clothing are only a few of the physical characteristics that can spawn a stereotype.

Reform Should Make Room for Dad

Joseph Perkins

In this essay, Joseph Perkins examines the problems faced by young unmarried fathers, single-mother households, and the welfare system. Combining the three, he traces both their causes and effects on his way to proposing changes that he believes will not only provide more "stable, intact families in America's inner cities," but less poverty as well. Joseph Perkins is a columnist for The San Diego Union-Tribune, *and this piece was reprinted in the* Rocky Mountain News, *June 23, 1993.*

WHAT TO LOOK FOR   *Getting started, that first sentence or paragraph, is often the hardest part of writing an essay, particularly one on a difficult subject such as the one Perkins tackles. A brief narrative, however, not only provides human interest but can also serve as an example. That's how Perkins starts his essay.*

KEY WORDS AND PHRASES

promiscuous 91)	*surrogate (13)*
incorrigible (2)	*perpetuates (14)*
inception (4)	*pathologies (15)*
legitimize (4)	*symptomatic (16)*
marginalization (10)	*cohesion (16)*
imbue (11)	*status quo (17)*
subsidy (13)	

1   Olie Mann was only 17 years old when he got a girl pregnant. At the time, the Cleveland youth hardly fit anyone's idea of a model father. "I was in a gang," he remembers. "I sold drugs. I was very promiscuous."

2   The teen-age mother of his child was whisked away to Texas by her mother, who wanted to put as much distance as possible between her daughter and incorrigible young Olie. But Olie wanted to have his child near him.

3   He turned to the National Institute for Responsible Fatherhood and Family Development, a Cleveland-based organization that began 10 years ago as a local support program for teen fathers.

4   Since its inception, the institute has reached almost 2,000 young fathers like Olie. the program is built on expectations: That the young dads will legitimize their children by acknowledging paternity. That they'll finish school. That they'll hold down a steady job.

5   The caseworker assigned to Olie, who himself had been through a similar experience, encouraged the young man to clean up his act. Olie went back to school and earned his high-school equivalency degree. He dropped out of the gang. He gave up drugs.

6   Now, three years later, he is married to the mother of his child. The family lives happily in Cleveland.

7   There are hundreds of thousands of young men like Olie in inner cities throughout the country. They want to be real fathers to their children, but most are unable to take advantage of the kind of program that helped Olie get on the straight and narrow.

8   While there are myriad public and private programs that provide aid and comfort to unwed mothers, there are precious few that support unwed fathers. That's because our culture tends to view the role of fathers in family life as less important than mothers.

9   Just look at television and film, says psychologist Jane Myers Drew, author of *Where Were You When I Needed You Dad?* "There often is such a sense of Dad being the fool, or not important, or that he's sort of a throwaway, or we can get along without him."

10   Ultimately, Drew says, the marginalization of fathers is detrimental to the development of children. "Dads have so much to do with building self-esteem, setting values, encouraging a child to find his or her place in the world," she says. "Without Dad there, it leaves a real gap."

11   This "gap" is probably even more pronounced in poor families. Not only are such families deprived of a breadwinner, they also lack a positive role model who can imbue poor young men, like Olie Mann, with character and a sense of responsibility.

12   The welfare system is no help. It tilts decidedly in favor of single mothers, at the expense of poor, young fathers. In California, for example, an unmarried mom may receive $500 to $600 a month through Aid to Families with Dependent Children, another $100 in food stamps, plus free medical care. If she has a man at home, she risks losing all of this.

13   The government's subsidy of single motherhood contributes mightily to the devaluation of fatherhood in poor families. In poor homes, the government acts as surrogate for the father, providing most of the family's material support. Poor children are virtual wards of the state.

14   The perverse irony is that by supporting unmarried mothers, and thereby marginalizing fathers, the government actually perpetuates poverty. Roughly half of all poor families are headed by unmarried mothers. Such families have a staggering 650% greater probability of being poor than families with a husband and wife present.

15   Moreover, the diminished role of fathers in poor families almost certainly has contributed to the rise of the various social pathologies that afflict many inner-city communities.

16   Teen pregnancies, school dropouts, drug and alcohol abuse, juvenile delinquency all are symptomatic of the breakdown of the family. If the welfare system were reformed to encourage family cohesion—or at least to not discourage poor mothers and fathers from getting and staying married—many of these social problems would improve.

17   Alas, for all the high-sounding blather about welfare reform emanating from the Clinton administration, the proposals floated will only perpetuate the status quo.

18   The Clintons hope to break the "cycle of dependency" by getting welfare moms off the rolls and into jobs. So they plan to offer poor moms government day care and job training and transportation and other such support.

19   But what welfare mothers really need are husbands and fathers. Whereas one in three female-headed families is poor, only one in 20 married-couple families falls below the poverty line.

20   If the government provided all poor men the kind of moral and material support that Olie Mann received from the National Institute for Responsible Fathers and Family Development, there would be far more stable, intact families in America's inner cities. In the long run, there would be fewer poor, too.

Thesis and Organization

1. The essay begins with the particular, the story of Olie Mann. At what point does it turn to the general?
2. Perkins points out that few programs are designed to help unwed fathers. What reasons does he cite for that fact?

3. What are the effects of the "marginalization of fathers" and the present welfare system?
4. What reforms does Perkins call for? What are their predicted effects?
5. Consider the problems Perkins addresses, the causes he cites, the reforms he proposes, and the effects he predicts. What is the essay's thesis?

Technique and Style

1. How does the story of Olie Mann relate to Perkins's thesis?
2. The paragraphing in the essay is typical of a newspaper format, one that calls for short paragraphs that can be read quickly. If you were to reformat the essay according to the paragraphing typical of books or magazines, what paragraphs would you combine and why?
3. Drew, the expert cited in paragraph 9, points her finger at television and film for their portrayal of fathers. In your experience, do you find her accusation accurate?
4. What is the irony in paragraph 14?
5. A glance at the vocabulary Perkins uses shows it to be formal. Choose a paragraph that uses formal diction and change it to a more conversational level. What is gained? Lost?

Suggestions for Writing

Make a list of problems and then pick the one you find most interesting to you. Think about it and jot down possible causes and possible effects. Select either cause or effect and write an essay that explains that part of the problem. If you want to write an essay closer to that of Perkins, consider other problems and the agencies designed to deal with them: career choice and your institution's counseling service; crime and neighborhood watch groups; dieting and Weight Watchers; problem children and Tough Love; the homeless and the Salvation Army; alcoholism and Alcoholics Anonymous. The odds are that any research you have to do will be easy; these groups and others like them usually publish material that will provide you with the necessary facts and information.

*T*he Education of Berenice Belizaire

Joe Klein

As conditions in less-developed countries worsen, the pressure on the United States to admit more immigrants increases. And as immigration, both legal and illegal, grows, so grows the resentment of many American citizens. This resentment commonly takes the form of prejudice and stereotyping, but Joe Klein disputes those attitudes as he relates the effect recent immigration has had on the city of New York, using one example—Berenice Belizaire—to support his point. Joe Klein is one the editorial staff of Newsweek, *where this essay first appeared in August 1993.*

WHAT TO LOOK FOR   When you read an essay by a professional writer and notice something odd about a sentence, what you see is intentional. Klein, for example, begins paragraph 2 with a fragment. Yet the fragment works because it is an answer that comes right on the heels of a question. The meaning is clear; the reader isn't confused. Perhaps your writing can also benefit by an occasional fragment, but only if its meaning is clear and you know you're using a fragment.

KEY WORDS AND PHRASES

Ruth Bader Ginsburg (3)	*fraternal (7)*
Buffalo (3)	*nuclear (7)*
retail (6)	*perverse (8)*
enlightened (6)	*propriety (8)*
hothouse (6)	*inebriated (8)*
median (7)	*phenomenon (8)*

1   When Berenice Belizaire arrived in New York from Haiti with her mother and sister in 1987, she was not very happy. She spoke no English. The family had to live in a cramped Brooklyn apartment, a far cry from the comfortable house they'd had in Haiti. Her mother, a nurse, worked long hours. School was torture. Berenice had always been a good student, but now she was learning a new

language while enduring constant taunts from the Americans (both black and white). They cursed her in the cafeteria and threw food at her. Someone hit her sister in the head with a book. "Why can't we go home?" Berenice asked her mother.

2   Because home was too dangerous. The schools weren't always open anymore, and education—her mother insisted—was the most important thing. Her mother had always pushed her: memorize everything, she ordered. "I have a pretty good memory," Berenice admitted last week. Indeed, the other kids at school began to notice that Berenice always, somehow, knew the answers. "The started coming to me for help," she says. "They never called me a nerd."

3   Within two years Berenice was speaking English, though not well enough to get into one of New York's elite public high schools. She had to settle for the neighborhood school, James Madison—which is one of the magical American places, the alma mater of Ruth Bader Ginsburg among others, a school with a history of unlikely success stories. "I didn't realize what we had in Berenice at first," says math teacher Judith Khan. "She was good at math, but she was quiet. And the things she didn't know! She applied for a summer program in Buffalo and asked me how to get there on the subway. But she always seemed to ask the right questions. She understood the big ideas. She could think on her feet. She could explain difficult problems so the other kids could understand them. Eventually, I realized: she wasn't just pushing for grades, she was hungry for *knowledge* . . . And you know, it never occurred to me that she also was doing it in English and history, all these other subjects that had to be much tougher for her than math."

4   She moved from third in her class to first during senior year. She was selected as valedictorian, an honor she almost refused (still shy, she wouldn't allow her picture in the school's yearbook). She gave the speech, after some prodding—a modest address about the importance of hard work and how it's never too late to try hard: an immigrant's valedictory. Last week I caught up with Berenice at the Massachusetts Institute of Technology where she was jump-starting her college career. I asked her what she wanted to be doing in 10 years: "I want to build a famous computer, like IBM," she said. "I want my name to be part of it."

5   Berenice Belizaire's story is remarkable, but not unusual. The New York City schools are bulging with overachieving immigrants.

The burdens they place on a creaky, corroded system are often cited as an argument against liberal immigration policies, but teachers like Judith Khan don't seem to mind. "They're why I love teaching in Brooklyn," she says. "They have a drive in them we no longer seem to have. You see these kids, who aren't prepared academically and can barely speak the language, struggling so hard. They just sop it up. They're like little sponges. You see Berenice, who had none of the usual, preconceived racial barriers in her mind—you see her becoming friendly with the Russian kids, and learning chess from Po Ching [from Taiwan]. It is *so* exciting."

6   **Dreamy hothouse:** Indeed, it is possible that immigrant energy reinvigorated not just some schools (and more than a few teachers)—but *the city itself* in the 1980s. "Without them, New York would have been a smaller place, a poorer place, a lot less vital and exciting," says Prof. Emanuel Tobier of New York University. They restored the retail life of the city, starting a raft of small businesses—and doing the sorts of entry-level, bedpan-emptying jobs that nonimmigrants spurn. They added far more to the local economy than they removed; more important, they reminded enlightened New Yorkers that the city had always worked best as a vast, noisy, dreamy hothouse for the cultivation of new Americans.

7   The Haitians have followed the classic pattern. They have a significantly higher work-force participation rate than the average in New York. They have a lower rate of poverty. The have a higher rate of new-business formation and a lower rate of welfare dependency. Their median household income, at $28,853, is about $1,000 less than the citywide median (but about $1,000 higher than Chinese immigrants, often seen as a "model" minority). They've also developed a traditional network of fraternal societies, newspapers and neighborhoods with solid—extended, rather than nuclear—families. "A big issue now is whether women who graduate from school should be allowed to live by themselves before they marry," says Lola Poisson, who counsels Haitian immigrants. "There's a lot of tension over that."

8   Such perverse propriety cannot last long. Immigrants become Americans very quickly. Some lose hope after years of menial labor; others lose discipline, inebriated by freedom. "There's an interesting phenomenon," says Philip Kasinitz of Williams College. "When immigrant kids criticize each other for getting lazy or loose, they say, 'You're becoming American'." (Belizaire said she and the Russians would tease each other that way at Madison.) It's ironic,

Kasinitz adds, "Those who work hardest to keep American culture at bay have the best chance of becoming American success stories." If so, we may be fixed on the wrong issue. The question shouldn't be whether immigrants are ruining America, but whether America is ruining the immigrants.

Thesis and Organization

1. What are the reasons behind the Belizaires' immigration?
2. What are the causes of Berenice Belizaire's success?
3. What are the effects of "immigrant energy" on New York City?
4. What are the effects of that energy on the Haitian community?
5. Consider Berenice Belizaire's success, the Haitian community in New York, and the last paragraph. What is Klein's thesis?

Technique and Style

1. Explain the irony in the last paragraph.
2. Klein could have picked another nationality instead of Haitian. What reasons can you think of for his choice?
3. Rather than telling the reader directly that Berenice Belizaire has become an academic success, Klein shows it through carefully selected details. What are some of those details?
4. What does Klein's use of quotations add to or take away form the essay?
5. Which paragraphs have a clearly stated topic sentence? Identify the sentences.

Suggestions for Writing

Like Klein, you can write about the causes and effects of success, focusing on any kind of success you can think of. One way to start is to consider an obstacle you or someone or some group you know has faced. Perhaps the obstacle was physical, such as a stutter, or economic, as in needing to get enough money together to go to school or to buy a car, or psychological, such as a fear of heights; or academic, such as a difficult course that you mastered. You might try making a list, first of causes, then of effects, and then use the list to draft your paper.

*P*ain, Not Pleasure, Now the Big Sell

George Felton

Today, according to Felton, the "sweat/pain motif" is being used to sell products, and "Healthism" is the latest craze. Felton, who teaches writing and copywriting at the Columbus College of Art and Design, explores why this is so in an essay that appropriately enough appeared in the "Living Today" section of the Miami Herald *(1989).*

WHAT TO LOOK FOR   *References to current events, people, or products tend to become out of date quickly while at the same time they provide solid detail. As you read Felton's essay, you'll find a number of references to products and the pitches behind them. Think about whether they add more than they detract.*

KEY WORDS AND PHRASES

admonitions (2)	self-actualization (13)
asceticism (3)	hedonism (13)
chic (8)	masquerading (14)
gingivitis (8)	William Blake (14)
voyeurs (10)	endorphin (14)
sculling (11)	

1   Advertising is a funny thing. We tell it our dreams, we tell it what to say, but after a while it learns the message so well, it starts telling us.

2   What are we being told now? Simply this: not only can we extend our life, we are required to. Nike, assuming responsibility for our physical and, by implication, our spiritual health, has raised the pitch of its admonitions, the newest campaign being "Just Do It." Bold type and bold people look up from the page or from their workouts and scold us for being our usual, sloppy selves. "Just Do It," we are warned, and as one of the players adds, "And it wouldn't hurt to stop eating like a pig, either." Ouch. Yes, ma'am.

3   We've asked for this, of course. Ever since the first jogger spurted out the back door, we've been headed on a course past

simple health and toward self-denial, asceticism, pain as pleasure. "Let's live forever," we say with no particular joy, and advertising couldn't agree more.

4   In the Era of healthism, any marketer with his finger in the wind knows that Nike need not be alone in selling the virtue of self-denial. "No Pain, No Gain" can now sell much more than workout gear.

5   Take food, for instance. Advertising has taught us that eating isn't fun anymore, not if we do it right. Breakfast has become the day's first moral test—will we or won't we do the right thing?

6   Quaker Oats' new pretty boy is not the smiling Quaker of the package but the noticeably unsmiling Wilford Brimley of *Our House* and *Cocoon,* who admonishes us to eat oatmeal, not because it tastes good, but because "it's the right thing to do." Casting a baleful eye upon us, he says. "First thing tomorrow morning, do something that brings down your cholesterol." We have our marching orders. Breakfast has been redefined as work: out of bed and on the job.

7   The cereal aisle at the grocery store now presents us with one trail mix after another designed for the long march through our large intestines, each another grainy way to combat cancer, cholesterol, our own weak desire for pleasure. I now walk down the aisle trying, not to satisfy my hunger, but to represent my colon. What would *it* like? What does *it* need? Even Cheerios has come to see its own name as deeply ironic, no longer a smiling matter. The current ad's headline straightens the minds of those inclined to play with their food: "The O stands for oat bran."

8   Everywhere, Healthism's central advertising strategy is to redefine the product away from fun and toward functionalism. Take shoes for instance. Forget stylish, sexy, chic—forget all that. A current Rockport campaign headlines itself: "Shoes that help you live longer," and the copy explains that shoes are really well-engineered things we stick on our feet for fitness walking. Similarly, we see watches sold, not as jewelry nor as fashion, but as ways to time our workout. Listerine mouth rinse, which could promise to make us more kissable, opts for health maintenance instead; a recent ad asks us to "Pick one: 'Gingivitis or Listerine.' "

9   Even gum chewing need not be idle amusement. Trident tells us it's really a fighter in the war for healthy teeth: "An ounce of

prevention" one ad claims. "Toothpaste should come in as many flavors," says another. In the war against sloth and decay, no product is unarmed, no movement without its purpose.

10   And our purpose, more and more ads tell us, is to sweat. Cher and Heather Locklear sell the sexiness of sweating at Scandinavian Health Spas. In harness in their machines, they fuse pain with pleasure until we the viewers/voyeurs see sex and sweat as indistinguishable.

11   Advertising also extends this glorification of sweat to other contexts. Hewlett Packard, for instance, in its celebrated "What if . . . ?" campaign, has equated sweating with thinking: its compulsive, driven types are out sculling on the river or doing laps in a pool, sweating inside and out, when the brilliant ideas strike hard enough to drive them to the phone with their inspiration, "What if . . .?" We admire them and trust them: good ideas and good people *are* sweaty, we say.

12   Cars are sweaty, too—recent Chevrolet advertising has featured cars driving past sweat-drenched runners and bikers, equating the glory of the car with the glory of their pain. More than a means to an end, sweat is becoming an end unto itself, a psychological destination.

13   This sweat/pain motif in recent advertising may signal new national restraint, a cultural move away from self-gratification and toward control, the awareness of limits, the virtue of a Just Say No trek to self-actualization. However, it might simply be good old-fashioned hedonism's greatest idea: through denial we can live forever and thus have everything.

14   There is, after all, nothing stronger than the Healthism promise. It's better than sex, it's better than money, it's even better than love, not least because it makes all these more possible with the extra time we'll have. In an era so health conscious that we apologize for not knowing our cholesterol count, what can be stronger than the me-too-ism of longer life? Much of this advertising is aimed at the late 30s-to-early–40s crowd, the Boomers, who overdid things in the sixties and may be overdoing them again. Self-indulgence could be masquerading as asceticism. The temper of our times, healthism first, is really an inverted hippie principle via William Blake: "The road of excess leads to the palace of wisdom." And the endorphin goblers, straining in their Gore-Tex, couldn't agree more.

Thesis and Organization

1. Summarize what paragraphs 1–3 say about advertising. What tentative thesis do you deduce for the essay that will follow?
2. Paragraphs 4–9 use example to trace cause-and-effect relationships. What are they?
3. Paragraphs 10–12 discuss the "glorification of sweat." What is the author's point?
4. The conclusion, paragraphs 13 and 14, analyzes the meaning of "Healthism." State that meaning in terms of cause and effect.
5. Reread paragraphs 1–3, 13, and 14. What is the thesis of the essay?

Technique and Style

1. Is Felton trying to persuade or inform the reader? Or is he merely telling the reader how he feels about "Healthism"? Explain your response.
2. The essay has a humorous tone, but how would you characterize the humor? Is it snide, sarcastic, exaggerated, understated, what?
3. Look over the essay, scanning it for Felton's use of capitals. What conclusions can you draw about his use of this device?
4. The author uses many brand names throughout the essay. What is lost or gained by this choice?
5. What examples can you find of formal diction? Slang? What reasons can you find for the author's wide range of diction?

Suggestions for Writing

Leaf through a magazine to see what advertisements fall into what categories; cars, cosmetics, clothes, educational products, and liquor are apt to be only a few. Pick one and consider the pitch behind the ads. What, in addition to the product, is being sold? What cause-and-effect relationships are involved?

Definition

When I use a word," said Humpty Dumpty, "it means just what I choose it to mean—neither more nor less." To that Alice replied, "The question is whether you can make words mean so many different things." Humpty Dumpty then pronounced, "The question is which is to be the master—that's all." Writers are the masters of their words, although not to the extent Humpty Dumpty would like, and often a discussion or argument boils down to the meaning of a crucial word. *Liberty, justice, civil rights, freedom,* and other similar concepts, for example, are all abstractions until they are defined.

If you had to write a paper on what *freedom* means to you, you might be tempted first off to look up the word in a dictionary, but you will discover more to say if you put aside the dictionary and first think about some basic questions, such as "whose freedom?" If it's your freedom that you are writing about, who or what sets limits on your freedom? The law? The church? Parents? Family responsibilities? After you mull over questions such as these, you are in a better position to make use of a dictionary definition. The dictionary is the most obvious place to find what the word means, but what you find there is only explicit meaning, the word's **denotation.** Look up *freedom* in a collegiate dictionary and you'll see the different ways in which the word can be used and also its etymology, but that won't convey the rich layers of meaning that the word has accumulated through the years.

The dictionary will not reveal the word's associative or emotional meanings, its **connotation**. One way to discover connotation is to ask yourself questions about the word, questions similar to those above that get at how the concept of freedom touches your life. The more specific your examples, the more concrete your definition can be, and the less the danger of slipping into clichés. Unless the word you are defining is quite unusual, most readers will be familiar with its dictionary definition; your own definition and your speculations on the word's connotation are of much greater interest.

A paper that defines a familiar word can hold just as much interest as one that examines an unfamiliar one or one that is particularly powerful. "What does *boredom* mean?" "Why is *synergism* a useful concept?" "What does it mean to be called *handicapped?*" Questions such as these can call upon almost any mode of thinking and writing, as the following list demonstrates.

Description
What details best describe it? What senses can you appeal to?

Narration
What story might best illustrate it? What kind of conflict might the word involve?

Example
What sorts of examples illustrate it? What different times and sources can you use to find examples?

Comparison and ContrasT
What is it similar to? What is it different from?

Analogy
What metaphor would make it vivid? What might the reader be familiar with that you can draw an analogy to?

Division and Classification
How can it be divided? What categories can it be placed in?

Process
What steps or stages are involved in it? Which are the crucial ones?

Cause and Effect
What are the conditions that cause it? What effect does it have?

When questions such as these are tailored to the particular word or concept under scrutiny, they will help you explore your subject.

AUDIENCE AND PURPOSE   For the most part, you can assume that your audience has a general understanding of the word or phrase that is to be defined. The nature of that general understanding, however, differs. For instance, the word *spinster* most often raises an image of a "little old lady," a picture possibly fleshed out with a cat or two and fussy furnishings. That image is a far cry from the feisty, spirited one Florence King portrays and lays claim to in her essay "Spinsterhood Is Powerful." She explores her subject, lets off steam, and argues for a more positive connotation.

In his essay "Discrimination Is a Virtue," Robert Keith Miller also wants to change his reader's understanding, to make his reader aware of how the changed meaning of *discrimination* is, in turn, reflected in our society. He argues for a redefinition of the word. Redefinition is also on Gloria Naylor's mind in her essay "The Myth of the Matriarch," but she goes a step further and attacks the effects of what she sees as the destructive myth of the "strong black woman."

J. Decker gives her readers yet another kind of essay, one that uses definition to explore what people know and don't know about her home state Wisconsin. She knows that most of her readers have never been there, but—thanks to cheese, football, and serial killers—they have nonetheless formed opinions about the place. In the course of examining some of those opinions, Decker argues that Wisconsin is a good place to be.

Garrison Keillor, in "O the Porch," calls not for redefinition but reexamination. He assumes that his audience is generally familiar with the old-fashioned porch, but he takes that familiarity and particularizes it, showing why the classic porch makes a house a home. William Raspberry also calls for reexamination, but his purpose is twofold—as is his audience. In "The Handicap of Definition," he seeks to inform his white readers and persuade his black audience. While blacks must instill a more positive image in their children, whites need to know just how limiting the present image is.

EXAMPLE   To flesh out the definition of a term, you can draw upon a number of sources. William Raspberry's initial examples come from the world around us, the world of the Boston Celtics' Larry Bird and of popular performers Tom Jones and Teena Marie, worlds where the adjective *black* is a compliment. Moving on to examples from education and business, Raspberry explores what black children mean when they call something "white." He then examines examples of "positive ethnic traditions," the Jews and Chinese, to argue that the black ethnic tradition is limiting, if not self-defeating.

OTHER MODES   Definition, perhaps more than any other rhetorical pattern, depends on other modes to serve its purpose. While example is the most obvious, as in Decker's essay, all the others also come into play. Process, cause and effect, and comparison and contrast enter into Gloria Naylor's "The Myth of the Matriarch," while narration introduces the essays by Florence King, and Robert Keith Miller. Miller also briefly uses process to trace the historical meaning of *discrimination,* turning from process to cause and effect to point out why the meaning shifted to the negative and the effects of that shift on our culture. Cause and effect provides impact in William Raspberry's "The Handicap of Definition," for he first shows the reader the harmful effects of a limited definition of *black* in order to argue for change.

THESIS AND ORGANIZATION   Although a definition can play a key role in an essay, it is not the essay's thesis. The thesis rises from the author's assertion about the definition. Most frequently, the reader can derive the essay's thesis by combining two or more of the author's statements, which is the case in the essays by Garrison Keillor, Gloria Naylor, and William Raspberry. Sometimes the barebones thesis is contained in one statement—in Miller's essay, the title. This kind of thesis is easy to identify. More elusive is the implied thesis, illustrated here by Florence King's "Spinsterhood Is Powerful."

An essay's organization can also be straightforward or somewhat complex. Robert Keith Miller uses a roughly chronological pattern of organization, starting with his childhood and an ancient tale similar to that of *King Lear,* moving through the seventeenth century into the nineteenth and finally the twentieth, where most of the essay is focused. Structuring an essay so that it moves from the least to the most important point is another obvious pattern, and it is the one used by William Raspberry. Perhaps the hardest to handle successfully is the organization that goes from the particular to the general, as illustrated by Garrison Keillor's "O the Porch."

USEFUL TERMS
Connotation   The meanings associated with and suggested by a
   word that add to its literal, explicit definition. The words *home* and

domicile have similar dictionary meanings, but they differ radically in their connotations.

Denotation   The dictionary meaning of a word, the literal meaning.

Diction   The writer's choice of words. Diction is often classified by level of formality: formal, technical, conversational, colloquial, and slang.

IDEAS FOR WRITING   Choose an abstract word that you have run across in one of your classes. You'll be using that word to try out definition as a means of explaining a term so that the results can be a journal entry or the draft of a paper. First look up the word in the index and glossary of the primary textbook you are using in the course, which will give you the specialized meaning and perhaps lead you to some examples. Jot down what you find. Then think about your connection with the word; that will give you some connotations to work with. Write down what you've thought of. Next, consider the audience you're writing to. If you're writing a journal entry, write it as thought you were going to read it ten years from now, and that will force you to explain clearly. If you're heading toward an essay, think of a particular audience such as your English class, whose members may or may not be familiar with the term.

■ **POINTERS FOR USING DEFINITION**

Exploring the Topic

1. **What are the denotations of your term?** You should consult an unabridged dictionary and perhaps a more complete or specialized one, such as the *Oxford English Dictionary* or a dictionary of slang.
2. **What are the connotations of your term?** What emotional reactions or associations does it elicit from people? What situations evoke what responses and why?
3. **What other words can be used for your term?** Which are similar?
4. **What are the characteristics, qualities, or components of your term?** Which are most important? Are some not worth mentioning?
5. **What other modes are appropriate?** What modes can you draw upon to help support your definition and the organization of the essay? Where can you use description? Narration? What examples can you use to illustrate your term?
6. **Has your word been used or misused in the past?** If so, might that misuse be turned into an introductory narrative? A closing one?

Drafting the Paper

1. **Know your reader.** Review your lists of denotations and connotations together with the characteristics related to your term to see how familiar they are to your reader. Check to see if your reader may have particular associations that you need to redirect or change. Or if your reader is directly related to your topic, make sure your definition does not offend.

2. **Know your purpose.** Unless your term is unusual, one of your biggest problems is to tell the reader something new about it. Work on your first paragraph so that it will engage the reader from the start. From that point on, keep your primary purpose in mind. If you are writing a paper that is basically self-expressive or persuasive, make sure you have an audience other than yourself. If you aim is informative, consider narration, example, cause and effect, and analogy as possible ways of presenting familiar material in a fresh light.

3. **Use examples.** Provide examples to illustrate what your key term means. Also consider using negative examples and setting out distinctions between the meaning of your word and others similar to it.

4. **Draw upon a variety of sources.** Define your term from several perspectives. Perhaps a brief history of the word would be helpful or maybe some statistical information is in order. See if a brief narrative might provide additional meaning for the term.

5. **Make a point.** Don't mistake your definition for your thesis. The two are certainly related, but one is an assertion, the other is not. Perhaps your definition is a jumping-off place for a larger point you wish to make or a key part of that point. Or perhaps your term evokes a single dominant impression you want to convey. Whatever purpose your definition serves, it supports your thesis.

the Porch

Garrison Keillor

Anyone who has heard "Prairie Home Companion" is familiar with Garrison Keillor, whose radio show made rural living downright attractive. It's no wonder we should pity the poor city dweller with no porch and therefore no company, no friends, no comfort, no grace. This essay by Keillor appeared in his 1989 collection We Are Still Married.

WHAT TO LOOK FOR   *Metaphor and simile come into play in definition because they help clarify the term under discussion and make it vivid. Keillor uses a simile in paragraph 8 to make the reader feel what a home without a porch is like. As you write your own definition paper, think of what metaphor and simile can add.*

KEY WORDS AND PHRASES
portico (2)   *rostrum (11)*
potentates (2)   *dais (11)*
decorous (4)   *parapet (11)*
chaise lounge (7)   *stockade (11)*

1   Of porches there are two sorts: the decorative and the useful, the porch that is only a platform and the porch you can lie around on in your pajamas and read the Sunday paper.

2   The decorative porch has a slight function, similar to that of the White House portico: it's where you greet prime ministers, premiers, and foreign potentates. The cannons boom, the band plays, the press writes it all down, and they go indoors.

3   The true porch, or useful porch, incorporates some of that grandeur, but it is screened and protects you from prying eyes. It strikes a perfect balance between indoor and outdoor life.

4   Indoors is comfortable but decorous, as Huck Finn found out at the Widow's. It is even stifling if the company isn't right. A good porch gets you out of the parlor, lets you smoke, talk loud, eat with your fingers—without apology and without having to run away from home. No wonder that people with porches have hundreds of friends.

219

5   Of useful porches there are many sorts, including the veranda, the breezeway, the back porch, front porch, stoop, and now the sun deck, though the veranda is grander than a porch need be and the sun deck is useful only if you happen to like sun. A useful porch may be large or not, but ordinarily it is defended by screens or large shrubbery. You should be able to walk naked onto a porch and feel only a slight thrill of adventure. It is comfortable, furnished with old stuff. You should be able to spill your coffee anywhere without a trace of remorse.

6   Our family owned a porch like that once, attached to a house overlooking the St. Croix River east of St. Paul, Minnesota, that we rented from the Wilcoxes from May to September. When company came, they didn't stop in the living room but went straight through to the porch.

7   You could sit on the old porch swing that hung from the ceiling or in one of the big wicker chairs or the chaise lounge, or find a spot on the couch, which could seat four or accommodate a tall man taking a nap. There was a table for four, two kerosene lanterns, and some plants in pots. The porch faced east, was cool and shady from midday on, and got a nice breeze off the river. A lush forest of tall ferns surrounded this porch so the occupants didn't have to look at unmowed lawn or a weedy garden and feel too guilty to sit. A brook ran close by.

8   In the home-building industry today, a porch such as that one is considered an expensive frill, which is too bad for the home buyer. To sign up for a lifetime of debt at a vicious rate of interest and wind up with a porchless home, a home minus the homiest room—it's like visiting Minnesota and not seeing the prairie. You cheat yourself. Home, after all, doesn't belong to the bank, it's yours. You're supposed to have fun there, be graceful and comfortable and enjoy music and good conversation and the company of pals, otherwise home is only a furniture showroom and you may as well bunk at the YMCA and get in on their recreation programs.

9   The porch promotes grace and comfort. It promotes good conversation simply by virtue of the fact that on a porch there is no need for it. Look at the sorry bunch in the living room standing in little clumps and holding drinks, and see how hard they work to keep up a steady dribble of talk. There, silence indicates boredom and unhappiness, and hosts are quick to detect silence and rush over to subdue it into speech. Now look at our little bunch on

this porch. Me and the missus float back and forth on the swing, Mark and Rhonda are collapsed at opposite ends of the couch, Malene peruses her paperback novel in which an astounding event is about to occur, young Jeb sits at the table gluing the struts on his Curtiss biplane. The cats lie on the floor listening to birdies, and I say, "It's a heck of deal, ain't it, a *heck* of a deal." A golden creamy silence suffuses this happy scene, and only on a porch is it possible.

10　　When passersby come into view, we say hello to them, but they don't take this as an invitation to barge in. There is something slightly *forbidding* about the sight of people on a porch, its grace is almost royal. You don't rush right up to the Queen and start telling her the story of your life, and you don't do that to porch sitters either. We are Somebody up here even if our screens are torn and the sofa is busted and we're drinking orange pop from cans. You down there are passersby in a parade we've seen come and go for years. We have a porch.

11　　It is our reviewing platform and observation deck, our rostrum and dais, the parapet of our stockade, the bridge of our ship. We can sit on it in silence or walk out naked spilling coffee. Whatever we do, we feel richer than Rockefeller and luckier than the President.

12　　Years ago, my family moved from that luxurious porch to a porchless apartment in the city. Our friends quit visiting us. We felt as if we had moved to Denver. Then we moved to a big old house with two porches, then to another with a long veranda in front and a small sleeping porch in back. Now we have arrived in Manhattan, at an apartment with a terrace. A porch on the twelfth floor with a view of rooftops, chimney pots, treetops, and the street below. A canvas canopy, a potted hydrangea, and two deck chairs. Once again, we're ready for company.

Thesis and Organization

1. Keillor introduces his essay in paragraphs 1–3. How does he use comparison and contrast? Cause and effect? What working thesis does the introduction establish?
2. In the body of the essay (4–11), how does Keillor use cause and effect? Comparison and contrast? Description? Example? Classification? What does each pattern of organization contribute to his definition?

3. In paragraphs 6 and 7, Keillor refers to where he has lived, a subject that comes up again in his conclusion (12). What do those references add to his definition?

4. Add up all the positive qualities Keillor attributes to the "true porch." What is his definition? Think about the cause-and-effect relationships in the essay and that definition. What is Keillor's thesis?

Technique and Style

1. Garrison Keillor is probably best known for his radio show "The Prairie Home Companion." If you are familiar with that show, describe the personality Keillor reveals there and compare it to the one in this essay. If you don't know that program, examine Keillor's use of diction, point of view, simile, and sentence structure and describe the personality he creates for himself.

2. In general, writers choose one point of view and stick with it, but here, Keillor keeps shifting his point of view from *you* to *we*. Analyze his point of view by figuring out exactly to whom the pronouns refer. For example, does the second person in paragraph 1 refer to the same person as the second person in paragraph 10? What justification can you find for the switching of point of view?

3. Examine the allusions Keillor makes: Huck Finn and the Widow Douglas (4), the Minnesota prairie (8), the Curtiss biplane (9), and Rockefeller and the president (11). What generalizations can you make about these allusions? What do they add to Keillor's tone?

4. In an earlier version of this essay, Keillor used three similes in paragraph 8: ". . . it's like ordering Eggs Benedict and saying 'Hold the hollandaise'; it's like buying a Porsche with a Maytag motor; it's like flying first-class and being seated next to a man who bores the eyeballs right out of you." He replaced those three with ". . . it's like visiting Minnesota and not seeing the prairie." What might account for Keillor's decision to rewrite this passage using just one simile? What function does the simile serve? Create one of your own that would fit with or substitute for the one Keillor uses.

5. Keillor relies heavily on description to make his point in paragraph 9. What do the descriptive details add to his tone? How are they framed?

Suggestions for Writing

Write your own "O the" essay, finding a topic among the everyday objects around you: easy chair, sofa, television set; hamburger, ice cream cone, pizza; tie, purse, cap, jogging shoes; backyard, barbecue grill, garage.

Picket Fences

J. Decker

When not donning a bite suit to prepare police dogs for duty or training dogs or helping friends cope with the peculiarities of their computers, J. Decker is working on her degree in advertising at the University of New Orleans. She was enticed away from Wisconsin by a Taylor scholarship, a generous award that provides full board and tuition as well as other benefits. The essay that follows was written in the spring of 1993 in response to an open-ended assignment—an essay about a person or place.

WHAT TO LOOK FOR   *While Decker does indeed define her central term—Wisconsin—she does it by using a variety of organizational strategies. As you read the essay, notice how she uses description, narration, example, comparison, and causal analysis to achieve her definition.*

KEY WORDS AND PHRASES
heritage (1)	Rorschach's ink blots (9)
steins (6)	guru (10)
deviant (9)	

1   When people ask me where I am from, I often hesitate. Should I admit, to a stranger, that I come from a state that named its professional baseball team after the beer-making industry? Should I admit to sharing a heritage with people who don foam cheese wedge hats and dance in the streets in October? It can be a difficult decision.

2   The first response to my admission that I come from Wisconsin is a tilt of the head. "Oh," they say, scanning their memory banks for a location, "isn't that in Canada?" I am constantly amazed that people who live at the southern end of the Mississippi River don't know the general location of where that same river starts. Even the learned are not immune. In my first semester at U.N.O., my geology professor talked about the "mountainous headwaters of the Mississippi River." There aren't any mountains in Wisconsin or Minnesota that I know of—just a few big hills left over from the

last ice age. Granted, Wisconsin is substantially above sea level. Maybe that confuses Louisianians.

3   If the public cannot correctly identify the country Wisconsin belongs to, it's a fairly safe bet that it isn't a holiday hot spot. Wisconsin is one of those places people don't purposely visit. You'll never hear a family coming back from vacation, "Ah, yes, we vacationed in Wisconsin this summer." Maybe they've switched planes at the (only) airport, but it wasn't an intentional visit. Travelers do sometimes drive through Wisconsin—to get somewhere else—but those who do cut through Wisconsin generally don't even know they've been there. In their minds, they've detoured straight from Illinois into Minnesota.

4   There may be some basis for this evasion. Wisconsin is the land of the Green Bay Packers, most of the serial killers you've seen on television, three cows for every person, and the Cheddar Heads. This alone is enough to scare many longtime residents away, let alone a visitor. Several years ago the state tourism department started a promotion campaign with the slogan "Escape to Wisconsin!" Not only was this slogan hard to fit on a bumper sticker, it was usually marked out to read "Escape Wisconsin!"

5   Perhaps one of the reasons travelers avoid Wisconsin is the way we name our towns. Sure, everyone has heard of Milwaukee, largely due to *Wayne's World* and Jeffrey Dahmer (definitely one of "Milwaukee's Best"). Now try to say Wonewoc, Oconomowoc, Sinsinawa, Memomonee, Chequamegon, or Kewaskum. Hooked on Phonics isn't going to help you here. Add to that the preponderance of people who don't live in any town at all, and you've got a direction-taker's nightmare. I've fielded those desperate calls many times. The conversation goes something like this:

CALLER: Hi, this is Dave. We're lost.
ME: Well, Dave, do you know where you are?
CALLER: The guy at the bar says I'm in Manitowoc.
ME: Are you sure that's not Manitowish, Dave?
CALLER: Oh, yeah, you're right. We're in Magnet Wish.
ME: Now Dave, think very hard. The sign above the bar—
           did it say Sal's, Hal's, or Big Al's?
CALLER (excitedly): It said Hal's! You mean you know where I
           am?

ME:	Well, Dave, I know where you are, but I don't know who you are.
CALLER (silent for a moment):	Is this 2148?
ME:	No, it's 2184, but I live just down the road from Bart's.
CALLER:	Oh, well maybe you an give me better directions than he did. . . .

Even if the names aren't all that hard to say, they can still be confusing. It's usually hard for non-natives to keep track of small towns that all sound like cheeses: Edam, Colby, Monterey, Edelweiss.

6   While it's not all rural, the entire state of Wisconsin has a reputation for being somewhat "hokey." By that, I mean that outsiders picture us milking cows named Betsy or Lola by hand while singing "What do the simple folk do?" But the state of Wisconsin is not entirely backwards, it just appears that way. After all, what is it that folks see on the news about our state? You see thousands of intoxicated people wearing orange cheese hats and holding steins as they run through the streets of Milwaukee during Oktoberfest. Or you might have had the good fortune to see a clip from the most recent cow chip-flinging contest. Yes, it really does go on, and no, gloves are not allowed. The secret is in selecting a well-shaped, thoroughly dried specimen. (Or so I've been told.)

7   Winter is another joy that keeps many people away. It is only a slight exaggeration to say that winter lasts three-quarters of the year. It begins in late September with vigor and ferocity, as if to chase those football fanatics inside, and ends, reluctantly, in mid-May when the tulips start bouncing their heads off the ice sheet that has covered our state.

8   This roughly corresponds to the school year, and for good reason. There's not much hope of skipping school when your bus driver has shovelled his way up your driveway, and besides, there's just no "cool" way to hang around town in snowshoes. The characteristic saunter of truants loses its effect when three feet of rawhide webbing is strapped to each foot.

9   Another tourist-banishing idea is Wisconsin's reputation for producing every serial killer and wacko that has graced the six o'clock news. That is absolutely not true. Just because our two most famous residents liked to upholster furniture with human skin and drill holes into skulls, respectively, there is no reason to classify ours as an overly deviant population. Though some researchers

have speculated that the abundance of Holstein cows and their resemblance to Rorschach's ink blots has something to do with this
"serial" trend. You might go crazy too if all you saw were grazing
cattle and cornfields.

10   In spite of the criticisms, people do leave the hustle and hassle
of big city life to "escape to Wisconsin." For every news clip show-
casing our problems or idiosyncrasies, there's a TV show reveling
in the normalcy ("Happy Days," "Flying High," "Step by Step"), a
good-hearted alien landing in our state forest (Star Man), or a su-
percomputer guru setting up shop (Cray). Wisconsin *is* a nice
place to live, but I wouldn't want to visit.

Thesis and Organization

1. Paragraphs 1 and 2 set out what some people do and do not know
   about Wisconsin. How do those ideas prepare the reader for the rest of
   the essay?
2. List all the negative features set out in paragraphs 3–9.
3. What positive qualities can you extract from the negative ones?
4. What does the last paragraph bring out? What would the effect of the
   essay be without it?
5. Given the positives, negatives, and the very last sentence, how does
   the author define Wisconsin?

Technique and Style

1. What does the dialogue in paragraph 5 add to the reader's impression
   of Wisconsin?
2. Reread the essay, looking for Decker's use of the second person pronoun *you*. To whom does it refer? What does this choice of pronoun
   add to the essay?
3. Look up the use of parentheses in a handbook of grammar and usage.
   Does Decker's use of them in paragraph 3, 5, 6, and 10 follow the explanation you find?
4. Given Decker's examples and her thesis, how would you describe the
   tone of the essay?
5. Throughout the essay, Decker uses details to make her points vivid.
   Which did you find particularly effective and why?

Suggestions for Writing

Chances are that people have some mistaken ideas about where you
live—the town, county, or state. Or perhaps you live in a large city or in a

rural area, both places that many people have false ideas about. Cities such as New York and Los Angeles are often thought of as having a mugger on every corner, and small towns and rural areas are considered so dull that watching a traffic light change is an event. Think of your reader as someone who has preconceived ideas about a place you know well and has never been there, and write an essay defining that place in such a way that you either reinforce or refute those ideas.

S pinsterhood is Powerful

Florence King

A prolific writer with more than enough to write about because she disagrees with so many opinions, Florence King's latest book is appropriately titled With Charity Toward None: A Fond Look at Misanthropy *(1992). Her articles have appeared in almost every major magazine, ranging from* Harper's *to* Cosmopolitan *to* Modern Romances. *"Spinsterhood Is Powerful" was originally published in the July 19, 1993, issue of the* National Review, *a conservative weekly, and was reprinted in the November/December issue of the* Utne Reader. *The essay is in the same spirit as one of King's better lines: "I don't suffer fools, and I like to see fools suffer."*

WHAT TO LOOK FOR   *Often when you write on a subject you feel strongly about, it's hard to move out of the personal and into the more general. As you read Florence King's essay, note how she does it.*

KEY WORDS AND PHRASES

marital (2)	*Elizabeth Peabody (5)*
unscathed (3)	*plangent (6)*
amok (3)	*renunciation (6)*
rancid (3)	*Adrienne Rich (6)*
Susan B. Anthony (5)	*preambles (7)*
Anna Dickinson (5)	*mendacious (9)*
Elizabeth Blackwell (5)	*unencumbered (9)*
Clara Barton (5)	*carte blanche (11)*
Dorothea Dix (5)	

1   It is typical of America that having invented efficiency apartments, singles bars, Soup for One, and That *Cosmopolitan* Girl, we have dropped *spinster* from the language and consider *old maid* a sexist slur.

2   I make a point of using both. If I fill out a form that asks for my marital status I skip the printed selections, write in *spinster,* draw a block beside it, and check it. When an aluminum siding telephone

salesman asked to speak to the "man of the house," I said, "There isn't any, I'm an old maid," and derived enormous satisfaction from his audible gulp.

3   Spinsterhood was powerful long before feminism hit the fan. Point to any area of "sex discrimination" and you will find that old maids have always sailed through unscathed. Businessmen know all too well that the hand that rocks the cradle rocks the boat. Most married women with children are no use to anybody unless the stock exchange is hiring amok runners, but spinsters give females a good name. We come to work on time with no visions of baby-sitters and day-care centers dancing like rancid sugar plums in our heads; we can work overtime on a moment's notice, and there is never any spit-up on our paperwork.

4   Credit ratings? An old maid and a divorcée with three children to support are both "single," but the resemblance ends there. Instead of urging women to conceal their marital status under the muzzy blanket of "Ms.," feminists should have encouraged the inclusion of *spinster* on applications. It would have pulled up women's overall credit rating and eliminated the automatic discrimination against them cause by the bill-paying problems of liberated divorcées.

5   Auto insurance? Old maids look at the road, not at what Jason did to Debbie's dress. As for life insurance, take a peek at the tombstones in Old Maid Gardens:

> Susan B. Anthony—1820–1906
> Anna Dickinson—1842–1932
> Elizabeth Blackwell—1821–1910
> Clara Barton—1821–1912
> Dorothea Dix—1802–1887
> Elizabeth Peabody—1804–1894

6   I wish my fellow conservatives would tone down their plangent testimonials to the Great God Family. I also wish that feminists would try to harden women, as real feminists should, by preaching renunciation, instead of tearing them apart by simultaneously promoting masculine work and condemning masculine work habits, e.g., Adrienne Rich: "I want to make it clear that I am *not* saying that in order to write well, or think well, it is necessary to become unavailable to others, or to become a devouring ego. This has been the myth of the masculine artist and thinker; and I repeat, I do not accept it."

7   Bull, madam, bull. If you really reject it, why not say so simply and briefly, instead of dragging in defensive preambles and italics?

8   The "myth" of the masculine artist and thinker—or any worker— is not myth but fact. Its real name is *concentration,* and it is achieved by making oneself unavailable to others. He travels fastest who travels alone, and that goes double for she.

9   Mendacious pep talks such as Miss Rich's keep married women in a perpetual state of conflict and make them jealous of unencumbered women. The jealousy crops up in a phrase I hear regularly: "If I could do what you do . . . ."

10   Write the same goddamn page 20 times? Write all day Christmas? Get halfway through a book only to realize that you started too late in dramatic time and the whole thing is turning into a flashback? Anybody who chose that moment to ask "When's dinner?" would get *killed,* ladies, and liberal Adrienne Rich knows it. She won't tell you; I just did.

11   Of all the benefits of spinsterhood, the greatest is carte blanche. Once a woman is called "that crazy old maid" she can get away with anything.

Thesis and Organization

1. The introduction makes clear society's and King's attitudes toward the word *spinster.* What are they?
2. What characteristics of spinsterhood does King explain in paragraphs 3–5?
3. What does King complain about in paragraph 6?
4. Concentration ranks high with King. Where does she indicate that concentration is not gender-related?
5. Consider both the denotative meaning and the connotations King supplies. How does she define *spinster?* Given that definition and the title, what is King's thesis?

Technique and Style

1. Use an unabridged dictionary or a dictionary of literary terms to look up *irony.* How is King's first paragraph ironic?
2. In paragraph 3 King twists the old saying "The hand that rocks the cradle is the hand that rules the world." What does her change add to the tone of the essay?
3. Paragraph 5 lists names and dates. What is King's point?

4. King begins both paragraph 4 and paragraph 5 with a question. Rewrite one so that you begin the paragraph with a complete sentence. What is gained? Lost?

5. How would you describe King's tone?

Suggestions for Writing

What one word can be used to define you? If you'd rather not write about yourself, then switch to someone you know well. The word you choose will probably be a characteristic—loyal, interesting, fun, loving, etc. Whatever that word is, it—not the person—is the subject of your essay. Like King, you can switch back and forth between the personal and the general, but remember that the idea here is to define that key word.

*T*he Myth of the Matriarch

Gloria Naylor

Best known for her novels, Gloria Naylor was born in Queens, a borough of New York City, and received her first library card at the age of 4. After graduating from Brooklyn College and earning a master's degree at Yale, she began her career as a writer. Her first novel, The Women of Brewster Place, *was published in 1982 and received the American Book Award for best first novel. Her most recent,* Bailey's Café, *rounds off what Naylor calls her "novel quartet." The essay that follows was published in* Life *in the spring of 1988. The neighborhood she grew up in and her travels have given her lots of opportunity to observe both the myth and the reality of the matriarch.*

WHAT TO LOOK FOR *Transitions between paragraphs usually flow fairly smoothly, but providing a transition from one major part of the essay to another is more difficult. Naylor does it by using a short paragraph in which she poses a question that she then answers in the paragraphs that follow.*

KEY WORDS AND PHRASES

Matriarch (title)	proximity (6)
Faulkner (1)	unstinting (6)
etiquette (1)	harbored (6)
permeated (1)	liaisons (6)
menial (3)	obesity (6)
Amazons (4)	precarious (7)
piety (5)	emancipation (7)
frailty (5)	protagonist (8)
benign (6)	impoverished (10)

1   The strong black woman. All my life I've seen her. In books she is Faulkner's impervious Dilsey, using her huge dark arms to hold together the crumbling spirits and household of the Compsons. In the movies she is the quintessential Mammy, chasing after Scarlett O'Hara with forgotten sunbonnets and shrill tongue-lashings about etiquette. On television she is Sapphire of *Amos 'n Andy* or a dozen variations of her—henpecking black men, herding white

children, protecting her brood from the onslaughts of the world. She is the supreme matriarch—alone, self-sufficient and liking it that way. I've seen how this female image has permeated the American consciousness to the point of influencing everything from the selling of pancakes to the structuring of welfare benefits. But the strangest thing is that when I walked around my neighborhood or went into the homes of family and friends, this matriarch was nowhere to be found.

2   I know the statistics: They say that when my grandmother was born at the turn of the century as few as 10 percent of black households were headed by females; when I was born at mid-century it had crept to 17 percent; and now it is almost 60 percent. No longer a widow or a divorcée as in times past, the single woman with children today probably has never married—and increasingly she is getting younger. By the time she is 18, one out of every four black unmarried women has become a mother.

3   But it is a long leap from a matrifocal home, where the father is absent, to a matriarchal one, in which the females take total charge from the males. Though I have known black women heading households in different parts of the country and in different social circumstances—poor, working class or professional—none of them has gloried in the conditions that left them with the emotional and financial responsibility for their families. Often they had to take domestic work because of the flexible hours or stay in menial factory or office jobs because of the steady pay. And leaving the job was only to go home to the other job of raising children alone. These women understood the importance of input from black men in sustaining their families. Their advice and, sometimes, financial assistance were sought and accepted. But if such were not forthcoming, she would continue to deal with her situation alone.

4   This is a far cry from the heartwarming image of the two-fisted black woman I watched striding across the public imagination. A myth always arises to serve a need. And so it must be asked, what is it in the relationship of black women to American society that has called for them to be seen as independent Amazons?

5   The black woman was brought to America for the same reason as the black man—to provide slave labor. But she had what seemed to be contradictory roles: She did the woman's work of bearing children and keeping house while doing a man's work at

the side of the black male in the fields. She worked regardless of the advanced stages of pregnancy. In the 19th century the ideal of the true woman was one of piety, purity, domesticity and submissiveness; the female lived as a wife sheltered at home or went abroad as a virgin doing good works. But if the prevailing belief was that the natural state of women was one of frailty, how could the black female be explained? Out in the fields laboring with their muscled bodies and during rest periods suckling infants at their breasts, the slave women had to be seen as different from white women. They were stronger creatures: they didn't feel pain in childbirth; they didn't have tear ducts. Ironically, one of the arguments for enslaving blacks in the first place was that as a race they were inferior to whites—but black women, well, they were a little _more_ than women.

6   The need to view slavery as benign accounted for the larger-than-life mammy of the plantation legends. As a house servant, she was always pictured in close proximity to her white masters because there was nothing about her that was threatening to white ideas about black women. Her unstinting devotion assuaged any worries that slaves were discontented or harbored any potential for revolt. Her very dark skin belied any suspicions of past interracial liaisons, while her obesity and advanced age removed any sexual threat. Earth mother, nursemaid and cook, the mammy existed without a history or a future.

7   In reality, slave women in the house or the field were part of a kinship network and with their men tried to hold together their own precarious families. Marriages between slaves were not legally recognized, but this did not stop them from entering into living arrangements and acting as husbands and wives. After emancipation a deluge of black couples registered their unions under the law, and ex-slaves were known to travel hundreds of miles in search of lost partners and children.

8   No longer bound, but hardly equal citizens, black men and women had access to only the most menial jobs in society, the largest number being reserved solely for female domestics. Richard Wright wrote a terribly funny and satirical short story about the situation, "Man of All Work." His protagonist is unable to find a job to support his family and save his house from foreclosure, so he puts on his wife's clothes and secures a position as a housekeeper. "Don't stop me. I've found a solution to our problem. I'm an army-

trained cook. I can clean a house as good as anybody. Get my point? I put on your dress. I looked in the mirror. I can pass. I want that job."

9   Pushed to the economic forefront of her home, the 19th century mammy became 20th century Sapphire. Fiery, younger, more aggressive, she just couldn't wait to take the lead away from the man of the house. Whatever he did was never enough. Not that he wanted to do anything, of course, except hang out on street corners, gamble and run around with women. From vaudeville of the 1880s to the advent of *Amos 'n Andy,* it was easier to make black men the brunt of jokes than to address the inequities that kept decent employment from those who wanted to work. Society had not failed black women—their men had.

10   The truth is that throughout our history black women could depend upon their men even when they were unemployed or underemployed. But in the impoverished inner cities today we are seeing the rise of the *unemployable.* These young men are not equipped to take responsibility for themselves, much less the children they are creating. And with the increasing youth of unwed mothers, we have grandmothers and grandfathers in their early thirties. How can a grandmother give her daughter's family the traditional wisdom and support when she herself has barely lived? And on the other side of town, where the professional black woman is heading a household, usually because she is divorced, the lack of a traditional kinship network—the core community of parents, uncles, aunts—makes her especially alone.

11   What is surprising to me is that the myth of the matriarch lives on—even among black women. I've talked to so many who believe that they are supposed to be superhuman and bear up under all things. When they don't, they all too readily look for the fault within themselves. Somehow they failed their history. But it is a grave mistake for black women to believe that they have a natural ability to be stronger than other women. Fifty-seven percent of black homes being headed by females is not natural. A 40 percent pregnancy rate among our young girls is not natural. It is heartbreaking. The myth of the matriarch robs a woman caught in such circumstances of her individuality and her humanity. She should feel that she has the *right* at least to break down—once the kids are put to bed—and do something so simple as cry.

Thesis and Organization

1. Paragraphs 1–3 introduce the essay. In what ways do they set the stage for what follows?
2. Paragraph 3 introduces the concepts of matrifocal and kinship relationships, and Naylor refers to these concepts again in paragraphs 7 and 10. What is her point?
3. Naylor states that "A myth always arises to serve a need" (4). Reread paragraphs 5–9 and explain the needs served by the myth of the matriarch.
4. How does Naylor's description of the present situation relate to the idea of the myth of the matriarch?
5. The essay concludes with the negative effects of the myth. What are they? Given those negative effects and the history of the myth explained in paragraphs 4–9, what is Naylor's thesis?

Technique and Style

1. The essay opens with allusions to fiction and television shows. How would you update them?
2. Paragraphs 2 and 11 introduce statistics into the essay. What do they contribute?
3. Naylor describes the role of black women in the days of slavery and the attitudes of whites toward them. Explain whether you find her tone more objective than subjective or the opposite.
4. What does the irony in paragraph 5 add to the idea of myth?
5. How would you describe Naylor's audience?

Suggestions for Writing

The myth of the matriarch is just one of the many myths in our culture that have given rise to stereotypes similar to the Mammies and Sapphires that Naylor points out. These stereotypes show up frequently in popular culture in films, books, and television shows, and thus further the myth. Mull over recent movies or television shows you've seen or popular fiction you've read. You may discover a myth of the hero, the supermom, the adorable child, the nightmare slasher, the happy homemaker, or some other myth. Once you've focused on a myth, search your memory for other examples of it and for how it may show up in real life. Your paper may turn out like Naylor's, defining the myth and showing its harmful and false side, or you may prefer a simpler route, exploring only the myth.

Discrimination Is a Virtue

Robert Keith Miller

By examining the connotations and denotations of the word dis-crimination, Robert Keith Miller shows us not only that we misuse it, but that its misuse points to a flaw in our "public policies." Miller's essay appeared in the "My Turn" column in Newsweek *in 1980. His argument still holds.*

WHAT TO LOOK FOR *Look up rhetorical questions in a handbook of grammar and usage and then be on the lookout for how Miller uses them. When you write your next paper, see if a rhetorical question or two can function as a transition or for emphasis.*

KEY WORDS AND PHRASES
hypocrites (3)   *euphemistically (12)*
preconceptions (8)   *arbitrary (14)*
bias (8)

1   When I was a child, my grandmother used to tell me a story about a king who had three daughters and decided to test their love. He asked each of them "How much do you love me?" The first replied that she loved him as much as all the diamonds and pearls in the world. The second said that she loved him more than life itself. The third replied "I love you as fresh meat loves salt."

2   This answer enraged the king; he was convinced that his youngest daughter was making fun of him. So he banished her from his realm and left all of his property to her elder sisters.

3   As the story unfolded it became clear, even to a 6-year-old, that the king had made a terrible mistake. The two older girls were hypocrites, and as soon as they had profited from their father's generosity, they began to treat him very badly. A wiser man would have realized that the youngest daughter was the truest. Without attempting to flatter, she said, in effect, "We go together naturally; we are a perfect team."

4   Years later, when I came to read Shakespeare, I realized that my grandmother's story was loosely based upon the story of King

Lear, who put his daughters to a similar test and did not know how to judge the results. Attempting to save the king from the consequences of his foolishness, a loyal friend pleads, "Come sir, arise, away! I'll teach you differences." Unfortunately, the lesson comes too late. Because Lear could not tell the difference between true love and false, he loses his kingdom and eventually his life.

5   We have a word in English which means "the ability to tell differences." That word is *discrimination.* But within the last 30 years, this word has been so frequently misused that an entire generation has grown up believing that "discrimination" means "racism." People are always proclaiming that "discrimination" is something that should be done away with. Should that ever happen, it would prove to be our undoing.

6   Discrimination means discernment; it means the ability to perceive the truth, to use good judgment and to profit accordingly. The *Oxford English Dictionary* traces this understanding of the word back to 1648 and demonstrates that for the next 300 years, "discrimination" was a virtue, not a vice. Thus, when a character in a nineteenth-century novel makes a happy marriage, Dickens has another character remark, "It does credit to your discrimination that you should have found such a very excellent young woman."

7   Of course, "the ability to tell differences" assumes that differences exist, and this is unsettling for a culture obsessed with the notion of equality. The contemporary belief that discrimination is a vice stems from the compound *discriminate against.* What we need to remember, however, is that some things deserve to be judged harshly: we should not leave our kingdoms to the selfish and the wicked.

8   Discrimination is wrong only when someone or something is discriminated against because of prejudice. But to use the word in this sense, as so many people do, is to destroy its true meaning. If you discriminate against something because of general preconceptions rather than particular insights, then you are not discriminating—bias has clouded the clarity of vision which discrimination demands.

9   One of the great ironies of American life is that we manage to discriminate in the practical decisions of daily life, but usually fail to discriminate when we make public policies. Most people are very discriminating when it comes to buying a car, for example, because they realize that cars have differences. Similarly, an in-

creasing number of people have learned to discriminate in what they eat. Some foods are better than others—and indiscriminate eating can undermine one's health.

10   Yet in public affairs, good judgment is depressingly rare. In many areas which involve the common good, we see a failure to tell differences.

11   Consider, for example, some of the thinking behind modern education. On the one hand, there is a refreshing realization that there are differences among children, and some children—be they gifted or handicapped—require special education. On the other hand, we are politically unable to accept the consequences of this perception. The trend in recent years has been to group together students of radically different ability. We call this process "mainstreaming," and it strikes me as a characteristically American response to the discovery of differences: we try to pretend that differences do not matter.

12   Similarly, we try to pretend that there is little difference between the sane and the insane. A fashionable line of argument has it that "everybody is a little mad" and that few mental patients deserve long-term hospitalization. As a consequence of such reasoning, thousands of seriously ill men and women have been evicted from their hospital beds and returned to what is euphemistically called "the community"—which often means being left to sleep on city streets, where confused and helpless people now live out of paper bags as the direct result of our refusal to discriminate.

13   Or to choose a final example from a different area: how many recent elections reflect thoughtful consideration of the genuine differences among candidates? Benumbed by television commercials that market aspiring officeholders as if they were a new brand of toothpaste or hair spray, too many Americans vote with only a fuzzy understanding of the issues in question. Like Lear, we seem too eager to leave the responsibility of government to others and too ready to trust those who tell us whatever we want to hear.

14   So as we look around us, we should recognize that "discrimination" is a virtue which we desperately need. We must try to avoid making unfair and arbitrary distinctions, but we must not go to the other extreme and pretend that there are no distinctions to be made. The ability to make intelligent judgments is essential both for the success of one's personal life and for the functioning of society as a whole. Let us be open-minded by all means, but not so open-minded that our brains fall out.

Thesis and Organization

1. Paragraphs 1–4 use narration. What is the "lesson" of the narrative? Why might Miller have chosen a narrative to introduce the essay?

2. Paragraph 5 deals with the popular connotations of *discrimination*. What are they? What other paragraph or paragraphs bring out the misuse of the word?

3. Paragraph 6 presents the denotative meaning of the word. What other paragraph or paragraphs emphasize that meaning?

4. Where does Miller maintain that the idea of differences runs counter to our notion of equality? How is that idea related to paragraphs 9–13?

5. Paragraph 14 concludes the essay. Consider the essay's title and the last paragraph. What is a full statement of Miller's thesis? Is the essay primarily expressive, informative, or persuasive?

Technique and Style

1. Consult a handbook of grammar and usage for discussion of the rhetorical question. Where in the essay do you find examples of this device? To what extent do the examples fit the handbook's definition?

2. What modes does Miller use to define his central terms? Which does he use most frequently?

3. Note all the times Miller uses quotation marks. What different functions do the quotation marks serve?

4. What sort of a person does Miller seem to be? In what ways does his persona fit his tone? How would you characterize his tone?

5. What sources does Miller draw his examples from? Group them according to the generalizations they support. In what ways are they appropriate or inappropriate to the generalizations? What do the examples add to Miller's persona?

Suggestions for Writing

Think of a word that is commonly misused or has outworn its meaning and make a case for its linguistic correction or restoration. Commonly misused words can be found in a handbook of grammar and usage, usually in the glossary of usage. You might come up with *virtually, disinterested, flaunt, irritate,* or words formed with the suffice *pre-,* as in *preheat, prewrite, pre-owned.* As for outworn words, they are all around us, particularly in advertisements: *fabulous, lovely, elegant.* Or your might consider how words once considered inappropriate to everyday conversation have now become more or less accepted. No matter what the topic, bring out its significance so that you use definition to make a larger point.

*T*he Handicap of Definition

William Raspberry

The terms black *and* white *have connotations that we don't often think about. William Raspberry shows us that if we stop to think about* black, *we'll see that it has so narrow a definition that it is "one of the heaviest burdens black Americans—and black children in particular—have to bear." Not much has changed since 1982, when this essay first appeared in William Raspberry's syndicated column.*

WHAT TO LOOK FOR   *Somewhere along the line, we've all been warned never to begin a sentence with a conjunction such as* and, but, *and the like. But as long as you know to avoid the trap of a sentence fragment, beginning a sentence with a conjunction can lend a conversational tone to your essay. As you read Raspberry's essay, notice how often he uses this technique.*

KEY WORDS AND PHRASES
deprivation (1)   *elocution (10)*
academia (6)   *ethnic (11)*
devastating (7)   *inculcated (11)*
infect (9)   *perverted (13)*
myth (9)

1   I know all about bad schools, mean politicians, economic deprivation and racism. Still, it occurs to me that one of the heaviest burdens black Americans—and black children in particular—have to bear is the handicap of definition: the question of what it means to be black.

2   Let me explain quickly what I mean. If a basketball fan says that the Boston Celtics' Larry Bird plays "black," the fan intends it—and Bird probably accepts it—as a compliment. Tell pop singer Tom Jones he moves "black" and he might grin in appreciation. Say to Teena Marie or The Average White Band that they sound "black" and they'll thank you.

3   But name one pursuit, aside from athletics, entertainment or sexual performance in which a white practitioner will feel complimented to be told he does it "black." Tell a white broadcaster he

talks "black," and he'll sign up for diction lessons. Tell a white reporter he writes "black" and he'll take a writing course. Tell a white lawyer he reasons "black" and he might sue you for slander.

4   What we have here is a tragically limited definition of blackness, and it isn't only white people who buy it.

5   Think of all the ways black children can put one another down with charges of "whiteness." For many of these children, hard study and hard work are "white." Trying to please a teacher might be criticized as acting "white." Speaking correct English is "white." Scrimping today in the interest of tomorrow's goals is "white." Educational toys and games are "white."

6   An incredible array of habits and attitudes that are conducive to success in business, in academia, in the nonentertainment professions are likely to be thought of as somehow "white." Even economic success, unless it involves such "black" undertakings as numbers banking, is defined as "white."

7   And the results are devastating. I wouldn't deny that blacks often are better entertainers and athletes. My point is the harm that comes from too narrow a definition of what is black.

8   One reason black youngsters tend to do better at basketball, for instance, is that they assume they can learn to do it well, and so they practice constantly to prove themselves right.

9   Wouldn't it be wonderful if we could infect black children with the notion that excellence in math is "black" rather than white, or possibly Chinese? Wouldn't it be of enormous value if we could create the myth that morality, strong families, determination, courage and love of learning are traits brought by slaves from Mother Africa and therefore quintessentially black?

10   There is no doubt in my mind that most black youngsters could develop their mathematical reasoning, their elocution and their attitudes the way they develop their jump shots and their dance steps: by the combination of sustained, enthusiastic practice and the unquestioned belief that they can do it.

11   In one sense, what I am talking about is the importance of developing positive ethnic traditions. Maybe Jews have an innate talent for communication; maybe the Chinese are born with a gift for mathematical reasoning; maybe blacks are naturally blessed with athletic grace. I doubt it. What is at work, I suspect, is assumption, inculcated early in their lives, that this is a thing our people do well.

12   Unfortunately, many of the things about which blacks make this assumption are things that do not contribute to their career success—except for that handful of the truly gifted who can make it as entertainers and athletes. And many of the things we concede to whites are the things that are essential to economic security.

13   So it is with a number of assumptions black youngsters make about what it is to be a "man": physical aggressiveness, sexual prowess, the refusal to submit to authority. The prisons are full of people who, by this perverted definition, are unmistakably men.

14   But the real problem is not so much that the things defined as "black" are negative. The problem is that the definition is much too narrow.

15   Somehow, we have to make our children understand that they are intelligent, competent people, capable of doing whatever they put their minds to and making it in the American mainstream, not just in a black subculture.

16   What we seem to be doing, instead, is raising up yet another generation of young blacks who will be failures—by definition.

Thesis and Organization

1. Examine paragraphs 1–4 as a unit. What sentence functions as the major assertion for this group of paragraphs? What examples support that assertion? What conclusion does Raspberry draw from the examples? How is that conclusion related to the paragraphs that follow?
2. Take paragraphs 5–7 as a unit and analyze it also, looking for the controlling assertion, the examples, and the conclusion.
3. Paragraphs 8–11 also form a paragraph block. What is its controlling assertion? What examples support it? What conclusion does Raspberry draw?
4. Examine paragraphs 12–16 as a concluding paragraph block. What is the relationship between paragraph 12 and the paragraphs that precede it? In what way is the point raised in paragraph 13 an analogy? Is the analogy apt or false? What is the function of paragraph 14? Paragraphs 15 and 16 look to the future an assess the present. What cause-and-effect relationship do they point out?
5. Consider the controlling ideas that guide the paragraph blocks and the conclusions Raspberry draws from the examples that support those assertions. Stated fully, what is Raspberry's thesis? Do you agree or disagree with this thesis? Why or why not?

Technique and Style

1. This essay was one of Raspberry's syndicated columns; as a result, it appeared in a large number of newspapers with equally large readerships, mostly white. What evidence can you find that Raspberry is trying to inform his white audience and persuade his black readers?

2. How and where does Raspberry establish his credibility as a writer on this subject? What grammatical point of view does he use? What is the effect of that point of view?

3. Where in the essay does he qualify or modulate his statements? What is the effect of that technique?

4. Many techniques can be used to give a paragraph coherence, but an often neglected one is syntax. Examine paragraphs 2, 3, 5, and 9 to discover the similar sentence structure at work. What do you find?

5. Paragraphs 3, 7, 13, and 14 all begin with a conjunction. What effect does this technique achieve? Consult a handbook of grammar and usage for a discussion of this device. To what extent does Raspberry's usage conform to the handbook's advice?

6. Paragraph 16 is an example of a rhetorical paragraph, a one-sentence paragraph that gives dramatic emphasis to a point. If you eliminate the dash or substitute a comma for it, what happens to the dramatic effect? What does the pun add?

7. A militant who read this essay would argue that Raspberry is trying to make blacks "better" by making them white. Is there any evidence to support this view? Explain.

8. A feminist who read the essay would argue that it is sexist. Is there any evidence to support this view? Explain.

Suggestions for Writing

Find a word that has accumulated broad connotations and then see what definitions have evolved and their effect. Like Raspberry, you may want to consider two terms but emphasize only one. Possibilities: *man, hero, student, woman, worker, lover, politician.*

Argument

*I*n everyday speech, ***argument*** is so closely associated with *quarrel* or *fight* that it has a negative connotation, but that connotation does not apply to the word as it is used in the writing of essays. If you were to analyze an essay by examining its argument, you would be looking at the writer's major assertion and the weight of the evidence on which it rests. That evidence must be compelling, for the aim of all argumentative writing is to move the reader to adopt the writer's view. In writing argumentative papers, sometimes you might want to go further than that and call for a particular action, but most of the time you'll probably work at convincing your reader to share your position on the issue. Often, however, it's possible to get so involved in a subject you feel strongly about that you end up writing only to readers who already share you views.

One way to avoid that trap is to start work on your topic by brainstorming on the subject, not your position on it. Phrase the subject as a question and then list the pros and cons. If you are writing on gambling, for instance, you would ask, "Should gambling be legalized?" Then you would define your terms: Who would be legalizing it—the federal government, the state, the county, the city? What kind of gambling—betting, gaming, playing a lottery? Answer those kinds of questions and you can draw up your pros and cons more easily because your focus will be more specific. Once you've listed the arguments that can be used, you can then sort through them, noting the evidence you can cite and where to find it. Having done all that, you then are in a position to choose which side you wish to take, and you know the arguments that can be used against you.

The next step is to think about the ways in which you can appeal to your readers. Citing facts and precedents will appeal to their reason; exploring moral issues will appeal to their emotions; and presenting yourself as a credible person will appeal to their sense of fairness. *Reason* is the primary appeal in most argumentative writing, and to use it successfully, you may need to do some research on your subject. Once your argument begins to take shape, however, you will find that dealing with one or two of the opposing views will not only strengthen your own case but also earn you some points for fairness.

Argumentative writing ranges from the personal to the abstract and draws upon the various patterns that can be used to structure an essay. For instance, waiting tables in a restaurant may have convinced you that tips should be automatically included in the bill. To make the case that the present system is unfair to those in a service trade, you might draw primarily on your own experience and that of others, though to avoid a **hasty generalization** you need to make sure that your experience is representative. A quick check among others similarly employed or a look at government reports on employment statistics should suffice and should also help you generalize logically from the particular.

Hasty generalization is one of many **logical fallacies** in argument. If you were to argue that the reader should only consider the present system of tipping or the one you propose, you will be guilty of either-or reasoning, which is false because it permits no middle ground. Quote William "The Refrigerator" Perry on the subject and you will be citing **false authority**; he knows football but not the restaurant industry. And obviously if you call a 5-percent tipper a cheap idiot, you will be accused quite rightly of name-calling, the **ad hominem** fallacy.

Post hoc reasoning is harder to spot in that it is tied to the claim that a temporal relationship is really a causal one. Say you noticed that as closing time loomed, your tips got smaller. Is that because people who dine late tip minimally or because your customers felt rushed? Assume the former and you fall into the *post hoc* trap.

You will find that if you are assigned an argumentative topic, it is often best to shape it so that you have a direct connection to it. Because you already know something about the subject, you have done some thinking about it instead of having to start from scratch or to use secondhand opinions. Even abstract topics such as euthanasia can be made concrete and will probably be the better for it. Though you may have never been confronted directly by the issue of mercy killing, you probably have had a member of your family who was terminally ill. Would euthanasia be an appropriate alternative? Should it be? In addition to using your own experience, consider using your local newspaper. Newspaper accounts and editorials can also help give form and focus to the abstract, and in addition to the book and periodical sources you consult, they will help you delineate your topic more clearly.

AUDIENCE AND PURPOSE   Audience plays a greater role in argument than in any other type of writing, and therein lies a problem: you must adapt both form and content to fit your audience, yet at the same time maintain your integrity. If a writer shapes an argumentative position according to its probable acceptance by the audience rather than its belief by the writer, the result is propaganda, not argument. Knowingly playing false with an audience by omitting evidence or shaping it to fit an assertion, by resorting to logical fallacies, or by stacking the deck are all dishonest tricks.

Within honest bounds, however, you have much to draw upon, and a sense of what the audience may or may not know and of what the audience believes about a topic can guide you. In their essays, Susan Shown Harjo and Ellen Goodman rely heavily on example to familiarize the audience with their topics. Jack Shaheen and Suz Duren, however, deal with well-worn subjects, Shaheen with stereotyping, Duren with curriculum. Yet what's new in the essays is the authors' perspectives on the issues and their own experience with them.

Whether the writers start with their audience's beliefs or lack of information, or with reviewing current situations, all aim at convincing the audience to adopt their convictions, perhaps even to act on them. Not all readers will be convinced, of course, but if they at least respond, "Hmm, I hadn't thought of that" or "Well, I may have to rethink my position," the essay has presented an effective argument.

APPEAL TO REASON   Logical thinking must undergird all argumentative essays, even those that stress an emotional appeal. Thomas B. Stoddard opens "Gay Marriages: Make Them Legal" with an emotion-laden narrative. But he then continues by appealing to reason, using definition and causal analysis to make his case. Cause and effect, definition, analogy, and various other patterns of development can all aid the writer in appealing to reason.

APPEAL TO EMOTION   Example, description, and narration are the basic tools of the emotional appeal. Fidel "Butch" Montoya begins his essay by describing his response to a recent newspaper column that he believed was fanning the "flames of isolationism and ignorance" by disparaging "multiculturalism" and "diversity." Montoya goes on to list examples of "intellectual and emotional apartheid" that have affected Native Americans, Hispanics, African-Americans, Japanese-Americans, Jews, and the gay community. For Montoya, the theory that the United States is a melting pot is a "phony argument." He uses his experience and that of other minorities to argue forcefully in favor of diversity, eliciting the reader's emotions as he makes his case.

APPEAL OF PERSONA   The appeal of **persona**, known in classical rhetoric as *ethos* (which translates somewhat ambiguously as "the ethical appeal"), is more subtle than the others; the writer is not appealing directly to the reader's emotions or intellect but instead is using his or her persona to lend credence to the essay's major assertion. The point gets tricky. A fair and honest writer is one who is fair and honest with the reader. Such a writer takes on a persona, not like donning a mask to hide behind but like selecting a picture to show those elements in the personality that represent the writer at his or her best. Henry Louis Gates, Jr., for example, projects the persona of a cool-headed, reasonable, fair-minded person who is a scholar, yes, but also someone with a good sense of humor and strong belief in the value of "free inquiry."

LOGICAL FALLACIES   **Logical fallacies** abuse the various appeals. Slips in the use of cause and effect, example, analogy, and so on can result in logical fallacies. Ellen Goodman, for instance, accuses Justices Burger and Stewart of several errors in logic in their ruling on the rights of children versus the rights of parents, citing them for **false analogy.** Logical fallacies are, as the term implies, flaws in the appeal to reason, and they are usually classified according to type, such as begging the question, misuse of authority, false analogy, non sequitur, shifting definition, straw man, either-or oversimplification, and *post hoc, propter hoc.* Argument *ad hominem* or *ad populem,* Latin terms for name-calling, are errors in reason as well as an abuse of the appeal to emotions. (See the Glossary of Terms for a fuller discussion of these fallacies.)

THESIS AND ORGANIZATION   The thesis of an argumentative essay should be readily identifiable: it is the conviction that you want an audience to adopt. Sometimes the thesis may be stated in the title, as in Stoddard's "Gay Marriages: Make Them Legal." More often, however, the essay states the position early on, then backs it up with evidence.

This kind of organization that moves from the general (the thesis) to the particular (the evidence) is called *deduction*. Deductive reasoning guides the organization of Suzan Shown Harjo's "Last Rites for Indian Dead" and Fidel "Butch" Montoya's "Multiculturalism and Diversity Are What Make America Great." The opposite kind of reasoning that moves from the particular to the general, from evidence to thesis, is called *induction*. Inductive reasoning is used by Ellen Goodman and Molefi Kete Asante. As for the other essays, you'll have to decide for yourself.

USEFUL TERMS

Ad hominem argument   Name-calling, smearing the person instead of attacking the argument. A type of logical fallacy.

Ad populum argument   Name-calling, smearing the group the person belongs to instead of attacking the argument. A type of logical fallacy.

Appeal to emotion   Playing or appealing to the reader's emotions.

Appeal to persona   The appeal of the writer's moral character that creates the impression that the writer can be trusted and therefore believed.

Appeal to reason   Presenting evidence that is logical, well thought out, so as to be believed.

Argument   The writer's major assertion and the evidence on which it is based.

Begging the question   Arguing off the point, changing direction. A type of logical fallacy.

Deductive reasoning   Reasoning that moves from the general to the particular, from the thesis to the evidence.

Either-or reasoning   Staking out two extremes as the only alternatives and therefore excluding anything in between. A type of logical fallacy.

False analogy   An analogy that does not stand up to logic. A type of logical fallacy.

False authority   Citing an expert on one subject as an expert on another. A type of logical fallacy.

Hasty generalization   Reasoning based on insufficient evidence, usually too few examples. A type of logical fallacy.

Inductive reasoning   Reasoning that moves from the particular to the general, from the evidence to the thesis.

Logical fallacy   An error in reasoning, a logical flaw that invalidates the argument.

Non sequitur   Literally, it does not follow. No apparent link between points. A type of logical fallacy.

Persona   The character of the writer that comes through from the prose.

Post hoc reasoning   Assuming a causal relationship where a temporal one exists. A type of logical fallacy.

Shifting definition   Changing the definition of a key term, a form of begging the question. A type of logical fallacy.

Straw man   Attacking and destroying an irrelevant point instead of the main subject.

IDEAS FOR WRITING   Jot down any issues that you feel strongly about. What's important here is that you have a connection with the subject, so how large or small that subject may be is irrelevant. Perhaps you are intolerant about intolerance, care passionately about adding a salad bar to the college cafeteria, support a particular political candidate. Whatever list you come up with, look over it carefully to see what might work best for an argument. Once you've selected a subject, make up two columns, one for arguments in favor and the other for arguments against. Next, see which side you want to take and then number the arguments you want to use as evidence in order of their strength. You probably want to build your case dramatically, so save your best argument till last. For a conclusion, try taking up one of the arguments that can be used against you, summarize it and destroy it.

POINTERS FOR USING ARGUMENT

Exploring the Topic

1. **What position do you want to take toward your subject?** Are you arguing to get your audience to adopt your conviction or to go further and take action? What is your conviction? What action is possible?

2. **How is your audience apt to respond to your conviction if you state it baldly?** How much background do they need you to provide? Do you need to use definition? What arguments can the reader bring against your assertion?

3. **What examples can you think of to illustrate your topic?** Are all of them from your own experience? What other sources can you draw upon?

4. **How can you appeal to your readers' emotions?** How can you use example, description, and narration to carry your emotional appeal?
5. **How can you appeal to your readers' reason?** How can you use example, cause and effect, process, comparison and contrast, analogy, or division and classification to strengthen your logic?
6. **What tone is most appropriate to the kind of appeal you want to emphasize?** Does your persona fit that tone? How can you use persona to support your argument?

Drafting the Paper

1. **Know your reader.** Estimate how familiar your reader is with your topic and how, if at all, the reader may react to it emotionally. Keeping those ideas in mind, review how the various patterns of development may help you contend with your audience's knowledge and attitudes, and decide whether your primary appeal should be to emotion or reason. Description, narration, and example lend themselves particularly well to emotional appeal; process, cause and effect, comparison and contrast, analogy, example, and division and classification are useful to rational appeal. Use definition to set the boundaries of your argument and its terms as well as to clear up anything the reader may not know.
2. **Know your purpose.** Depending on the predominant appeal you find most appropriate, your essay will tend toward persuasion or argument; you are trying to get your reader not only to understand your major assertion but also to adopt it and perhaps even act on it. Short of that, a successful writer of argument must settle for the reader's "Well, I hadn't thought of it that way" or "Maybe I should reconsider." The greatest danger in argumentative writing is to write to people like yourself, ones who already agree with you. You need not think of your audience as actively hostile, but to stay on the argumentative track, it helps to reread constantly as you write, playing the devil's advocate.
3. **Acknowledge the opposition.** Even though your reader may be the ideal, someone who holds no definite opposing view and indeed is favorably inclined toward yours but hasn't really thought the topic through, you should bring out one or two of the strongest arguments against your position and demolish them. If *you* don't, the reader may, and there goes your essay. The ideal reader is also the thinking reader who says, "Yes, but. . . ."
4. **Avoid logical pitfalls.** Logical fallacies can crop up in unexpected places; one useful way to test them is to check your patterns of development. If you have used examples, does your generalization or assertion follow? Sometimes the examples are too few to support the assertion, leading to a hasty generalization; sometimes the examples don't

fit, leading to begging the question or arguing off the point or misusing authority; and sometimes the assertion is stated as an absolute, in which case the reader may use an example as the exception that destroys your point. If you have used analogy, double-check to see that the analogy can stand up to scrutiny by examining the pertinent aspects of the things compared. If you have used cause and effect, you need to be particularly careful. Check to see that the events you claim to have a causal relationship are not related instead by a temporal one, or else you fall into the *post hoc, ergo propter hoc* fallacy. Also examine causal relationships to make sure that you have not merely assumed the cause in your statement of effect. If you claim that "poor teaching is a major cause of the high dropout rate freshman year in college," you must prove that the teaching is poor; if you don't you are arguing in a circle or begging the question. Non sequiturs can also obscure cause-and-effect relationships when an element in the relationship is missing or nonexistent. The reader's response is "It does not follow," in Latin *non sequitur*. Definition also sets some traps. Make sure your definition is not only fully stated but also commonly shared and consistent throughout. (All of the logical fallacies referred to in this section are defined more fully in the Glossary of Terms.)

5. **Be aware of your persona.** The ethical appeal, the rational appeal, and the emotional appeal are fundamental concepts of argument, and it is the persona, together with tone, that provides the ethical appeal. To put it simply, you need to be credible. If you are writing on an issue you feel strongly about and, for example, are depending primarily on an appeal to reason, you don't want to let your dispassionate, logical persona slip and resort to name-calling (formally known as arguing *ad hominem* or *ad populem*). That's obvious. Not so obvious, however, is the same slip in diction or tone that reveals the hot head behind the cool pen. Your reader may feel manipulated or use the slip to discount your entire argument, all because you lost sight of the ethical appeal. Tone should vary, yes, but never to the point of discord.

6. **Place your point where it does the most good.** Put each of your paragraphs on a separate piece of paper so that you can rearrange their order as you would a hand of cards. Try out your major assertion in different slots. If you have it at the beginning, try it at the end and vice versa. Or extend the introduction so that the thesis comes closer to the middle of the paper. See which placement carries greater impact. You may want to organize your material starting with examples that lead up to the position you wish to attack and to the conviction you are arguing for; in that case your thesis may occur somewhere in the middle third or at the end of the paper. On the other hand, you may want to use deduction, starting with the opposition, stating your position, and then

spending 90 percent of the remaining essay supporting your case. Remember that you want to win over your reader, so put your thesis where it will do the greatest good.

Dangerous Shelter

Suz Duren

Suz Duren was enrolled in a composition class at the University of New Orleans that culminates in a proficiency examination—an argumentative essay on a choice of two statements. "Dangerous Shelter" is Duren's essay written in response to a practice test: "Some parents have argued that they should have veto power over which books may be taught in public high schools. (In various states, parents have objected to such works as Adventures of Huckleberry Finn, Alice in Wonderland, The Catcher in the Rye, *and* The Shining.) *Argue for or against parents playing such a role in curriculum decisions."*

Born in Tulsa, Oklahoma, Suz Duren moved to New Orleans in 1988 and is majoring in Fine Arts with a concentration in painting. She intends to continue her education in an MFA program and to pursue a career as a professional artist. She describes her paintings as "mostly representational, using manipulations in color, size, and focal point to achieve emotional images on canvas." As you read her essay, you will find similar qualities.

WHAT TO LOOK FOR   *Choosing a title for an essay gives a writer an opportunity to shape the reader's expectations: a title can state or hint at the subject, suggest the writer's thesis, set up the tone, arouse the reader's curiosity. Duren hooks the reader with a paradox. As you read her essay, think about the ways in which the title fits.*

KEY WORDS AND PHRASES
empowering (1)   ramifications (4)
impending (2)   flounder (4)

1   One of the most empowering spaces in a public high school is the library. Shelves of ideas, volumes of brilliance, lie in wait to introduce the unknown, to broaden the imagination and to challenge the intellect. Often, teachers will choose books such as *The Adventures of Huckleberry Finn* or *Go Ask Alice* for class study. However, some parents find controversial issues in these and other books. Wanting to limit educational horizons strictly to their own

beliefs, these parents are arguing for the power to select which books can and cannot be taught in public high schools. Not only would this parental power be nonproductive in a practical sense, it would be counterproductive in an educational sense.

2   Practically, the impending debates over which books are not deemed appropriate for teenagers would be never-ending. One parent might argue that there is too much explicit information concerning drugs and drug use in *Go Ask Alice,* while another parent, perhaps concerned about the sexual matter in *Madame Bovary,* would feel her teenager could benefit from the content of *Go Ask Alice*. In other words, one parent's insult is another parent's lesson.

3   Also, it is simply not the job of parents to run our public high schools. Just as we have lawyers to speak for us in court, doctors to diagnose and treat our illnesses, and various other advisers to assist us in specific areas of our lives, so we have educators who are trained to give our youth a complete and balanced education. These educators should be allowed to create a varied and thought-friendly curriculum.

4   Most important, though, is the educational aspect. Secondary schooling is designed to prepare young adults for life in society. The ramifications of the censure-happy parents would be the sheltering of teenagers from reality. Imagine the teenager, upon high school graduation, who has never been exposed to extreme political ideas or information about culture, religious, and ethnic differences. How long will that individual have to flounder in the real world after the protective shield of "morality," the tunnel-vision, has been lifted? How easy will it be for her to find a balance without having had the preparation in more formative years?

5   And, finally, allowing parents to wield such power in decisions concerning printed material is a dangerous step toward censorship. We must make certain that all ideas are protected. Knowledge is power. Ideas are meant to be absorbed, dissected, analyzed, and challenged. The more information we have, the better equipped we are to make rational decisions. If we continue to make ideas of all sorts available to our youth, help them to understand the content, and trust them to build their lives based on that knowledge, then they have the advantage to be productive and successful adults.

Thesis and Organization

1. Identify the thesis. Where is it placed?
2. What point is Duren making with the examples of *Go Ask Alice* and *Madame Bovary?*
3. Paragraph 3 presents a series of analogies. To what extent are they accurate?
4. What would be a good topic sentence for paragraph 4? How necessary is it?
5. Does paragraph 5 function as another point, a conclusion, or both? How so?

Technique and Style

1. How does the writer establish her authority, the knowledge that gives her credibility?
2. Look up the term *rhetorical question* in a handbook of usage. To what extent does Duren use this type of question effectively?
3. To pinpoint the quality of voice, jot down your impressions of the writer. What sort of person does she seem to be?
4. What transitions does Duren use to guide the reader through the essay?
5. What principle can you discern behind Duren's sequencing of the points in her argument? Explain whether or not you find it effective.

Suggestions for Writing

If you agree with Duren, you can write an essay that takes your own approach to the subject, citing examples out of your experience to support your point. If you don't agree, then you can use the essay as a backboard that you bounce your own ideas off of, again citing examples to make your point. But if the subject doesn't hold much interest for you, think about writing on one related to education or censorship: required courses, the grading system, sex education, rating systems for films and recordings, violence on television, pornography. No matter what your subject, make up your own prompt and then respond to it with your essay.

Last Rites for Indian Dead

Suzan Shown Harjo

Writing as a Cheyenne, Suzan Shown Harjo points to a problem that affects Native Americans and, she argues, it raises an ethical issue for the rest of us. Her essay appeared on the editorial page of the Los Angeles Times *in September 1989.*

WHAT TO LOOK FOR   *Conclusions are often difficult to write, but one way of ending an argumentative essay is to call for a specified action. That is what Harjo does in her essay, and it's a technique you can adapt for your own argument.*

KEY WORDS AND PHRASES
archeological (2)	desecrated (7)
disinterred (3)	macabre (10)
Daniel Webster (4)	curation (11)
excruciating (5)	funerary (15)

1   What if museums, universities, and government agencies could put your dead relatives on display or keep them in boxes to be cut up and otherwise studied? What if you believed that the spirits of the dead could not rest until their human remains were placed in a sacred area?

2   The ordinary American would say there ought to be a law—and there is, for ordinary Americans. The problem for American Indians is that there are too many laws of the kind that make us the archaeological property of the United States and too few of the kind that protect us from such insults.

3   Some of my own Cheyenne relatives' skulls are in the Smithsonian Institution today, along with those of at least 4500 other Indian people who were violated in the 1800s by the U.S. Army for an "Indian Cranial Study." It wasn't enough that these unarmed Cheyenne people were mowed down by the cavalry at the infamous Sand Creek massacre; many were decapitated and their

257

heads shipped to Washington as freight. (The Army Medical Museum's collection is now in the Smithsonian.) Some had been exhumed only hours after being buried. Imagine their grieving families' reaction on finding their loved ones disinterred and headless.

4   Some targets of the Army's study were killed in noncombat situations and beheaded immediately. The officer's account of the decapitation of the Apache chief Mangas Coloradas in 1863 shows the pseudoscientific nature of the exercise. "I weighed the brain and measured the skull," the good doctor wrote, "and found that while the skull was smaller, the brain was larger than that of Daniel Webster."

5   These journal accounts exist in excruciating detail, yet missing are any records of overall comparisons, conclusions or final reports of the Army study. Since it is unlike the Army not to leave a paper trail, one must wonder about the motive for its collection.

6   The total Indian body count in the Smithsonian collection is more than 19,000, and it is not the largest in the country. It is not inconceivable that the 1.5 million of us living today are outnumbered by our dead stored in museums, educational institutions, federal agencies, state historical societies and private collections. The Indian people are further dehumanized by being exhibited alongside the mastodons and dinosaurs and other extinct creatures.

7   Where we have buried our dead in peace, more often than not the sites have been desecrated. For more than 200 years, relic hunting has been a popular pursuit. Lately, the market in Indian artifacts has brought this abhorrent activity to a fever pitch in some areas. And when scavengers come upon Indian burial sites, everything found becomes fair game, including sacred burial offerings, teeth and skeletal remains.

8   One unusually well-publicized example of Indian grave desecration occurred two years ago in a western Kentucky field known as Slack Farm, the site of an Indian village five centuries ago. Ten men—one with a business card stating "Have Shovel, Will Travel"—paid the landowner $10,000 to lease digging rights between planting seasons. They dug extensively on the 40-acre farm, rummaging through an estimated 650 graves, collecting burial goods, tools and ceremonial items. Skeletons were strewn about like litter.

9   What motivates people to do something like this? Financial gain is the first answer. Indian relic-collecting has become a multimillion-dollar industry. The price tag on a bead necklace can easily top $1000; rare pieces fetch tens of thousands.

10   And it is not just collectors of the macabre who pay for skeletal remains. Scientists say that these deceased Indians are needed for research that someday could benefit the health and welfare of living Indians. But just how many dead Indians must they examine? Nineteen thousand?

11   There is doubt as to whether permanent curation of our dead really benefits Indians. Dr. Emery A. Johnson, former assistant surgeon general, recently observed, "I am not aware of any current medical diagnostic or treatment procedure that has been derived from research on such skeletal remains. Nor am I aware of any during the 34 years that I have been involved in American Indian . . . health care."

12   Indian remains are still being collected for racial biological studies. While the intentions may be honorable, the ethics of using human remains this way without the full consent of relatives must be questioned.

13   Some relief for Indian people has come on the state level. Almost half of the states, including California, have passed laws protecting Indian burial sites and restricting the sale of Indian bones, burial offerings and other sacred items. Representative Charles E. Bennett (D-Fla.) and Sen. John McCain (R-Ariz.) have introduced bills that are a good start in invoking the federal government's protection. However, no legislation has attacked the problem head-on by imposing stiff penalties at the marketplace, or by changing laws that make dead Indians the nation's property.

14   Some universities—notably Stanford, Nebraska, Minnesota and Seattle—have returned, or agreed to return, Indian human remains; it is fitting that institutions of higher education should lead the way.

15   Congress is now deciding what to do with the government's extensive collection of Indian human remains and associated funerary objects. The secretary of the Smithsonian, Robert McC. Adams, has been valiantly attempting to apply modern ethics to yesterday's excesses. This week, he announced that the Smithsonian would conduct an inventory and return all Indian skeletal remains that could be identified with specific tribes or living kin.

16   But there remains a reluctance generally among collectors of Indian remains to take action of a scope that would have a quantitative impact and a healing quality. If they will not act on their own— and it is highly unlikely that they will—then Congress must act.

17   The country must recognize that the bodies of dead American Indian people are not artifacts to be bought and sold as collectors's

items. It is not appropriate to store tens of thousands of our ancestors for possible future research. They are our family. They deserve
to be returned to their sacred burial grounds and given a chance to
rest.

18   The plunder of our people's graves has gone on too long. Let
us rebury our dead and remove this shameful past from America's
future.

Thesis and Organization

1. Paragraphs 1 and 2 introduce the essay by presenting a "What if?" situation. Why might Harjo have chosen this kind of opening?
2. Harjo presents examples in paragraphs 3–8. Summarize them.
3. Paragraphs 9–12 explain why people dig up Indian burial sites. What
   reasons does Harjo give?
4. Harjo explains what is being done, and what needs to be done, about
   the situation in paragraphs 13–18. What solution does she call for?
5. Considering the situation Harjo describes, the steps that are being
   taken to address that situation, and what remains to be done, what is
   the thesis of the essay?

Technique and Style

1. Describe the audience the essay is aimed at as precisely as you can.
   What evidence do you base your description upon?
2. How would you characterize the diction Harjo uses in connection with
   her examples? Choose one or two examples and substitute more, or
   less, loaded words. What is gained? Lost?
3. Considering the way the essay is written, what kind of person does
   Harjo appear to be? How would you describe her?
4. To what extent does the essay rest its appeal on Harjo's persona? On
   emotion? On logic? Which appeal predominates?
5. The essay concludes with a call for action. Evaluate the effectiveness of
   that call.

Suggestions for Writing

Think of an action that in the past was considered acceptable but today is
either questionable or unacceptable. Years ago, for instance, no one
thought much about the hazards of smoking, or of cholesterol levels, or of
needing to inspect meat. Segregation was acceptable, as were other forms
of racism. Choose a subject and think about the ethics involved, how present knowledge has changed how we live, and what remains to be done.

Gay Marriages: Make Them Legal

Thomas B. Stoddard

What is traditional is not always what is right, so Thomas B. Stoddard argues in the essay that follows. He calls for a redefinition of marriage that accommodates the legal status of matrimony to the present times. Stoddard is an attorney and executive director of the Lambda Legal Defense and Education Fund, a gay rights organization.

Stoddard's essay was published as an opinion piece in the New York Times *in 1989. Since that time, the narrative Stoddard opens with has developed a different ending: Kowalski's parents stopped paying the bills for the nursing home, and she was then released into the care of Karen Thompson.*

WHAT TO LOOK FOR *Definition is a key element in argument. Note how careful Stoddard is to define* marriage *in paragraphs 4 and 5. When you write your own argumentative paper, first identify the most important term and then make sure early on in your paper that you define it carefully.*

KEY WORDS AND PHRASES
jurisdiction (1)   sanctimonious (10)
miscegenation (7)

1   "In sickness and in health, 'til death do us part." With those familiar words, millions of people each year are married, a public affirmation of a private bond that both society and the newlyweds hope will endure. Yet for nearly four years, Karen Thompson was denied the company of the one person to whom she had pledged lifelong devotion. Her partner is a woman, Sharon Kowalski, and their home state of Minnesota, like every other jurisdiction in the United States, refuses to permit two individuals of the same sex to marry.

2   Karen Thompson and Sharon Kowalski are spouses in every respect except the legal. They exchanged vows and rings; they lived

together until November 13, 1983—when Ms. Kowalski was se-
verely injured when her car was struck by a drunk driver. She lost
the capacity to walk or to speak more than several words at a time,
and needed constant care.

3   Ms. Thompson sought a court ruling granting her guardianship
over her partner, but Ms. Kowalski's parents opposed the petition
and obtained sole guardianship. They moved Ms. Kowalski to a
nursing home 300 miles away from Ms. Thompson and forbade all
visits between the two women. Last month, as part of a reevalua-
tion of Ms. Kowalski's mental competency, Ms. Thompson was
permitted to visit her partner again. But the prolonged injustice
and anguish inflicted on both women hold a moral for everyone.

4   Marriage, the Supreme Court declared in 1967, is "one of the basic civil rights of man" (and, presumably, of woman as well). The
freedom to marry, said the Court, is "essential to the orderly pursuit of happiness."

5   Marriage is not just a symbolic state. It can be the key to survival, emotional and financial. Marriage triggers a universe of
rights, privileges and presumptions. A married person can share in
a spouse's estate even when there is no will. She is typically entitled to the group insurance and pension programs offered by the
spouse's employer, and she enjoys tax advantages. She cannot be
compelled to testify against her spouse in legal proceedings.

6   The decision whether or not to marry belongs properly to individuals—not the government. Yet at present, all 50 states deny that
choice to millions of gay and lesbian Americans. While marriage
has historically required a male partner and a female partner, history alone cannot sanctify injustice. If tradition were the only measure, most states would still limit matrimony to partners of the
same race.

7   As recently as 1967, before the Supreme Court declared miscegenation statutes unconstitutional, 16 states still prohibited marriages between a white person and a black person. When all the
excuses were stripped away, it was clear that the only purpose of
those laws was, in the words of the Supreme Court, "to maintain
white supremacy."

8   Those who argue against reforming the marriage statutes because they believe that same-sex marriage would be "antifamily"
overlook the obvious: marriage creates families and promotes social stability. In an increasingly loveless world, those who wish to

commit themselves to a relationship founded upon devotion should be encouraged, not scorned. Government has no legitimate interest in how that love is expressed.

9   And it can no longer be argued—if it ever could—that marriage is fundamentally a procreative unit. Otherwise, states would forbid marriage between those who, by reason of age or infertility, cannot have children, as well as those who elect not to.

10   As the case of Sharon Kowalski and Karen Thompson demonstrates, sanctimonious illusions lead directly to the suffering of others. Denied the right to marry, these two women are left subject to the whims and prejudices of others, and of the law.

11   Depriving millions of gay American adults the marriages of their choice, and the rights that flow from marriage, denies equal protection of the law. They, their families and friends, together with fair-minded people everywhere, should demand an end to this monstrous injustice.

Thesis and Organization

1. Paragraphs 1–3 present an example that holds a "moral for everyone." What is it?
2. Paragraphs 4 and 5 define marriage. What point does Stoddard make about marriage?
3. Paragraphs 6–9 are aimed at countering arguments that can be used against Stoddard's view. Summarize them.
4. What is the effect of paragraph 10? What other paragraphs does it connect with?
5. The essay concludes with a statement of thesis and a call to action. Who should demand what and how?

Technique and Style

1. What paragraph or paragraphs appeal to the reader's emotions?
2. What paragraph or paragraphs appeal to the reader's reason?
3. Where in the essay can you identify an ethical appeal, an appeal based on the author's persona?
4. Stoddard cites the arguments that can be used against his. Does he cite obvious ones? Is his treatment of them fair? How so?
5. Stoddard's subject is a sensitive one and his views may not be shared by many readers. Where in the essay can you find evidence that he is aware of his readers and their potential sensitivity to the issue he writes about?

Suggestions for Writing

Think of an issue that ought to be covered by a law or one that is governed by law and should not be. For example, you may think some laws unjust—the 55 mph speed limit, the legal age, zoning or IRS regulations. Or you may think of something that should be required by law—car insurance, automobile safety seats for infants, helmets for motorcycle riders, neutering of pets.

Multiculturalism and Diversity Make America Great

Fidel "Butch" Montoya

The essay that follows appeared on the editorial page of Denver's Rocky Mountain News *in June 1993. Denver, where Montoya is a television news producer, is very much a multicultural city, having a large Hispanic and African-American population. It was the Hispanics who opposed the "English-only" movement that would have made English the official—and only— language in Colorado. Some of the resentment evident at that time spills over into the essay.*

WHAT TO LOOK FOR *It's often hard to write coolly about a hot issue, particularly one you feel strongly about. The problem is made all the more difficult if you are attacking a position held by another person. As you read Montoya's essay, notice how he tries to avoid offending the person whose position he attacks.*

KEY WORDS AND PHRASES
Balkanization (1)	paranoia (10)
articulate (1)	bigotry (10)
multiculturalism (2)	Manifest Destiny (11)
Bosnia (7)	Treaty of Guadalupe-Hidalgo (11)
apartheid (9)	

1   The headline, "The Balkanization of the United States," caught my attention, and so I read the recent column by *Rocky Mountain News* associate editor Clifford D. May. May is one of the brightest people I have met. He is thoughtful, informed, articulate and one of the best columnists around.

2   Needless to say, then, I was disappointed with May's misconception of multiculturalism and diversity.

3   Several years ago, former governor Richard Lamm fed the same flames of isolationism and ignorance by stating his reasons for essentially endorsing the English-only movement in Colorado. For his views, Lamm found out the hard way that Hispanics do not forget and didn't support his recent candidacy for the U.S. Senate.

4   Now we're hearing again the same misguided view of those who say "multiculturalism" or "diversity" are bad for the United States. May even goes on to question the patriotism of "blacks, Hispanics, Jews, females, gays and whatever" because of their pride in cultural, ethnic or gender backgrounds. May wants to know how many will "just as assertively stand up and say they are proud to be American?"

5   May does not understand the struggles and painful progress made by minority communities. It's easy to say "E pluribus unum—one out of many," when you are in the majority community or when you hold all the good cards in the card game.

6   I don't know of many "minorities" who wouldn't assertively stand up and say with pride, "We are Americans! Just because we may be different doesn't make us any less American!" Those who would refuse to stand up are those who have given up on the U.S. Constitution and its broken promises of liberty and guarantees of justice for everyone.

7   It's easy to draw parallels to Bosnia, especially when you have the most to lose. If I were a white, middle- to upper-class male, I'd be frightened, too. I would be afraid I could lose my good job, my nice home, my financial investments, my social standing in the community, my ability to influence opinions, and my ability to dictate political policy in the community.

8   "Those other people" might take it away from me if they were given the same opportunities, especially if they're different from me and proud of their diversity. If "those other people" who were different from me took over, they might follow their own social and political agenda and exclude me from it. A scary thought if you were a white, middle- to upper-class male, wouldn't you think?

9   May says, "An unrelenting emphasis on diversity, on the barriers between separate communities, can only lead to intellectual and emotional apartheid."

10   Those barriers, however, already exist, and they were forced on us by members of the majority community. If there is intellectual and emotional apartheid today, it's because paranoia, racism, ignorance and bigotry have been force-fed throughout our history to members of minority communities.

11   Ask the Native Americans about Manifest Destiny, the Spanish and Mexicans about the Treaty of Guadalupe-Hidalgo, the African-Americans about their heritage of slavery and bondage, the Japan-

ese about their treatment by this government during World War II, the Jewish people about their treatment at the hands of Nazi Germany and America's reluctance to enter the war. Go and ask the gay community about the effects of Amendment 2, and you will find that intellectual and emotional apartheid already exists—and it wasn't born in our communities.

12   Diversity and multiculturalism, and the ability to retain the richness of our cultural heritage is what makes America a great country. The theory of the melting pot taught in our history classes was a phony argument. We're a country that needs to be able to tolerate and appreciate the need for diversity.

13   It's when we hear the call to devalue the richness of diversity and multiculturalism that we must take a stand as proud Americans and put to rest the folly of the ignorant.

Thesis and Organization

1. Montoya is writing in response to a column by Clifford May. Where in the essay does he summarize what May said? To what extent does the summary seem fair?
2. Much of the essay focuses on what it means to be an American. What is May's answer? What is Montoya's?
3. Montoya argues that barriers among ethnic groups exist because of the way minorities have been treated, citing examples of that treatment (11). Choose one of these examples, look it up in an encyclopedia, and be prepared to explain it to the class. How apt is the example?
4. What relationship do you find between the examples in paragraph 11 and the last sentence of paragraph 6? What does the link add to the essay?
5. The title of the essay clearly states its thesis, yet you know that often an introduction or conclusion contains the thesis. How effective do you find Montoya's placement?

Technique and Style

1. In paragraphs 5, 7, and 8, Montoya tries to convey to the majority how it feels to be a minority. How well does he succeed?
2. Montoya obviously feels strongly about his topic, and a conviction can be expressed in many ways. How would you describe Montoya's tone—is he angry or cool-headed, passionate or reasoned, more emotional or more rational? What examples can you find to support your opinion?

3. Montoya uses "we" in paragraph 13. Reread the essay noting the times he uses *we*. Is he always referring to the same group? Who is the "we" in paragraph 13?

4. The first sentence of paragraph 6 illustrates two uses of quotation marks. Describe how they differ.

Suggestions for Writing

Think of a word that identifies you (or someone you know well) so you can write an "I am a _____" paper. The possibilities are almost endless, depending on how you see yourself (or someone close to you) at any given time. Perhaps, like Montoya, you see yourself as an American and a member of a specific ethnic group, but instead you may see yourself as a mother, father, brother, or sister; republican, democrat, independent, liberal, or conservative; overworked student, jaded voter, or blitzed TV viewer. Choose examples that clearly illustrate your point. As an alternative, look through the editorial page of your local newspaper and choose a letter or editorial that you disagree with. Write an essay attacking that position and arguing for your own, using examples to support your view.

*T*he Media's Image of Arabs

Jack G. Shaheen

Surprisingly, Jack G. Shaheen's essay appeared in February 1988, almost three years before the Gulf War when anti-Arab emotions in the U.S. were at their height. Although, ironically, back in 1988 Shaheen saw some shifts toward a more positive portrayal of Arabs in the media, his essay shows us that the seeds of that anti-Arab feeling had been planted for some time. Shaheen should know. He keeps track of the media for a living, teaching mass communications at Southern Illinois University. His essay was published in the "My Turn" column in Newsweek.

WHAT TO LOOK FOR   *Evidence to be used as support for a thesis can come from a number of sources, the most accessible of which is personal experience. Yet an essay that uses only personal experience to make its point runs the risk of having too narrow a base—one person's experience may not be representative. To avoid that danger, you may follow Shaheen's example, introducing your essay with what you have experienced first hand and then relying on other sources for the bulk of your argument.*

KEY WORDS AND PHRASES
caricatures (3)	scimitars (6)
humane (5)	Valhalla (8)

1   America's bogyman is the Arab. Until the nightly news brought us TV pictures of Palestinian boys being punched and beaten, almost all portraits of Arabs seen in America were dangerously threatening. Arabs were either billionaires or bombers—rarely victims. They were hardly ever seen as ordinary people practicing law, driving taxis, singing lullabies or healing the sick. Though TV news may portray them more sympathetically now, the absence of positive media images nurtures suspicion and stereotype. As an Arab-American, I have found that ugly caricatures have had an enduring impact on my family.

2   I was sheltered from prejudicial portraits at first. My parents came from Lebanon in the 1920s; they met and married in America. Our home in the steel city of Clairton, Pa., was a center for

ethnic sharing—black, white, Jew and gentile. There was only one major source of media images then, at the State movie theater where I was lucky enough to get a part-time job as an usher. But in the late 1940s, Westerns and war movies were popular, not Middle Eastern dramas. Memories of World War II were fresh, and the screen heavies were the Japanese and the Germans. True to the cliché of the times, the only good Indian was a dead Indian. But when I mimicked or mocked the bad guys, my mother cautioned me. She explained that stereotypes blur our vision and corrupt the imagination. "Have compassion for all people, Jackie," she said. "This way, you'll learn to experience the joy of accepting people as they are, and not as they appear in films. Stereotypes hurt."

3   Mother was right. I can remember the Saturday afternoon when my son, Michael, who was seven, and my daughter, Michele, six, suddenly called out: "Daddy, Daddy, they've got some bad Arabs on TV." They were watching that great American morality play, TV wrestling. Akbar the Great, who liked to hear the cracking of bones, and Abdullah the Butcher, a dirty fighter who liked to inflict pain, were pinning their foes with "camel locks." From that day on, I knew I had to try to neutralize the media caricatures.

4   It hasn't been easy. With my children, I have watched animated heroes Heckle and Jeckle pull the rug from under "Ali Boo-Boo, the Desert Rat," and Laverne and Shirley stop "Sheik Ha-Mean-Ie" from conquering "the U.S. and the world." I have read comic books like the "Fantastic Four" and "G.I. Combat" whose characters have sketched Arabs as "lowlifes" and "human hyenas." Negative stereotypes were everywhere. A dictionary informed my youngsters that an Arab is a "vagabond, drifter, hobo and vagrant." Whatever happened, my wife wondered, to Aladdin's good genie?

5   To a child, the world is simple: good versus evil. But my children and others with Arab roots grew up without ever having seen a humane Arab on the silver screen, someone to pattern their lives after. Is it easier for a camel to go through the eye of a needle than for a screen Arab to appear as a genuine human being?

6   Hollywood producers must have an instant Ali Baba kit that contains scimitars, veils, sunglasses and such Arab clothing as *chadors* and *kufiyahs*. In the mythical "Ay-rabland," oil wells, tents, mosques, goats and shepherds prevail. Between the sand dunes, the camera focuses on a mock-up of a palace from "Ara-

bian Nights"—or a military air base. Recent movies suggest that Americans are at war with Arabs, forgetting the fact that out of 21 Arab nations, America is friendly with 19 of them. And in "Wanted Dead or Alive," a movie that starred Gene Simmons, the leader of the rock group Kiss, the war comes home when an Arab terrorist comes to the United States dressed as a rabbi and, among other things, conspires with Arab-Americans to poison the people of Los Angeles. The movie was released last year.

7   **Racial slurs:** The Arab remains American culture's favorite whipping boy. In his memoirs, Terrel Bell, Ronald Reagan's first secretary of education, writes about an "apparent bias among mid-level, right-wing staffers at the White House" who dismissed Arabs as "sand niggers." Sadly, the racial slurs continue. At a recent teacher's conference, I met a woman from Sioux Falls, S.D., who told me about the persistence of discrimination. She was in the process of adopting a baby when the agency staffer warned her that the infant had a problem. When she asked whether the child was mentally ill, or physically handicapped, there was silence. Finally, the worker said: "The baby is Jordanian."

8   To me, the Arab demon of today is much like the Jewish demon of yesterday. We deplore the false portrait of Jews as a swarthy menace. Yet a similar portrait has been accepted and transferred to another group of Semites—the Arabs. Print and broadcast journalists have started to challenge this stereotype. They are now revealing more humane images of Palestinian Arabs, a people who traditionally suffered from the myth that Palestinian equals terrorist. Others could follow that lead and retire the stereotypical Arab to a media Valhalla.

9   It would be a step in the right direction if movie and TV producers developed characters modeled after real-life Arab-Americans. We could then see a White House correspondent like Helen Thomas, whose father came from Lebanon, in "The Golden Girls," a heart surgeon patterned after Dr. Michael DeBakey on "St. Elsewhere," or a Syrian-American playing tournament chess like Yasser Seirawan, the Seattle grandmaster.

10   Politicians, too should speak out against the cardboard caricatures. They should refer to Arabs as friends, not just as moderates. And religious leaders could state that Islam like Christianity and Judaism maintains that all mankind is one family in the care of God. When all imagemakers rightfully begin to treat Arabs and all other

minorities with respect and dignity, we may begin to unlearn our prejudices.

Thesis and Organization

1. Paragraph 1 introduces the essay by stating an assertion in the first sentence and then ending with the essay's thesis. What principle guides the organization of the paragraph?
2. Shaheen focuses on the image of Arabs in popular culture, using examples to illustrate his point. What paragraphs deal with what examples?
3. Think about the order in which Shaheen presents his examples. Why do you think he presents them in that order?
4. What paragraph or paragraphs provide a conclusion to the essay? What reasons can you find for your choice?
5. Reread the introduction and conclusion. What sentence best states the essay's thesis and why?

Technique and Style

1. Argumentative essays rely on appeals to reason, emotion, and the writer's credibility. Which appeal to you think dominates Shaheen's essay, and why?
2. In paragraph 8, Shaheen uses a comparison. Why might he have chosen that particular example?
3. Where in the essay does the writer use very short sentences? What is their effect?
4. Look up *irony* in the Glossary of Terms or in an unabridged dictionary. What examples can you find of Shaheen's use of this device. What effect does it have?
5. Shaheen draws his examples from different sources. To what extent does the variety of sources support the essay's appeal to reason?

Suggestions for Writing

Justly or unjustly, many people have criticized television programming and commercials for stereotyping and for presenting a biased view of various groups—women, old people, minorities, teenagers, lawyers, and so on. With a particular group that you identify with in mind, watch a day's worth of television to see if you think the charge of stereotyping or bias (choose one or the other) is justified. Using what you saw as evidence together with your personal experience, write a letter to the editor of your local paper, taking a stand on the issue of bias in television.

C hecks on Parental Power

Ellen Goodman

In a syndicated column published in 1981, Ellen Goodman reacts to a Supreme Court ruling, attacking the position taken by the Court and arguing the opposing view. Note the essay's appeals both to emotion and to reason.

WHAT TO LOOK FOR   *Often a certain amount of summary is necessary in argumentative writing, particularly if you're writing in response to a specific action or ruling. When you hit that problem, you would do well to refer to Goodman's essay to see how to handle summary smoothly.*

KEY WORDS AND PHRASES
truant *(3)*   pathologically *(7)*
promiscuous *(5)*   incarceration *(9)*
incorrigible *(5)*   infringement *(9)*

1   First. consider the stories.

2   An 11-year-old retarded boy was brought to a mental hospital with a teddy bear under his arm. His parents were, they said, going on a two-week vacation. They never came back.

3   A 12-year-old "tomboy" and truant was committed to a mental hospital by her mother after school authorities threatened the woman with prosecution.

4   A 7-year-old boy's mother died one year, and he was committed the next year by his father—two days before the man's remarriage. The diagnosis: a reaction of childhood.

5   Consider, too, the story of one child committed because he had "school phobia," another because she was "promiscuous," a third and fourth because they were "difficult" or even "incorrigible."

6   Then, when you've heard the stories, listen to Justice Warren Burger insist that the "natural bonds of affection lead parents to act in the best interests of their children."

7   Last Wednesday the Supreme Court assured all parents—the confused and the pathologically indifferent as well as the caring and concerned—an equal right to put their kids in mental hospi-

tals. Last Wednesday they denied all children—the odd and the unwanted as well as the ill—an equal right to a hearing before being institutionalized.

8 And they did it on a wish and a myth: that parents—and those bureaucratic "parents," state agencies—know best. It took seven years and four separate Supreme Court hearings to achieve this disappointing decision.

9 Lawyers from Pennsylvania and Georgia, and children's advocates, argued that minors deserve the same treatment adults have: a simple hearing before incarceration. They argued that children facing a mental institution deserved the same treatment as children facing a penal institution: a hearing.

10 But the justices, especially Burger and Potter Stewart, were convinced that these children didn't need any advocate other than their parents, or any check on parental power other than the institution's own medical team. In roughly 38 states, they left the fate of children up to parents and hospitals.

11 "That some parents may at times be acting against the interest of their child creates a basis for caution, but is hardly a reason to discard wholesale those pages of human experience that teach that parents generally do act in the child's best interest," wrote Burger.

12 The conflict was between the right of the parents to make decisions about bringing up their children, and the rights of children to their liberty, and to due process. Burger and Stewart, both ardent advocates of extreme parental supremacy, interpreted the Constitution to read, Families First.

13 I agree that most parents do want to act in the "child's best interest." But the law is not necessary to protect children from wise and sensitive parents. Nor is it made to "interfere" with families functioning smoothly on their own.

14 As David Ferleger, the Pennsylvania lawyer who argued this case, put it: "We all want to protect the integrity of a family where it exists. But when the family wants to incarcerate a member, it has already created a break. There is no longer a united family to protect."

15 At that point, the question is whether it's more important to protect a possible, and devastating, infringement of the child's liberty, or to protect the right of a parent or state guardian to dispose of that child's fate.

16 A family in stress may not have the information and emotional stability to make good judgment. A state agency may not care. Nor

can we trust the hospital for an impartial judgment. If surgeons have a bias toward surgery, institutional psychiatrists often have a bias toward institutional psychiatry. Psychiatry is hardly an infallible science, as Burger knows, and there are many children in hospitals now who are simply not mentally ill.

17   The justices compared signing a child into a mental hospital with signing him into a general hospital to have his tonsils out. But a tonsillectomy takes hours, not years. And it does less harm.

18   Parents obviously have and must have a wide range of decisions over their children's lives. But they don't have absolute power and never have. They cannot refuse immunization for their kids or keep them uneducated. They cannot (at least yet) forcibly sterilize them, order them to become a transplant donor, commit incest or abuse them.

19   Nor should they have the right, without another impartial source, to deprive children of something equally as fundamental as their liberty, by putting them away in an institution. In this case (which bodes badly for other children's rights cases coming before the Court), the majority of the justices have sided with a parental power that is virtually unchecked.

20   Chalk one up for the folks who dropped off the boy with the teddy bear.

Thesis and Organization

1. What paragraphs introduce the essay? What elements do the examples in those paragraphs have in common?
2. What paragraphs focus on the Supreme Court's ruling? Which paragraph sums up the issues in the case?
3. What paragraphs present Goodman's analysis of the ruling? Which paragraph sets out her own position? What future actions are at stake? Is the essay's purpose to influence those actions directly or indirectly? How so?
4. Consult a handbook of grammar and usage for an explanation of the rhetorical paragraph. Do paragraphs 1 and 20 fit that explanation? How or how not? Evaluate the effectiveness of those paragraphs in providing a framework for the essay.

Technique and Style

1. Where in the essay does Goodman rely on emotional appeal? On logical appeal? Which predominates? Why might she have started with one and then gone to the other? In which category does the last paragraph fit?

2. What characteristics can you infer about Goodman as a person? What evidence can you cite for your assumptions? How would you describe Goodman's tone? In what ways is it in keeping with her persona? With the effect she wishes to have on her audience?

3. On what point or points does the author agree with Burger and Stewart? What effect does that agreement have on her credibility as a sound arguer?

4. Why might Goodman have chosen to quote from the Supreme Court decision? Where does she quote and what effects does she achieve? Where does she paraphrase? How else does she use quotation marks and to what effect?

5. Where does Goodman fault the justices for a false analogy? How is her own analogy a correct one? Why might she have selected the examples she does?

Suggestions for Writing

Look around for concrete examples of a particular kind of abuse. For instance, leafing through a few days of newspapers may turn up examples of unprovoked violence, abandoned children, white-collar crime, political graft, or terrorist attacks. Using one category of examples, mull over their moral, political, or legal ramifications figuring out what argumentative point you can make based on them. Or go about the assignment as a short research paper. Start with a recent Supreme Court decision with which you disagree and then work backwards through resource material to find examples that you can use for an emotional appeal.

*P*utting Africa at the Center and Beware of the New Pharaohs

Molefi Kete Asante and Henry Louis Gates, Jr.

Both Asante and Gates are scholars who specialize in African-American studies, yet as these two essays point out, their approaches to their field are quite different. Asante sees "cultural stability" as the crucial goal, but Gates finds it to be "free inquiry." Asante's view concentrates on African-Americans, Gates welcomes all comers. What they have in common is a belief in Afrocentricity, but the similarity stops there. The two essays appeared side-by-side in the September 23, 1991, issue of Newsweek *as part of a larger story on the black experience.*

Asante chairs the Department of African-American Studies at Temple University and is the author of a number of books, including The Afrocentric Idea *(1988) and* Afrocentricity *(1990). Gates chairs Afro-American Studies at Harvard University. Gates has written a number of scholarly books of which the best known is probably* The Signifying Monkey *(1989). Most recently, however, he has written for a more general audience in* Loose Canons: Notes of the Culture Wars *(1992) and his autobiography* Colored People: A Memoir *(1993).*

WHAT TO LOOK FOR   *The vocabulary in Asante's essay may at first put you off, but bear with it, for he is using the specialized diction of academic prose.* Subject *and* object *take on special meanings here. A group or person in the* subject *position commands center stage as the one who acts, does, causes things to happen; conversely, a group or person in the* object *position is a bit player who is acted upon or done to. Once you think about it, the terms makes sense. Gates's vocabulary is also formal, academic. As you read the essays, figure out whether or not the specialized language is necessary.*

KEY WORDS AND PHRASES   —ASANTE

Afrocentricity (1)	*pejoratives (3)*
misorientation (2)	*anti-Semitic (4)*
Mayflower (2)	*resonates (6)*

KEY WORDS AND PHRASES—GATES

Pharoahs (title)	*stigmatized (3)*
polemicists (2)	*shibboleths (3)*
proliferation (2)	*diaspora (3)*
methodologies (2)	*Milton (4)*
ideological (2)	*acculturation (5)*
conformity (2)	*labile (5)*
fundamentalism (2)	*resurrects (6)*
porous (3)	

Putting Africa at the Center

Molefi Kete Asante

1   Afrocentricity is both theory and practice. In its theoretical aspect it consists of interpretation and analysis from the perspective of African people as subjects rather than as objects on the fringes of the European experience. When Afrocentric methods are used to explain an issue, the aim is to look for areas where the idea or person is off-center in terms of subject position and suggest appropriate solutions. For example, young African-American males who may be engaged in violent behavior are often off-center. It is the aim of Afrocentric intervention to relocate them in a place of values and cultural stability.

2   Since Africans in America have been dislocated—that is, taken off their own terms for the past 345 years—we seldom operate as the subjects of our own historical experiences. We often operate based on an illusion that creates disillusionment and self-alienation, the most fundamental alienation a person can have. Afrocentricity is a struggle against extreme misorientation, where many of us believe that we share the same history as whites; indeed, that we came across on the Mayflower.

3   In its practical implications, Afrocentricity aims to locate African-American children in the center of the information being presented in classrooms across the nation. Most African-American children sit in classrooms, yet are outside the information being discussed. The white child sits in the middle of the information, whether it is literature, history, politics or art. The task of the Afrocentric curriculum is finding patterns in African-American history and culture that help the teacher place the child in the middle of the intellectual experience. This is not an idea to replace all things European, but to expand the

dialogue to include African-American information. An Afrocentric curriculum covers kindergarten through 12th grade in every subject area. It can then be infused into an academic program cleansed of pejoratives like "Bushman" and "wild Indian" in order to have a truly multicultural curriculum.

4   Afrocentricity is neither racist nor anti-Semitic; it is about placing African people within our own historical framework. In none of the major works of Afrocentricity has there ever been a hint of racism, ethnocentrism or anti-anybody. Indeed, Afrocentricity believes that in order to have a stable society, we must always have a society that respects difference. One cannot argue that there is no difference—or that difference necessarily means hostility. One may be alien and yet not hostile. We only have to witness "E.T." to see the truth of that proposition.

5   **Imitative history:** Recent African-American history has shown that we have frequently been imitative of whites, following in the path of Europeans without understanding our own identities. Few African-American students or adults can tell you the names of any of the African ethnic groups that were brought to the Americas during the Great Enslavement; and yet prior to the Civil War there were no African-Americans, merely enslaved Africans. We know European ethnic names, but not these names, because we have seldom participated in our own historical traditions.

6   Afrocentricity resonates with the African-American community because it is fundamental to sanity. It is the fastest growing intellectual and practical idea in the community because of its validity when tested against other experiences. What could be any more correct for any people than to see with their own eyes?

Beware of the New Pharaohs

Henry Louis Gates Jr.

1   There's a scene in Woody Allen's "Bananas" in which the luckless hero, played by Allen, bemoans the fact that he dropped out of college. "What would you have been if you'd have finished school," a co-worker asks him. "I don't know," he sighs, "I was in the black-studies program. By now, I could have been black."

2   The truth is, too many people still regard African-American

studies primarily as a way to rediscover a lost cultural identity—or invent one that never quite existed. And while we can understand these impulses, those in our field must remember that we are scholars first, not polemicists. For our field to survive, we need to encourage a true proliferation of rigorous methodologies, rather than to seek ideological conformity. African-American studies should be the home of free inquiry into the very complexity of being of African descent in the world, rather than a place where critical inquiry is drowned out by ethnic fundamentalism.

3   We need to explore the hyphen in African-American, on both sides of the Atlantic. We must chart the porous relations between an "American" culture that officially pretends that an Anglo-American *regional* culture is the true, universal culture, and the black cultures it so long stigmatized. We must also document both the continuities and discontinuities between African and African-American cultures, rather than to reduce the astonishing diversity of African cultures to a few simple-minded shibboleths. But we should not lay claim to the idea of "blackness" as an ideology or religion. Surely all scholars of Africa and its diaspora are, by definition, "Afrocentric," if the term signals the recognition that Africa is centrally in the world, as much as the world is in Africa. But this is a source of the problem: all Afrocentrists, alas, do not look alike.

4   In short, African-American studies is not just for blacks; our subject is open to all—to study or to teach. The fundamental premise of the academy is that all things ultimately are knowable; all are therefore teachable. What would we say to a person who said that to teach Milton, you had to be Anglo-Saxon, Protestant, male . . . and blind! We do nothing to help our discipline by attempting to make of it a closed shop, where only blacks need apply. On the other hand, to say that ethnic identity is the product of history and culture is not to say that it is any less real. Nor is it to deny our own personal histories, to pretend that these are not differences that make a difference.

5   Nobody comes into the world as a "black" person or a "white" person: these identities are conferred on us by a complex history, by patterns of social acculturation that are both surprisingly labile and persistent. Social identities are never as rigid as we like to pretend: they're constantly being contested and negotiated.

6   For a scholar, "Afrocentrism" should mean more than wearing Kente cloth and celebrating Kwanzaa instead of Christmas. (Kwanzaa, by the way, was invented in Los Angeles, not Lagos.) Bogus

theories of "sun" and "ice" people, and the invidious scapegoating of other ethnic groups, only resurrects the worst of 19th-century racist pseudoscience—which too many of the pharaohs of "Afrocentrism" have accepted without realizing.

7   We must not succumb to the temptation to resurrect our own version of the thought police, who would determine who, and what, is "black." "Mirror, mirror, on the wall, who's the blackest one of all?" is a question best left behind in the '60s.

Thesis and Organization

1. How do Gates's and Asante's definitions of Afrocentricity differ?
2. How do the two writers view the African-American culture?
3. Both essays contain attacks. Who is attacking what?
4. Who is defending what?
5. Both writers argue for changes in curriculum. What does each want?

Technique and Style

1. The audience for *Newsweek* can be described as college educated, middle-class, predominantly white and male. Which essay is apt to have more appeal to that audience? To an African-American audience?
2. Select a paragraph that uses formal vocabulary and rewrite a sentence or two, using more conversational words. What is gained? Lost?
3. Of the two writers, which would you rather take a class with and why?
4. What examples can you think of that fit Asante's statement that "Most African-American children sit in classrooms, yet are outside the information being discussed"?
5. How does the term *New Pharaohs* fit Gates's essay?

Suggestions for Writing

Gates maintains "Nobody comes into the world as a 'black' person or a 'white' person: these identities are conferred on us by a complex history, by patterns of social acculturation that are both surprisingly labile and persistent." Write an essay in which you argue for or against requiring a college course that focuses on how cultural identities are formed.

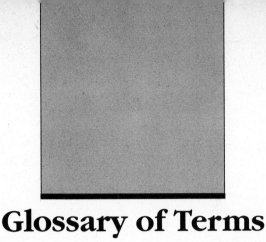

Glossary of Terms

Active voice See *Voice.*

Ad hominem A logical fallacy in which the argument is directed at the person, not the view held by the person. Name-calling.

Ad populem A logical fallacy in which the argument is directed at the group the opponent belongs to, not the views held by the opponent. Name-calling.

Aim See *Purpose.*

Allusion A reference to a real or fictitious person, place, or thing. An allusion is a concise form of association that carries the meaning of the thing alluded to and uses it to enhance the writer's own meaning.

Analogy One of the patterns used to develop an idea. Analogy examines a topic by comparing it point by point to something seemingly unlike but more commonplace and less intricate. Analogy extends a metaphor, concentrating on one subject; comparison and contrast explores the similarities and differences of two or more subjects within the same class.

Antithesis The use of opposite words or phrases to emphasize contrasting ideas that are usually stated in balanced or parallel terms.

Argumentative appeals The three classical appeals central to argument: *logos,* the appeal to reason; *pathos,* to emotion; and *ethos,* to the writer or speaker's persona. For a fuller discussion, see Chapter 9.

Argumentative writing One of the four major purposes of writing. Argument attempts to move the reader to action or to adopting the writer's conviction. Many teachers distinguish between argumentative and persuasive writing: argumentative writing appeals primarily to reason, persuasive writing to emotion.

Assertion A statement that is debatable, as opposed to a fact. Sometimes the author's major assertion appears in the essay's title (Robert Keith Miller's "Discrimination Is a Virtue"), sometimes in a key sentence. Often, however, the reader deduces the writer's assertion by considering the essay's most important statements, most of which appear as topic sentences.

Audience The intended readership for a given work. The audience can be general, as in Joe Klein's "The Education of Berenice Belizaire;" specific, as in Naomi Wolf's "A Woman's Place"; or multiple, as in Robert C. Maynard's "Of Prophets and Protestors." No matter what the audience, a writer should keep in mind A. D. Van Nostrand's summary of the "Common Reader": a person who does not know the thesis, is impatient, shares the writer's level of maturity and education, and knows something about the subject.

Balanced sentence See *Sentence.*

Begging the Question A logical fallacy in which the major line of argument is dodged and a lesser line taken up instead.

Cause and effect Of the patterns used to develop an idea. Cause and effect examines the topic to discover, explain, or argue why a particular action, event, situation, or condition occurred.

Chronological organization See *Organization.*

Classification One of the patterns used to develop an idea. Classification examines a class of things according to shared characteristics, grouping the things according to a similar feature.

Coherence Literally the quality of sticking together. To communicate ideas clearly to the reader, the writer must present material in a logically integrated, understandable, and consistent manner; in short, words, phrases, clauses, sentences, and paragraphs must relate to each other. Coherency can be achieved by using appropriate transitions, logical sequences, and interlocking ideas.

Comparison and contrast One of the patterns used to develop an idea. Comparison and contrast examines two or more subjects by exploring their similarities and differences. Similarities are usually developed through literal and logical comparisons within similar categories:

small cars such as Ford Escort and Honda Civic, popular music such as rock and reggae. Figurative comparisons usually come under analogy. In contrasting subjects, differences fall into two categories: differences in kind, such as Yale has a football team and the University of Chicago does not; or differences in degree, such as the University of Michigan has a better football team than the University of Texas.

Complex sentence See *Sentence.*

Compound sentence See *Sentence.*

Conflict An element essential to narrative. Conflict involves pitting one force against another: a student against the educational system in "Angels on a Pin," a woman against a potential mugger in "I Have a Gun."

Connotation The meanings associated with and suggested by a word that augment its explicit denotative or dictionary definition. The words *home* and *domicile* have a similar denotative value, but they differ radically in their connotations.

Cumulative sentence See *Sentence.*

Declarative sentence See *Sentence.*

Deductive reasoning The method of argument whereby the author first gives the assertion and then explores the reasoning behind it. Suzan Shown Harjo's "Last Rites for Indian Dead" is organized deductively.

Definition One of the patterns used to develop an idea. Definition examines a word or phrase by exploring its meaning, determining its essence. Simple definition employs synonyms, antonyms, and etymology; extended definition may use classification, comparison, description, and example as well as other patterns in order to expand upon the connotations of a word or phrase.

Denotation See *Connotation.*

Description One of the patterns used to develop an idea. Description explores the subject by breaking it down into parts in order to better understand the whole. It draws upon the senses to paint vivid images usually set in time and space, employing repetition, enumeration, spatial development, perspective, and imagery. Description can be classified according to what is described—a person, place, or thing—or according to how it is described—subjectively or objectively.

Detail A precise description—"Six feet four inches" instead of "tall," for example.

Diction The writer's choice of words. The level of diction (colloquial, slang, informal, technical, formal) along with denotation, connotation, and sound determine the writer's judgment of a word's appropriateness to the work's audience and the writer's purpose.

Division The process of separating, usually associated with classification. First a subject is divided into groups, then examples can be sorted out—classified—into the groups or categories.

Dramatic organization See *Organization.*

Either-or reasoning A logical fallacy in which the central term is claimed to be either one thing or another, omitting any possibility of middle ground. A writer who agues that a person is a believer in either democracy or communism is guilty of either-or thinking.

Ethos See *Argumentative appeals.*

Example One of the patterns used to develop an idea. Example explores an assertion by illustrating it, showing how the assertion applies in particular instances. Example is used to provide evidence to support generalizations.

Exclamatory sentence See *Sentence.*

Expository writing See *Informative writing, Purpose.*

Expressive writing One of the four major purposes of writing. Expressive writing emphasizes the author's feelings or attitudes toward the subject.

Fallacy See *Logical fallacies.*

False analogy A logical fallacy in which the analogy does not hold true. Ellen Goodman, in "Checks on Parental Power," accuses Justices Burger and Stewart of using false analogy when they "compared signing a child into a mental hospital with signing him into a general hospital to have his tonsils out."

Hasty generalization A logical fallacy in which a conclusion is reached on the basis of inadequate examples or sampling.

Imperative mood See *Mood.*

Imperative sentence See *Sentence.*

Indicative mood See *Mood.*

Inductive reasoning The method of argument whereby the author first presents information and then moves from explanation and evidence to a logical conclusion. Ellen Goodman uses inductive reasoning in her argumentative essay.

Informative writing (expository writing) One of the four major purposes of writing. Informative writing attempts to further the reader's understanding about the topic.

Interrogative sentence See *Sentence.*

Irony A statement or action in which the intended meaning or occurrence is the opposite of the surface one. Shana Alexander, for instance, cites a judgment that the funerary customs among tribes in New Guinea are "bizarre in the extreme" and then contrasts them with a technological society's high-rise mortuary. The ironic juxtaposition raises questions as to which is the more "bizarre."

Journalistic questions The traditional questions: *who, what, where, when, why,* and *how.*

Logical fallacies Errors in reasoning. See *Ad hominem, Ad populem, Begging the question. Either-or reasoning, False analogy, Hasty generalization, Misusing authority, Non sequitur, Post hoc, propter hoc, Shift in definition, Straw man.*

Logos See *Argumentative appeals.*

Loose sentence See *Sentence.*

Metaphor An implied but direct comparison in which the primary term is made more vivid by associating it with a quite dissimilar term.

Middle premise See *Syllogism.*

Misusing authority A logical fallacy in which a person's skill or knowledge in one area is assumed to exist in another. A successful baseball player may be a valid authority on makes of baseball gloves, for instance, but not on after-shave lotion.

Modes Common patterns of thought used to explore, develop, and organize a topic. The various modes or patterns can be classified according to their function: those that sequence information are narration, process, and cause and effect; those that compare are analogy and comparison and contrast; and those that divide are classification, description, definition, and example.

Mood   An aspect of the verb that reveals the attitude of the writer. The indicative mood states fact or asks a question; the subjunctive mood states a matter of possibility, desire, contradiction, or uncertainty; the imperative mood states a command or request.

Name-calling   See *Ad hominem* and *Ad populem*.

Narration   One of the patterns used to develop an idea. Narration explores a topic by presenting a story or account of an experience bounded by time and space. Whereas cause and effect emphasizes *why*, and process emphasizes *how*, narration emphasizes *what*. Narration can be factual, grounded in an actual event, or fictional, grounded in the imagination.

Non sequitur   A logical fallacy in which the causal relationship claimed does not follow: "The essay was published in the *New York Times*, so it must be accurate."

Organization   The manner in which a paragraph or essay is put together. Essays are usually organized by several principles: the various modes, and chronological, dramatic, and spatial order. Chronological order is determined by time, dramatic order by emotional effect, and spatial order by physical location.

Paradox   A statement that appears to be contradictory yet may in fact be true; an apparent contradiction.

Paragraph   A cohesive unit of thought or emphasis set off by indention. Most paragraphs develop a controlling assertion or topic sentence, explicit or implied, and therefore run to 150 words or so; other shorter paragraphs function as transitions or as rhetorical devices.

Paragraph block   A group of paragraphs that taken together develop a controlling assertion or topic sentence. William Raspberry's "The Handicap of Definition" illustrates paragraph blocks.

Parallelism   The repetition of words or grammatically similar phrases, clauses, or sentences to emphasize coherence.

Parody   An exaggerated imitation that treats a serious subject in an absurd manner, ridiculing both form and content. James Gorman's "Man,

Bytes, Dog" is a parody.

Passive voice See *Voice*.

Pathos See *Argumentative appeals*.

Patterns of organization Common patterns of thought used to explore, develop, and organize a topic. The various patterns can be classified according to their function. Those that sequence material are cause and effect, process, and narration; those that compare are analogy and comparison and contrast; those that divide are classification, description, definition, and example. Patterns of organization are also called *modes*.

Periodic sentence See *Sentence*.

Persona The mask or character assumed by the writer to engage the intended audience. While the most obvious persona is an ironic one (as in the case of James Gorman), to achieve credibility, focus, and emphasis, all writers assume personas to greater or lesser degrees.

Persuasive writing See *Argumentative writing* and *Purpose*.

Point of view The perspective from which the work is related. In nonfiction, point of view usually refers to the writer's use of personal pronouns (*I, you, he, she, we, they*, etc.); in fiction, point of view is usually further divided into first person, limited omniscient, omniscient, and objective.

Post hoc, propter hoc A logical fallacy in which a temporal relationship is mistaken for a causal one: if all your lights went out just as you plugged in your new television set and you then assume you are the cause of the power failure, you must be in a *post hoc* trap.

Process One of the patterns used to develop an idea. Process examines the topic to discover the series of steps or acts that brought or will bring about a particular result. Whereas cause and effect emphasizes *why* and depends primarily on analysis, process emphasizes *how* and depends primarily on classification. For example, the topic "leaving the teaching profession" can be developed by cause and effect, explaining *why* by providing an analysis of the various reasons that lay behind the decision, or by process, explaining *how* by showing the steps that were involved, steps that may be put in categories such as first doubts, the brink of decision, and tidying up. Process can be further divided into historical, practical, and scientific: historical process deals with topics such as how the United States will carry out foreign policy or how

Levi's became big business; practical process deals with topics such as how to make butter; scientific process deals with topics such as how the body reacts to starvation.

Purpose The intention that drives the text; its function. Most written work can be classified into one of four categories according to its purpose: expressive writing, such as journal entries and diaries that analyze, record, relate the writer's feelings and ideas; informative or expository writing, such as explanations and analyses that further the reader's understanding about the topic; persuasive or argumentative writing, such as narratives, descriptions, and analyses that try to move the reader to action or to share the writer's conviction; and literary writing, such as poems, plays, short stories, and novels that create fictional worlds out of the interplay of language. In general, expressive writing emphasizes the writer, informative writing the subject, persuasive writing the reader, and literary writing the language itself.

Sarcasm A caustic or sneering remark or tone that is usually ironic as well.

Satire The use of wit, sarcasm, irony, and parody to ridicule or expose some folly or evil.

Sensory detail Detail relating to one or more senses. See *Detail.*

Sequence See *Organization.*

Sentence One or more words that convey meaning. In grammar, sentences can be classified as simple, compound, and compound-complex. A simple sentence has one main clause and no subordinate clauses; a complex sentence has a main clause and a subordinate clause; a compound sentence has two or more main clauses and no subordinate clause; and a compound-complex sentence has two or more main clauses and one or more subordinate clauses.

In rhetoric, sentences can be classified as declarative, stating facts; as interrogative, asking questions; as imperative, giving commands; and as exclamatory, expressing feeling.

Also in rhetoric, certain types of sentences achieve certain effects; the cumulative or loose sentence, in which the main clause comes first, occurs most frequently and allows for modification without sacrificing clarity; the less used periodic sentence, in which the main clause comes last, achieves dramatic tension; and the balanced sentence, in which phrases are parallel, usually emphasizes contrast.

Shift in definition A logical fallacy in which the meaning of a term central to the argument is changed. A person who shifts the definition of lying from intention to deceive to the far narrower meaning of verbal untruth is guilty of a shift in definition, a form of *begging the question*.

Simile A stated but removed comparison in which the primary term is made vivid by associating it with a quite dissimilar one. Simile differs from metaphor in that simile uses a term of comparison such as *like* or *as*.

Simple sentence See *Sentence*.

Spatial organization See *Organization*.

Straw man A logical fallacy in which the argument is shifted to an insignificant or unrelated point, which is then attacked and destroyed in hopes that some of the destruction will carry over to the main point. The use of an extreme example is a popular form of straw man argument.

Subjunctive mood See *Mood*.

Syllogism A form of deductive reasoning composed of a major premise, a minor or middle premise, and a conclusion: All Labrador retrievers are gentle; Beartrap is a Labrador retriever; therefore Beartrap is gentle. Note that a syllogism can be logical but false, as above.

Syntax The way in which words are put together to form phrases, clauses, and sentences; the grammatical relationship between the words.

Thesis A statement about a subject that accounts for the relevant information about it; a statement or assertion of the subject's significance. An essay's thesis is its umbrella statement, the assertion at the highest level of generality under which all the essay's other assertions fit.

Tone A writer's attitude toward the subject and the audience. An author's tone can be contemplative (Sue Hubbell), intense (Sandra Cisneros), tongue-in-cheek (James Gorman), and so on.

Topic sentence A statement of the topic of a paragraph and an assertion about the topic. A topic sentence is to the paragraph what the thesis is to the essay. Whether implicit or explicit, the topic sentence conveys the paragraph's controlling idea.

Transition A word, phrase, sentence, or paragraph that carries the reader smoothly from point A to point B. Some transitions, such as time markers and semantic guideposts—*therefore, however, but,* and so on—are overt; others are more subtle—a repeated word or phrase, a synonym for a key term, a shift in tense. All, however, provide coherence and unity.

Voice In grammar, forms of the verb. If the subject performs the action, the verb is in the active voice; if the subject is acted upon, the verb is in the passive voice: "I bit the dog" versus "The dog was bitten by me."

In rhetoric and composition, voice refers to the reader's sense of the writer as a real person. A writer's voice is a combination of tone and persona.

Wordplay A clever phrasing of words, a pun.

Acknowledgments

Ellery Akers, "Left Sink" by Ellery Akers. Copyright © 1990 by Ellery Akers. Used by permission.

Shana Alexander, "Fashions in Funerals" from *Talking Women* by Shana Alexander, pp. 120–121. Copyright © 1976 by Shana Alexander. Reprinted by permission.

Kurt Andersen, "Not the Best of Times, Not the Worst" by Kurt Andersen from *Rollingstone,* May 18, 1989 by Straight Arrow Publishers, Inc. 1989. Copyright © 1992 All Rights Reserved. Reprinted by permission.

Molefi Kete Asante, "Putting Africa at the Center" by Molefi Kete Asante. Copyright © 1991 by Molefi Kete Asante. *Newsweek,* September 23, 1991. Used by permission.

Russell Baker, "The Plot Against People" by Russell Baker. *The New York Times,* June 18, 1968. Copyright © 1968 by the New York Times Company. Reprinted by permission.

Suzanne Britt, "The Lean and Hungry Look" by Suzanne Britt, *Newsweek,* October 9, 1978. Copyright © 1978 by Suzanee Britt. Used by permission of the author.

Alexander Calandra, "Angels on a Pin" by Alexander Calandra from *Saturday Review,* December 21, 1968. Copyright © 1968 by Saturday Review. All rights reserved. Reprinted by permission.

Sandra Cisneros, "Who Wants Stories Now?" by Sandra Cisneros. Copyright © 1993 by The New York Times Company. Reprinted by permission.

Laurel Dewey, "Gad's Its Garlic" by Laurel Dewey. First appeared in *Valley Journal,* October 1993. Used by permission.

George Felton, "Pain, Not Pleasure, Now the Big Sell" by George Felton. Reprinted by permission of the author.

J. Merill-Foster, "At 85, Frightened by a Loss of Power" by J. Merill-Foster. The *New York Times,* January 31, 1988. Copyright © by The New York Times Company. Reprinted by permission.

Maneka Gandhi, "You Sure You Want to Do This?" by Nameka Gandhi. Third World Network Features.

Tania Nyman, "I'm Frightened Angry and Ashamed: I Have a Gun" by Tania Nyman. *The Times-Picayune,* April 21, 1990. Reprinted by permission of The Times Picayune Publishing Corporation.

Joseph Perkins, "Reform Should Make Room for Dad" by Joseph Perkins. Copyright © 1993 by Joseph Perkins. Reprinted by permission.

Perry James Pitre, "The Writer" by Perry James Pitre. Reprinted by permission of the author.

Anna Quindlen, "Mom, Dad and Abortion" by Anna Quindlen, *The New York Times,* July 1, 1990. Copyright © 1990 by The New York Times Company. Reprinted by permission.

William Raspberry, "The Handicap of Definition" from "Instilling Positive Images" by William Raspberry. Copyright © 1982 by Washington Post Writers Group. Reprinted by permission.

Patricia Raybon, "A Case of Severe Bias" by Patricia Raybon. Copyright © 1989 by Patricia Raybon. Appeared in *Newsweek,* October 2, 1989. Reprinted by permission of the author.

Gary Soto, "The Pie" from *A Summer Life,* copyright © 1990 by University Press of New England. Used by permission of the University Press of New England.

Brent Staples, "Black Men and Public Space" by Brent Staples. Reprinted by permission of the author. "When Only Monsters Are Real" by Brent Staples. Copyright © 1993 by The New York Times Company. Reprinted by permission.

Thomas B. Stoddard, "Gay Marriages: Make Them Legal" by Thomas B. Stoddard, The *New York Times,* March 4, 1989. Copyright © 1989 by The New York Times Company. Reprinted by permission.

Mario Suarez, "El Hoyo" by Mario Suarez for *Arizona Quarterly,* Summer 1947, vol. III, no. 2. Copyright © by the Arizona Quarterly. Reprinted by permission.

Brad Wackerlin, "Against All Odds, I'm Just Fine" by Brad Wackerlin. Appeared in *Newsweek,* June 1990. Reprinted by permission of the author.

Barbara H. Wilson, "Erased Edges" by Barbara H. Wilson. Copyright © 1988 by Barbara H. Wilson. Used by permission.

Naomi Wolf, "A Woman's Place" by Naomi Wolf. The *New York Times,* May 31, 1992. Copyright © 1992 by The New York Times Company. Reprinted by permission.

"Taking the Hard Road with Black Athletes" by The *New York Times Sports.* The New York Times Sports, November 13, 1988. Copyright © 1988 by The New York Times Company. Reprinted by permission.

Index